I0643694

ART STARTS WITH A *Line*

a creative and interactive guide to THE ART OF LINE DRAWING

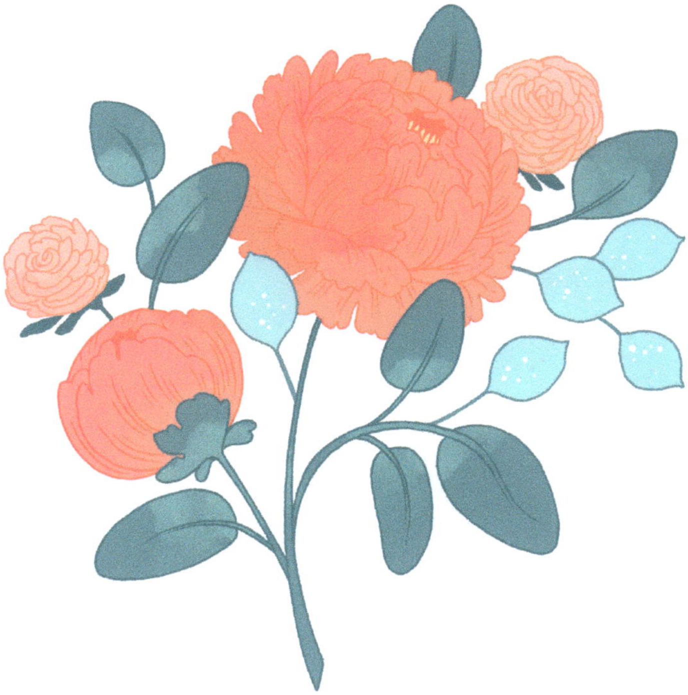

Written and Illustrated By Erin McManness
of Paper Raven Co.

Walter Foster

Quarto.com
WalterFoster.com

First published in 2018 by Walter Foster Publishing, an imprint of The Quarto Group.
100 Cummings Center, Suite 265D, Beverly, MA 01915, USA.
T (978) 282-9590 **F** (978) 283-2742

ISBN: 978-1-63322-481-0

Digital edition published in 2018
eISBN: 978-1-63322-482-7

Acquiring and Project Editor: Stephanie Carbajal
Page Layout: Melissa Gerber
Copy Editor: Elizabeth T. Gilbert

TABLE OF CONTENTS

INTRODUCTION

Hello there! Welcome to *Art Starts with a Line*. I am so glad you picked up this book! I'm Erin, a full-time illustrator. My brand, Paper Raven Co., is a line of stationery, greeting cards, home decor, and other fun illustrated things! My favorite things to draw are flowers and plants, decorative elements, and hand lettering. I also love symmetry, folk art, and clean lines! Illustration has been my job for more than five years, and I'm so excited to join you on this journey.

Perhaps you really enjoy art and want to hone your illustration skills further, learn a new style, or strengthen your draftsmanship muscle. Or maybe you're considering drawing and illustration for the first time and want to learn some good foundational techniques. Either way, you're in the right place! This book works well for those familiar with everyday drawing, and it is also a great tool if you're just starting out.

Whether you enjoy art as a hobby or are considering it as a possible career path, there are so many resources and avenues available online to share, sell, and create illustration work. This is a thrilling time to be a creative person! Illustration is a rewarding discipline, and I'm here to give you tools and techniques to help you build a solid skillset in line-based illustration. Drawing is simply the honing of hand-eye coordination, combined with a different way of viewing the world around you. Develop these two "muscles," and you can draw anything. By the time you have finished this book, you'll be familiar with how to draw a multitude of subjects—lettering, plants and flowers, architecture, animals, and everyday objects. Let's get started!

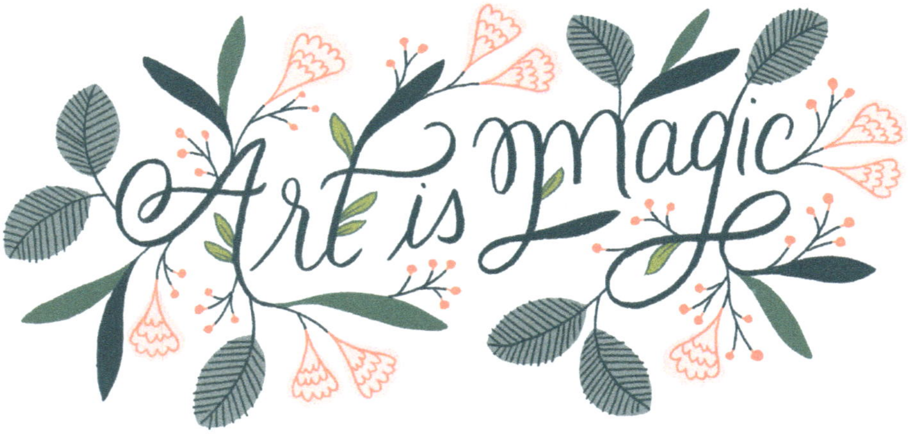

LINE ART HAS SO MANY WONDERFUL APPLICATIONS—IT'S PERFECT FOR EMBELLISHING YOUR LIFE PLANNER, BULLET JOURNAL, SCRAPBOOK, AND MORE. YOU CAN MAKE YOUR OWN STATIONERY OR DESIGN A LOGO FOR YOUR BLOG...THE POSSIBILITIES ARE ENDLESS!

HOW TO USE THIS BOOK

This book is divided into five main sections: Borders, Banners & Letters; Botanicals; Architecture & City Life; Animals & Insects; and Everyday Life. Each section is designed to teach you how to draw different types of objects within that theme. Most sections start with basic objects and become more advanced as you progress.

You'll also find step-by-step instructions on how to draw a variety of objects and give them unique features and personality by adding details. These instructions are meant to be used as a guide—you don't have to draw exactly what I draw, but you can if you like! And you can always follow the foundational principles in building the illustration and add your own personal twist in the details. I highly encourage you to doodle in this book, draw in the margins, make notes, and practice the different techniques in your own sketchbook. Practice really does make perfect!

You'll find practice pages where you can try your hand at what you've learned. Explore anything that fits the theme! Want to practice drawing the paws of animals? Go for it. Really want to draw a llama? Pull up a reference and try it! This is your free space.

Each section also includes a creative prompt to spark the imagination and encourage you to take what you've learned and get really creative.

By the time you've worked your way through this book, you'll feel more confident about incorporating drawing into your everyday life and more self-assured about illustrating complex items and objects—and hopefully you will have had a lot of fun!

Are you ready to begin? Onward!

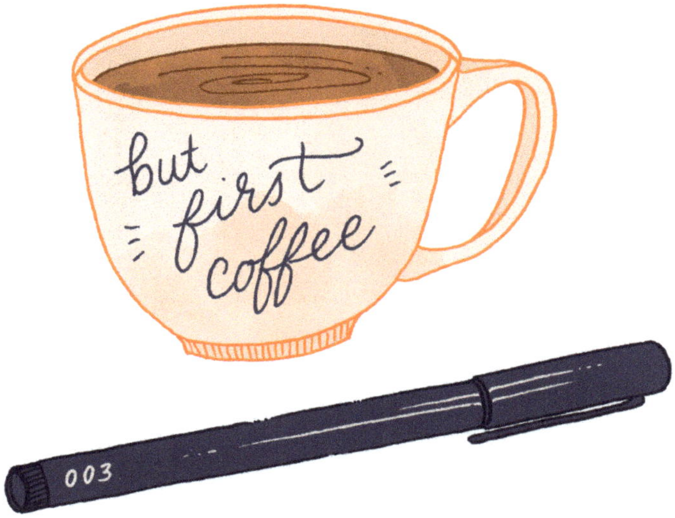

DRAWING TOOLS & MATERIALS

These are some of the drawing tools I use every day. You'll notice a variety of pens, pencils, and erasers. I feel that the greater the variety of utensils you have for mark-making, the better and more flexible your work will be! Of course, you don't need all of these tools to make great art. All you really need are a few trusty supplies.

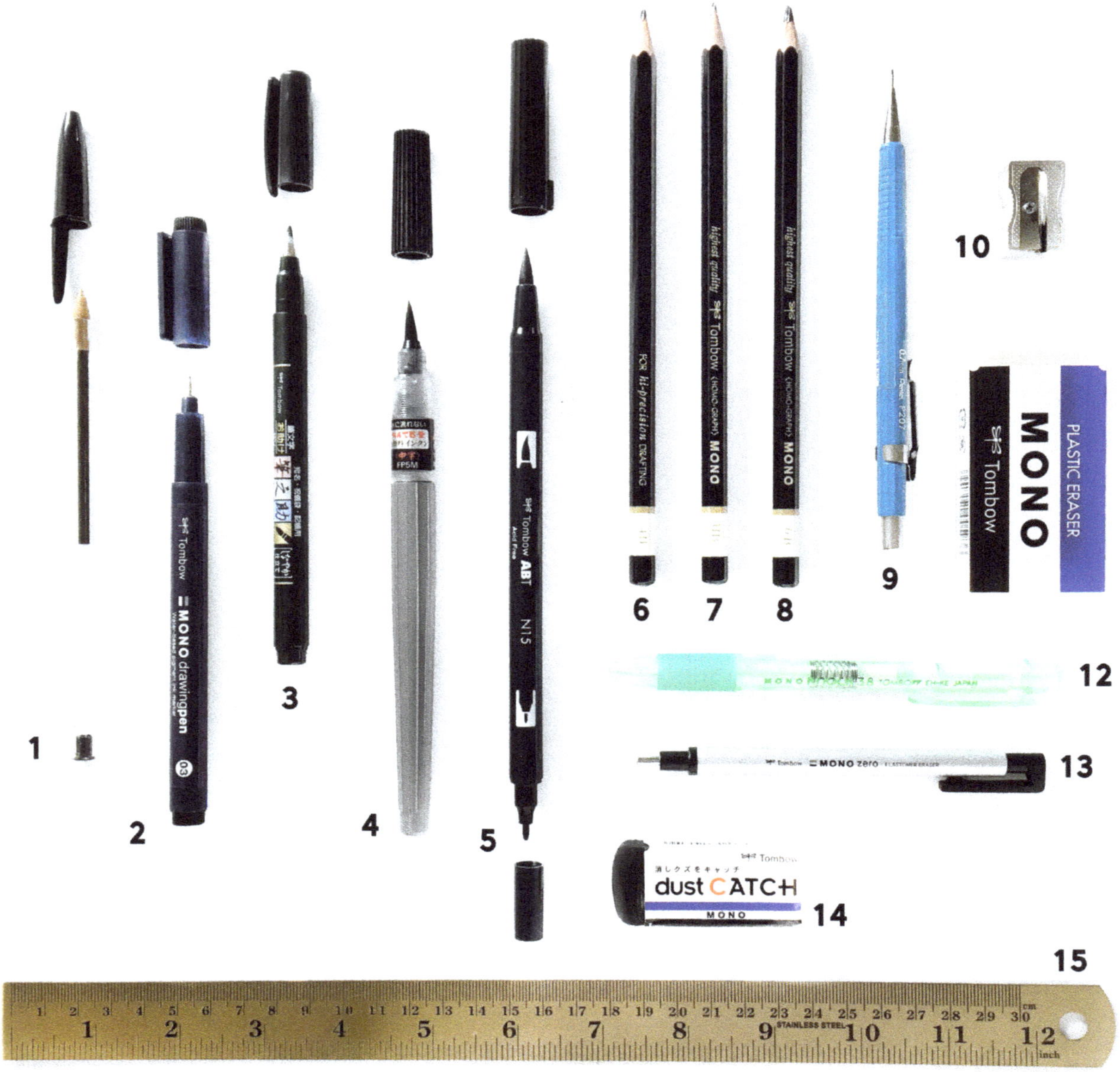

1. Ballpoint Pen
I like to use a BIC® ballpoint. This pen is great for loose sketching, doodling, and taking along for travel. It creates a light, single-weight line and can be used with different pressure to achieve some subtle shading effects.

2. Tombow® MONO Drawing Pen, Size 03
This is my favorite inking pen—I use it in almost all of my final illustrations. This is a felt-tip pen with a small nib. It delivers a single-weight line (hence the name, "MONO") that is rich with ink and won't scrub up when you erase lines underneath. The MONO pens come in three sizes: 01 (very fine), 03 (fine), and 05 (medium).

3. Tombow Fudenosuke Calligraphy Pen, Soft Tip
I love this pen for lettering! For reference, the lettering section of this book was done almost exclusively with this calligraphy pen. This pen has a sturdy brush tip, but the bristles stay together for a bouncy tip that allows for great variation in line weight. It's also available with a hard tip.

4. Pentel® Brush Pen
This pen has a bristly, thick tip that is great for lettering and making inkier, sweeping marks. Every brushstroke has natural edges, creating a beautiful, organic feel.

5. Tombow Dual Brush Pen
This pen is perfect for both traveling and as a mainstay in your drawing kit. One side uncaps to reveal a flexible brush tip that allows for great line variation, while the other side uncaps a fine tip that is ideal for detailing and fixing little inconsistencies. I love this pen for its versatility.

6. 4H Pencil
In the next section, we will discuss basic drawing techniques and how to achieve them with different tools. This pencil is at the hard end of the HB graphite spectrum. It creates a very lightweight, precise line.

7. HB Pencil
This pencil is in the middle of the HB graphite spectrum; it has some give and thickness. It's great for shading!

8. 6B Pencil
This pencil is at the soft end of the HB graphite spectrum. It's very easy to use and provides a very dark mark with little pressure.

9. Pentel Mechanical Pencil
Sometimes for loose sketching or sketches that will be inked, I use a simple mechanical pencil. They are easy to use and easy to erase—and they pack perfectly with the built-in eraser.

10. Standard Sharpener
I like a basic sharpener for my pencils, but if you're on the go frequently or are in school, you can use one that has a plastic cover for catching shavings.

11. Tombow MONO Eraser
This is a great, large plastic eraser that works well on light sketches.

12. Tombow MONO Knock Eraser
I love this eraser. It comes in pen form with a clicking bottom that pushes up the eraser like the lead of a mechanical pencil. It has a small, soft tip that is ideal for erasing small areas. And the lead pickup is great!

13. Tombow MONO Zero Eraser
If you love putting detail into your sketches, this is the perfect eraser for you. It has a tiny but flexible tip, allowing you to erase the smallest of areas cleanly.

14. Tombow MONO Dust Catch Eraser
This eraser is excellent for traveling! It's a black plastic eraser that clings to itself. It erases naturally, but instead of creating little "pills" of eraser material, it rolls together to drastically reduce the amount of eraser dust left on the page.

15. Ruler
I always like to keep a ruler handy. You never know when you'll need it. In this book, there are several sections that require a ruler or straightedge!

COLOR TOOLS & MATERIALS

There are so many great options for adding color traditionally to your drawings. Many of these supplies are portable and easy to use, so I highly recommend picking some up the next time you're at an art supply store. Shown here are some of the coloring tools I use in my work.

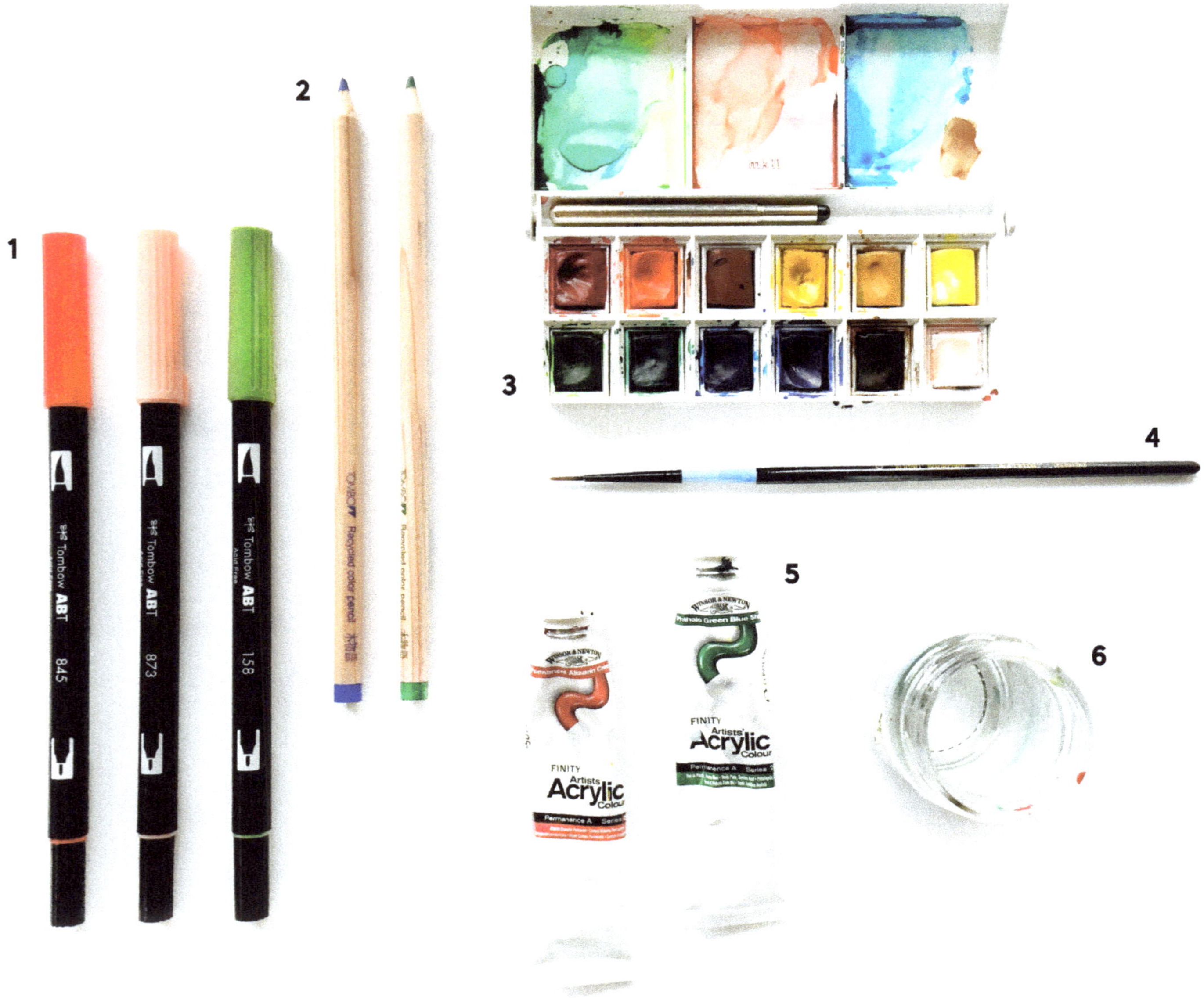

1. Tombow Dual Brush Pens
These pens come in almost 100 different colors, and all are outfitted with a thick brush tip and a fine felt tip. Grab a few mainstay color combinations for your drawing toolkit or pouch, and you will always be ready to make some gorgeous work. These pens blend into each other, making the possibilities endless (you'll learn more about this in the next section}.

2. Tombow Recycled Colored Pencils
Colored pencils are so easy to use and require only occasional sharpening. I like their rich color and the way they blend so well into each other.

3. Winsor & Newton™ Watercolor Travel Palette
This watercolor set comes in a little folding box that houses twelve paints, making it very easy to use. As long as you have access to a little water—or invest in a water brush, available at any art supply store—this will work great for you!

4. Watercolor Brush
Even if your watercolor set comes with a brush, it's always handy to have an extra!

5. Winsor & Newton Tube Acrylics
These acrylic paints come as liquid in individual tubes, as well as in sets.

6. Small Jar
Finally, for watercolor and acrylic painting, you'll need a little jar for holding water.

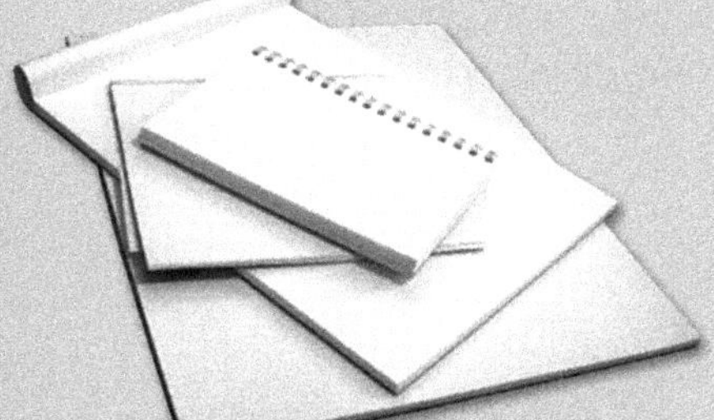

THERE ARE A FEW EXTRA SUPPLIES YOU MAY WANT TO CONSIDER:

1. Get yourself a trusty sketchbook. I like the 9" x 12" Mixed Media Strathmore® sketchbook. The pages hold up to various media, and it's not too big. It fits comfortably in a bag or backpack, as well as on your lap.
2. I also recommend a drawing pouch or bag to keep your supplies in. There are so many fun options! Get one that speaks to and inspires you.

• ARTIST'S TIP •

IT'S A GOOD IDEA TO EXPERIMENT WITH DIFFERENT TOOLS TO DISCOVER THE BRANDS AND TYPES OF DRAWING IMPLEMENTS YOU LIKE BEST. MANY BRICK-AND-MORTAR ART SUPPLY RETAILERS ALLOW YOU THE OPPORTUNITY TO TEST PENCILS, PENS, AND MARKERS RIGHT IN THE STORE.

BASIC DRAWING TECHNIQUES

In this section, we'll cover some basic drawing and mark-making techniques with various drawing pen and pencil suggestions. Mastering techniques to achieve different results in your drawings is key to a solid illustration style. As you experiment, notice which techniques you really enjoy, as well as those you don't.

MARK-MAKING WITH PEN

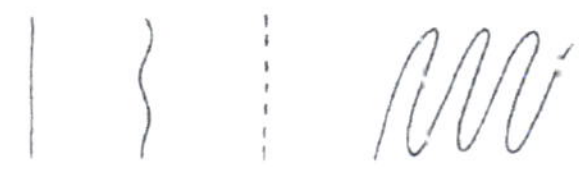

MONO Drawing Pen
I drew these lines with a Tombow MONO Drawing Pen in size 03. A MONO drawing pen is great for finishing illustrations with consistent, thin line weight. This works well with detailed pieces!

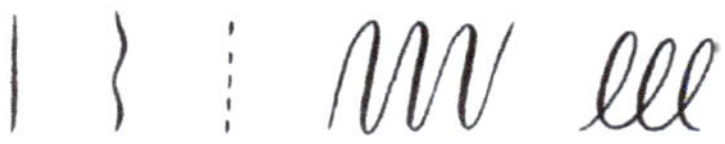

Calligraphy Pen
A calligraphy pen is a wonderful tool for lettering. Notice how it creates nice thick and thin lines. Here I used a Tombow Calligraphy Pen.

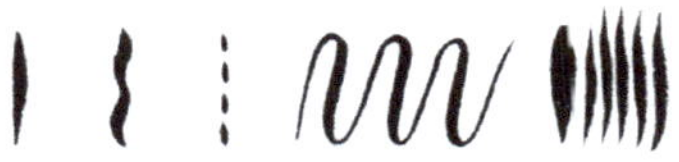

Brush Pen
Brush pens are great for loose illustrations, organic lines, and fills. Shown here are marks made with a Pentel Brush Pen, which creates very inky, thick strokes.

Once you know what types of strokes to expect from the different tools, you can combine mark-making techniques to achieve unique results.

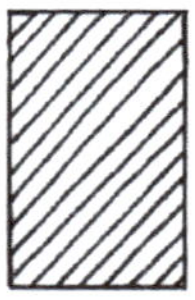

Hatching is when you fill an area with close, parallel lines. You can draw them vertically, horizontally, or diagonally. Draw the lines in the same direction and at the same distance apart.

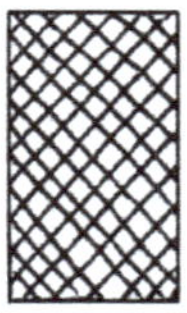

Crosshatching is very similar to hatching. To achieve this look, simply lay down hatch marks, and then redraw them in the opposite direction. You can do this diagonally (as shown here), vertically, or horizontally.

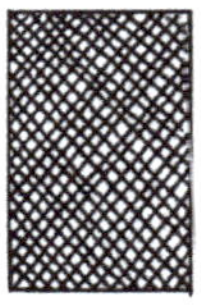

Tight Crosshatching is the same technique as crosshatching, but the lines are much closer together. Notice how this box looks darker. Experiment with the distance between the lines, and you can get some really interesting results!

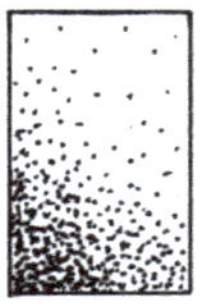

Stippling is the act of tapping your pen on the paper in an upright position to create a sea of dots. For darker areas, place the dots closer together; for lighter areas, place the dots farther apart.

MARK-MAKING WITH PENCIL

Using pencil in your illustrations can give your work a wonderful variety of tone. Here, we'll explore the different options you have in selecting the right type of lead for your drawings. As always, it's great to pick up a pack of pencils and experiment to learn what you really enjoy using.

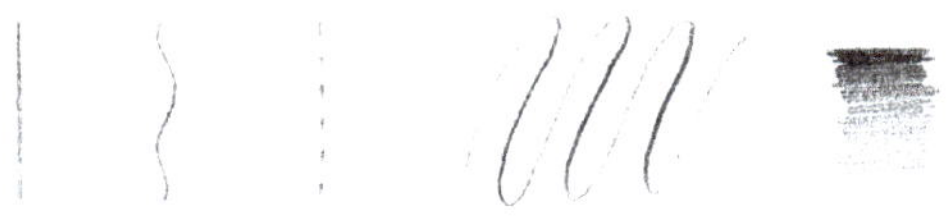

Mechanical Pencil
This tool holds thin sticks of lead and allows for consistent, predictable strokes. When used with hard lead, it yields fine, light lines that are great for sketches or illustrations you plan to ink.

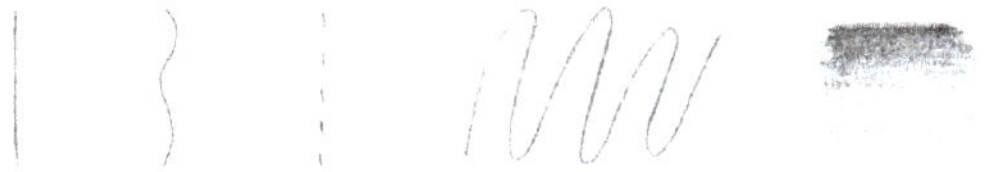

4H Drawing Pencil
This pencil contains very hard lead, which produces a thin, light line that is excellent for drawing with precision. "H" stands for "hard." The higher the number in front of the H, the harder the lead. The shading effect is very light.

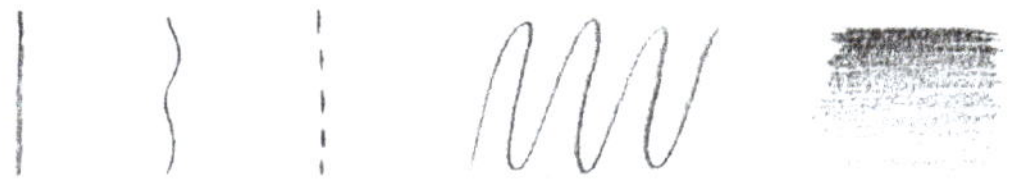

HB Drawing Pencil
This pencil contains lead that is in the middle of the graphite spectrum. It's softer than the 4H pencil, creating a thicker, denser line and a darker shading effect.

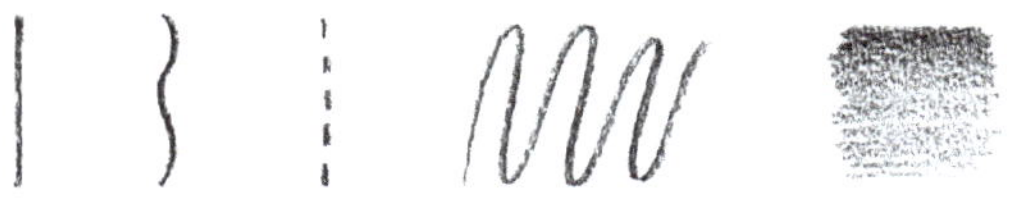

6B Drawing Pencil
This pencil is on the very soft side of the graphite spectrum. It produces a dark mark and is great for shading. "B" stands for "black." The higher the number in front of the B, the softer and blacker the lead.

ADVANCED SHADING WITH PEN

Crosshatch

Practice this technique with pen. In my example, I used crosshatching on a sphere, which has a highlight on one side (usually near the top), and a shadow that scoops around it. Start by hatching in one direction on the bottom left side of the sphere. Then hatch the other way. Keep hatching and crosshatching until you have built up darker tones along the bottom of the sphere and light, separated marks at the top where the light is. Draw your own sphere in the space provided.

PRACTICE HERE

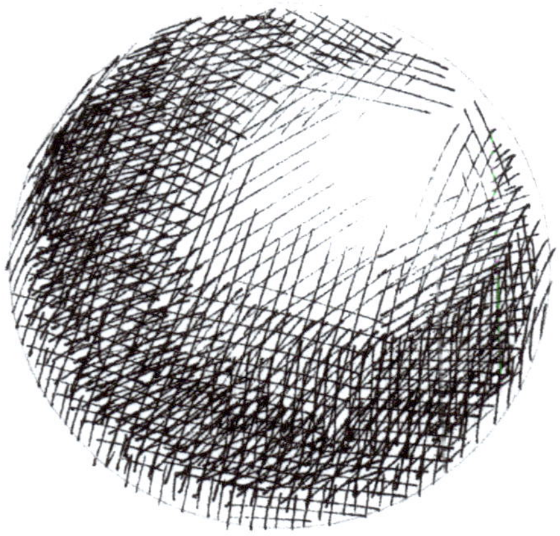

Stipple

Now try stippling. Keeping the same principles of basic lighting in mind, add dots around the surface of the sphere to create the illusion of volume. Where the shadow falls on the bottom section of the sphere, keep stippling until you have started to build a gradient of dark to light. Draw your own stippled sphere in the space provided.

PRACTICE HERE

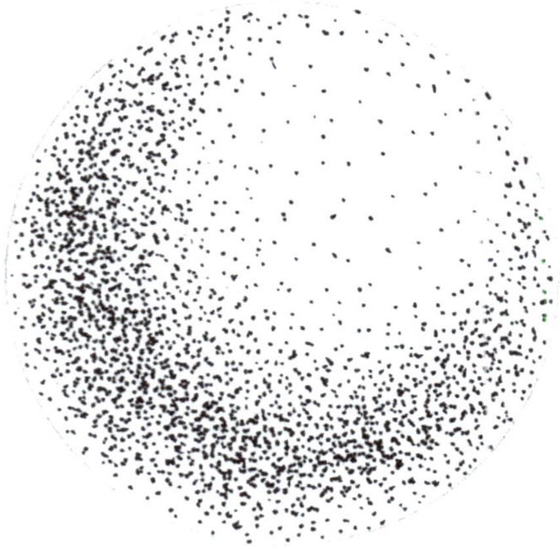

ADVANCED SHADING WITH PENCIL

Hard Pencil

Using pencil to shade is different than mark-making techniques with pen. You can vary the amount of pressure you use to achieve darker or lighter tones. Use light, even strokes toward the highlighted part of the sphere. As you near the bottom, press harder to achieve darker values. In this example, I used a 4H drawing pencil, which has hard lead. Notice how the darkest areas are not very dark at all, and the lighter areas are very light. Practice shading your own sphere in the space provided.

PRACTICE HERE

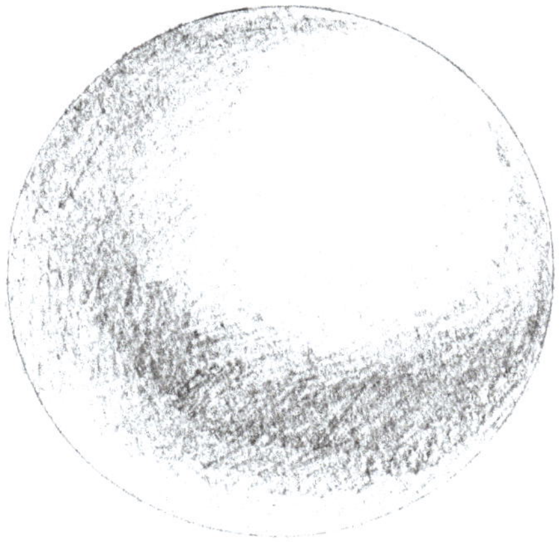

Soft Pencil

Now try the sphere with a soft drawing pencil, such as a 6B. Because of the softness and blackness of the lead, you need to press very lightly to achieve the highlight. Filling in the shadows will be much easier. Notice how much darker this sphere is compared to the above sphere. Practice shading your own sphere in the space provided.

PRACTICE HERE

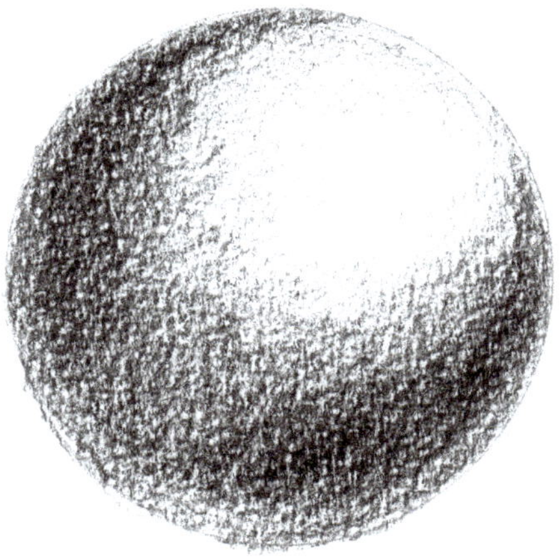

ADDING COLOR

In this section, we'll explore several options for adding color to a line drawing, including marker, colored pencil, watercolor, acrylic, and even mixed-media techniques. For this section, you will need the following:

- A small container of water
- A paper towel or napkin
- A small paintbrush
- Thick art paper or a mixed-media sketchpad

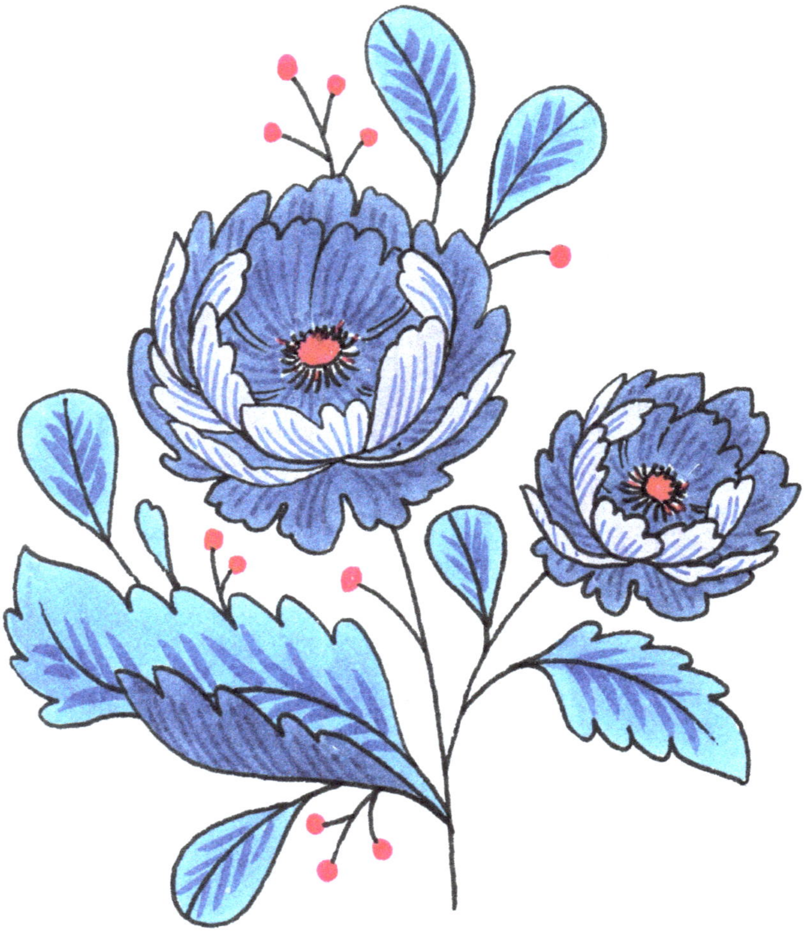

MARKERS

Working with markers is fun and easy. Markers don't require any extra tools or cleanup, so they're also ideal for working outside of the studio, such as at a coffee shop or school. In this demonstration, I used Tombow Dual Brush Pens in bright red, pink, and grass green.

Basic Fill
Simply fill each area with solid color. Avoid applying too many layers or using too much pressure, which can disturb the paper's surface.

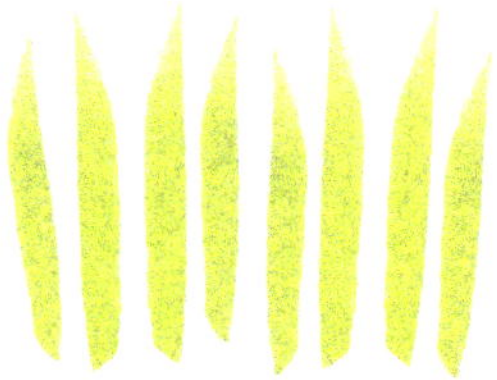

Stroke
Pull the marker from the center of the leaf to the outside, creating a stroke effect that gives depth and interest to the leaf. Experiment with the types of strokes you can create with different marker tips. I like to make a few practice strokes before applying then to my final illustration.

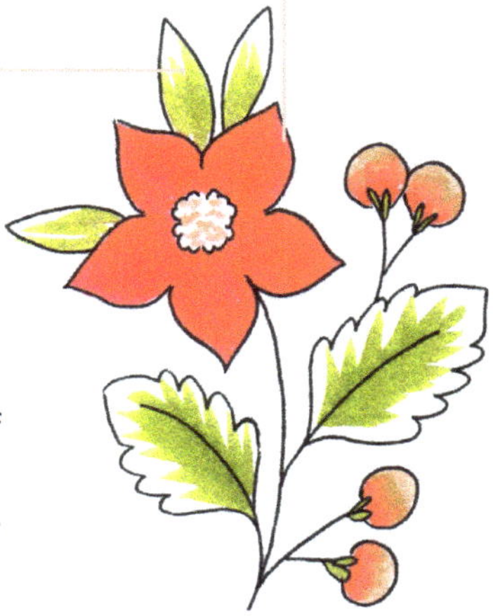

Blending
I love Tombow Dual Brush Pens because they can blend into each other with just a couple simple steps. First lay down a small amount of the darker or more saturated color. Then lay down a large amount of the lighter color, pushing it right up to the edge of the darker color. Then, using the lighter color, swivel back and forth into the deeper color, and pull it back into the lighter color to form a gradient. I used this technique on the buds in this illustration.

PRACTICE HERE

Use this space to practice what you've learned.

COLORED PENCILS

Colored pencils are also great to have in your drawing toolkit. Like markers, they don't require any additional tools to use. You may want to have a sharpener handy, though! There are many quality colored pencil brands available. I recommend Prismacolor®, Faber Castell®, or Tombow colored pencils. In this example, I used Tombow Recycled Colored Pencils.

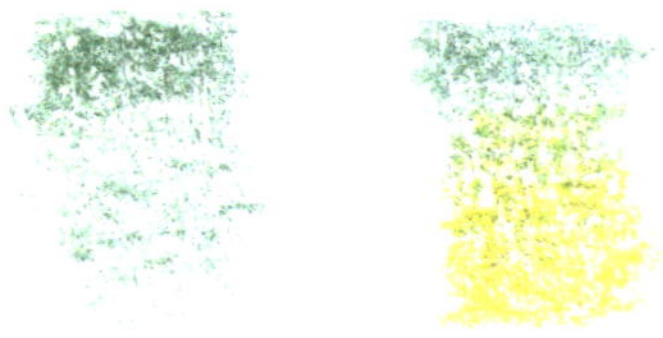

Color Blending
Start with your darker color. In this case, I placed the darker color at the base of the leaves. I shaded while applying pressure; then I lightened the tone as I shaded toward the tip of each leaf. Now switch to your lighter color. I switched to a light green and started at the tip of the leaf, creating a gradient in the opposite direction. The result is a beautiful seamless merging of colors.

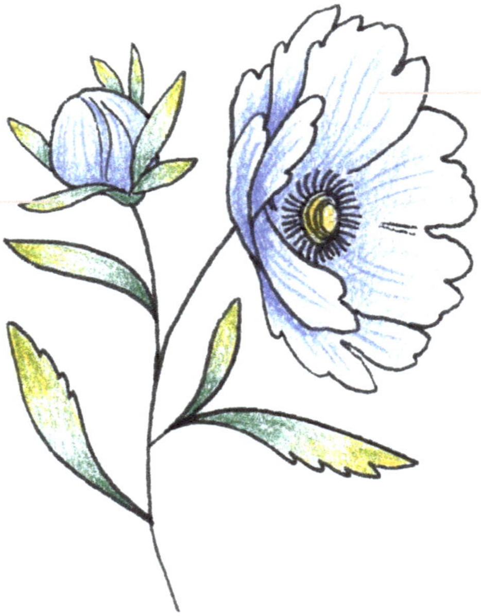

Color Washes
To get a light wash of color, push your pencil back and forth with a light touch. To make a darker mark, gradually increase the pressure. In this flower, I made the center of the flower deep blue, decreasing my pressure to lighten the blue as I moved toward the tips of the petals. I also used this technique in the yellow buds.

In the space here, draw a simple flower or object with pen, and then color it using the above colored pencil techniques.

WATERCOLOR

Watercolor is a very organic, versatile medium. It does require some extra tools, including a jar of water, a palette, and a paintbrush, but it's a favorite among artists due to its flexibility and forgiving nature. Watercolors are available in cake palettes or individual tubes. I personally love the flow of watercolor, and there are a number of techniques you can use to create luminous, lively results.

Wet-on-Wet Blending
Thoroughly wet the brush and apply a layer of water to the paper, allowing it to soak in a bit. Then dip the brush in paint. Once the paint touches the water on the page, it will spread, creating beautiful, organic variation. Try this with a few different colors! I used this technique in the main flower, using reds, pinks, and yellows. Use less water for brighter colors and more water for muted colors.

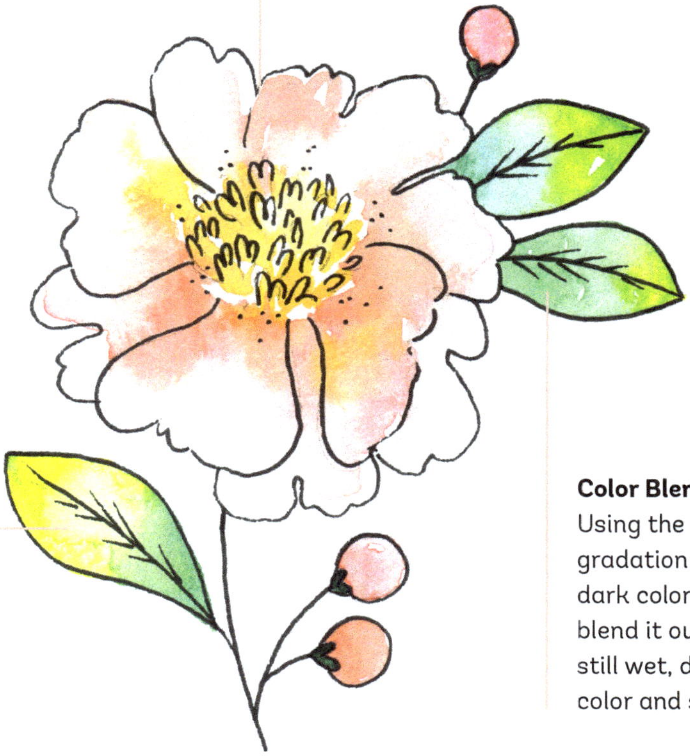

Color Gradation
Start by laying down a heavy amount of color. Then dip your brush in water and blend outward to create a soft, light tone.

Color Blending
Using the same methods as the gradation technique, lay down a dark color of paint and use water to blend it out. Then, while the paint is still wet, dip your brush in another color and stroke back into the first.

ACRYLIC

Acrylic is another versatile medium that requires a few tools, but it's very accessible for beginning artists. Unlike oils, acrylic is water-based, so it's very easy to clean up and doesn't contain any harsh chemicals. Acrylic does dry quickly, so you need to work quickly! If you like opaque, deep colors, add very little water to achieve handsome textures on your paper or canvas. You can make it more pliable and translucent by adding more water. In this example, I blocked in the flower with acrylic, using varying amounts of water.

Thick Application
Notice the intensity of this green paint application (top right). I used more layers of paint and just a little bit of water. In the flower example below, I also used a thicker application of paint in the flower petals. The strokes are almost undetectable.

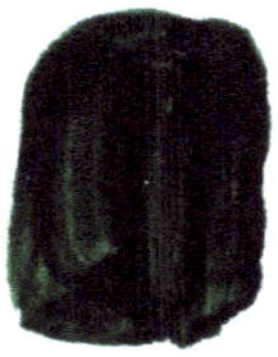

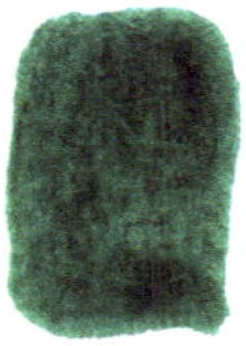

Thin Application
This application (below left) was painted with green acrylic paint mixed with a good amount of water. It's both lighter and brighter. I painted the leaves of the flower this way, and the brushstrokes are more visible. It all depends on what look you prefer in your own work!

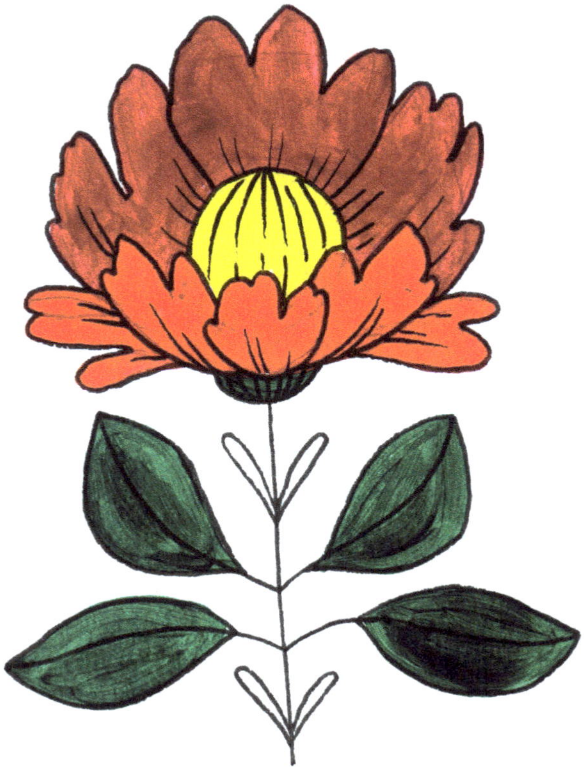

COMBINING MEDIA

You can combine media if you like! This example combines watercolor and fine-tipped markers.

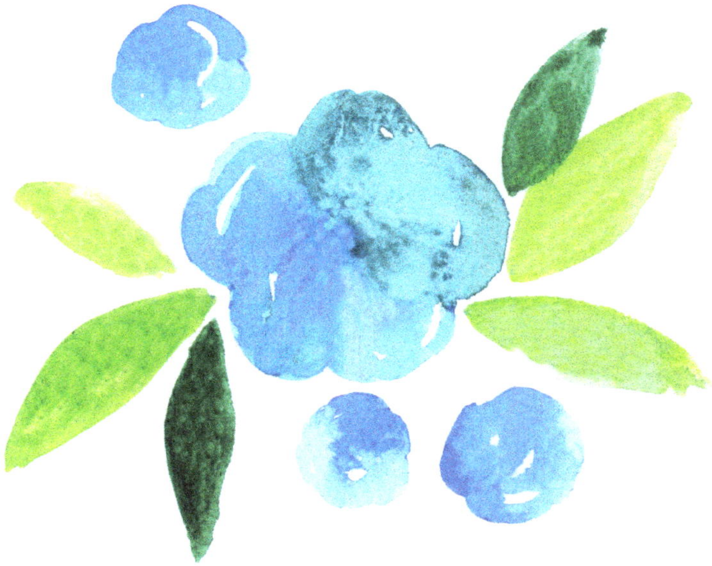

First choose a color palette and lay down organic, circular shapes to represent flowers. This doesn't have to be precise or planned—just have fun! Try to vary the shapes and sizes, and use the wet-on-wet technique to achieve some color mixing in the flowers. Next clean the brush in your water jar, and paint some leaf shapes. Feel free to vary the colors here too!

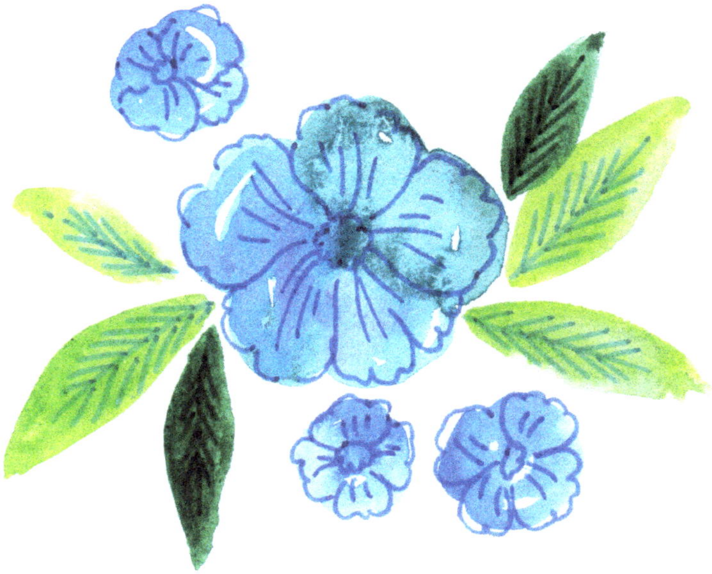

After the watercolors dry (very important!), select some complementary marker colors. Then, using the fine tip of the marker, draw the centers of the flowers, followed by the petals and leaves. Get creative! This is what experimentation is about.

WORKING DIGITALLY

Working traditionally offers so many options for creating work with color. However, if you'd like the option of creating multiple colorways or more freedom to experiment, working digitally is a good alternative.

In this section, you'll learn how to prepare your artwork for scanning and how to convert your artwork to a digital file. Then we'll jump into Adobe® Photoshop®, where I'll show you how to separate and colorize your line work, how to fill in with color, and how to create layers of colors and textures. It may sound daunting, but once you understand a few tools, you'll get the hang of working digitally very quickly!

PREPARING & SCANNING ARTWORK

The best way to scan artwork to be colorized is to scan in black and white. Draw your illustration roughly to the size you would like it to be. Once you have inked the illustration, erase any pencil marks. The cleaner your illustration is from the start, the less you will have to clean up during the digital process.

Put the drawing facedown in your scanner, and open your scanning program. (I use the Epson® Perfection V7 Scanner.) Every scanner has its own software for bringing the image into your computer. Once the program opens, select the black-and-white scanning mode and 300 dpi for the resolution.

Select preview. The scanner will show an image of your artwork. I recommend going into the Levels/Contrast tab in your software and using the sliders to create the most contrast possible. Scan the image.

The scanner will typically ask you to select a scanning destination on your computer, where the software will automatically drop all files scanned. I created a "Scans" folder on my desktop for this purpose.

If you want to scan in color, repeat this process in the color mode.

WHAT IS DPI?

Dpi means "dots per inch." It's the size at which your artwork will print. The minimum size required for printing is 300 dpi. I recommend always scanning at 300 dpi or above.

- 72 dpi is for screen resolution. Your image will appear great on screen but will print blurry and pixelated. Never scan at this size!
- 300 dpi is standard print resolution. This is considered best practice. Your drawing will print crisply and clearly up to the size you have originally drawn it.
- 600 dpi is very high resolution, double the size of standard. If you draw an illustration at 4" wide, scanning at 600 dpi will ensure that the illustration can be printed crisply and clearly at up to 8" wide.
- 1200 dpi is for really large printing needs, and it's typically the highest resolution available on a home scanner.

• ARTIST'S TIP •

IF YOU DON'T OWN A SCANNER, YOU CAN GO TO YOUR SCHOOL, LOCAL LIBRARY, OR A FEDEX® OFFICE LOCATION TO SCAN. BE SURE TO BRING A FLASH DRIVE WITH YOU SO YOU CAN SAVE YOUR FILE AND TAKE IT HOME WITH YOU!

CLEANUP & SEPARATING LINE WORK

Once the image has been scanned, go to your saved location and drag the file into Photoshop or the photo-editing software of your choice.

Once the image is in Photoshop, make sure it's set to the right orientation. If it isn't, correct it by going to the top bar and selecting Image > Image Rotation. Select the magnifying glass tool from the toolbar, and zoom in on your artwork by clicking on the image. It will most likely appear dirty, and you'll be able to see marks from the texture of the paper. We'll eliminate these, leaving just the black tones of the illustration.

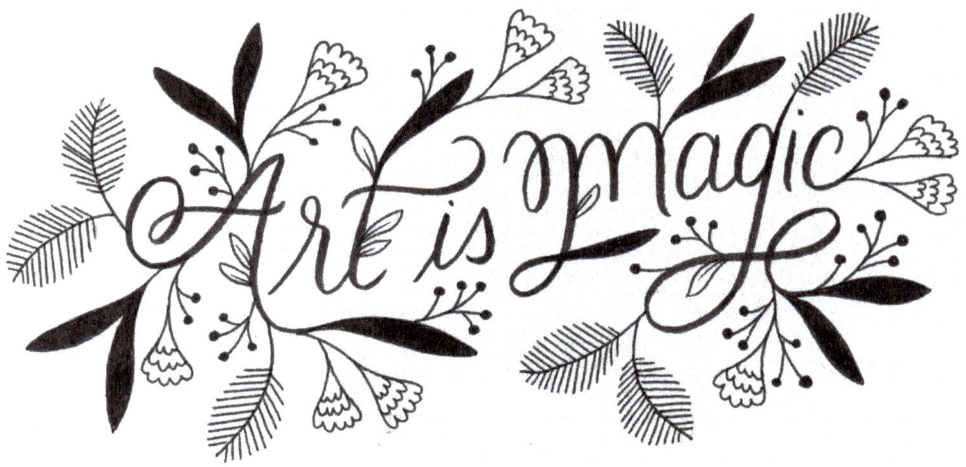

CLEANUP & SEPARATING LINE WORK

To start, go to the top menu bar and select Image > Adjustments > Levels. With the levels tool you can adjust the whites and blacks of an image. The black slider is on the left, and the white slider is on the right. Slide the white slider slightly into the center, keeping an eye on your artwork. You'll see the paper texture disappear! Be sure not to slide too far, or you'll start to erode the black tones. Then slide the black slider into the center. You should see the black tones become more robust. Do this a few times until you can no longer see paper texture, and the blacks look solid.

Next clean the image. Scanning sometimes leads to little dust particles and other debris getting into the drawing. Use the eraser tool from the toolbar to erase any remaining blemishes in your work. You can also use this time to correct any mistakes in the drawing.

If you make a mistake at any point, go up to the main toolbar, and select Edit > Undo!

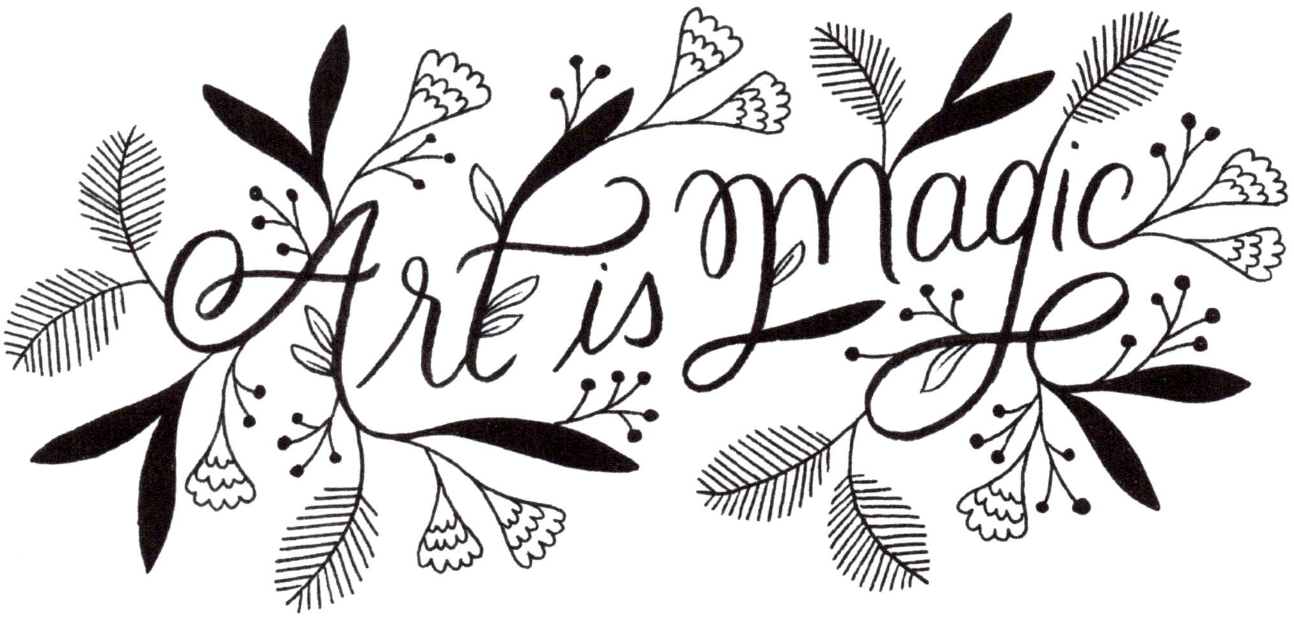

Now you should have a very clean, pristine black-and-white illustration that is ready to be separated from the background so you can color it. This process may seem complicated, but once you get the hang of it, it will become second nature!

Adobe offers a free thirty-day trial of Photoshop for new users!
Visit www.adobe.com/creativecloud/catalog/desktop.html.

Follow these steps:

- From the top menu, navigate to Select > Select All (or tap Command + A) to select the entire canvas.
- Then select Edit > Cut (or tap Command + X) to copy the selection and cut it out of the canvas.
- Go into Quickmask Mode by tapping Q on your keyboard. Tap it just once—nothing will change except for the screen mode icon in the bottom of the side toolbar.
- Select Edit > Paste (or tap Command + V) to paste the illustration into the Quickmask. You'll notice that your illustration is now in red, with a selection around the entire canvas. (Sometimes the selection is referred to as "Marching Ants," because that's what it looks like!)
- Tap Q again to exit Quickmask Mode. Now the red is gone, and all of the white areas of your original drawing are still selected. You should be able to see your drawing outlined with the "Marching Ants."
- Now invert the selection by going to Select > Inverse (or tap Command + Shift + I). You'll notice the "Marching Ants" move and condense around the drawing. Now the selection is on the black parts of your original drawing.
- Create a new layer by going to Layer > New > New Layer (or tap Command + Shift + N) or by tapping the square icon in the layers panel in the bottom right of the screen (next to the trashcan). We'll put the illustration on a new layer above the background layer so we can color it!
- Almost done! Notice that at the bottom left of the side toolbar are two swatches of color: black on top and white behind it. The top color is the active color. You can change the color by double-clicking on the swatch. For now, leave it as black. Fill with black by tapping Option + Delete on the keyboard. You will see your drawing appear!
- Finally, go to Select > Deselect (or tap Command + D). The "Marching Ants" will disappear. Now your artwork is separated away from the background and ready for color!

ADDING DIGITAL COLOR

The trick to adding color is separating the line work, like you just did. Before adding color, you need to lock the transparent pixels, which will ensure that you can only color on the active illustration. We've already separated it from the background, so go to the Layers panel in the bottom right side of your screen, and make sure the layer that has your artwork is selected. Above the layer is a set of four icons; the first icon is a checkerboard. Click on this. You'll see a lock icon appear on your artwork layer. Now the only thing you can color on is the artwork.

Select the brush tool from the side toolbar. To start, use the basic brush, which is already loaded. Go down to your color swatches, and double-click the top swatch. Use the Color Picker to select any color you like—except black or white! Click OK.

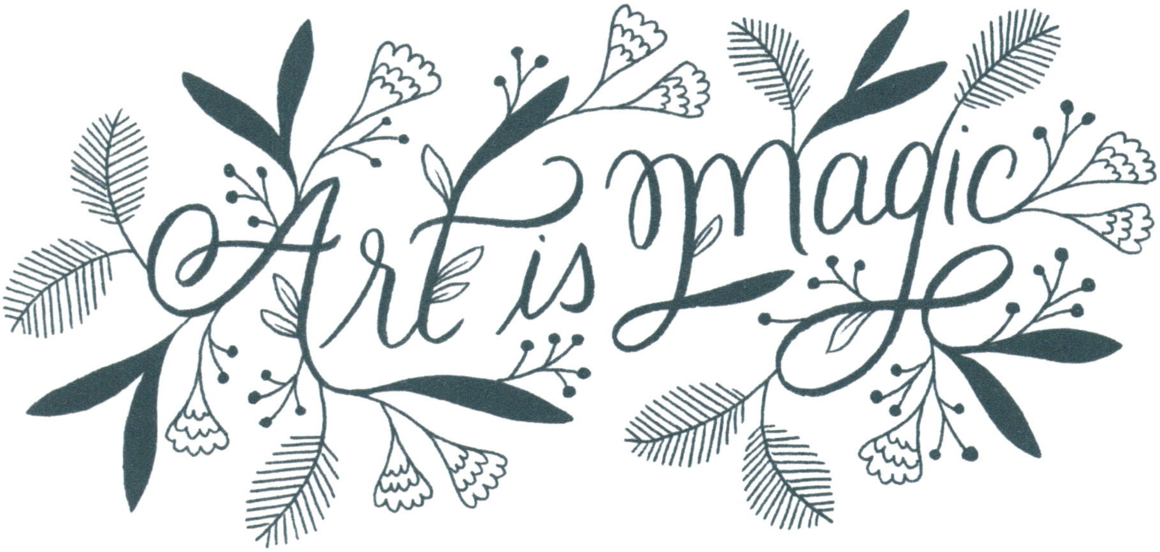

Now start to color over the illustration. Notice how only the black parts are recolored! That's because you told the program that you only want to change the active pixels—in this case, the drawing. Color until you've filled the whole illustration with new color. You can also tap Command + Delete to fill the entire illustration with the same color.

• ARTIST'S TIP •

IF YOU NEED TO INCREASE THE SIZE OF THE BRUSH, RIGHT-CLICK ON THE SCREEN AND USE THE SCRUBBER TO INCREASE THE BRUSH. YOU CAN ALSO TAP THE] BRACKET KEY ON YOUR KEYBOARD.

Next let's talk about clipping masks. Essentially, this technique means that we'll create a new layer with a different area of color, and then "clip" it to our illustration. I use this technique in all my finished illustrations so that I can utilize multiple colors with flexibility.

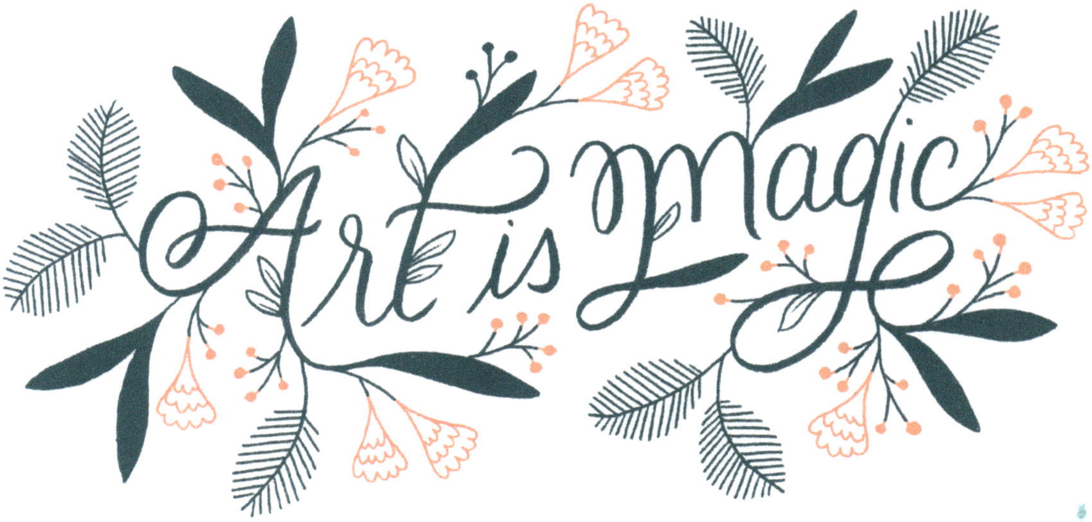

First create a new layer in the layers panel by clicking on the new layer icon in the bottom right corner of the panel. You'll see the new layer pop up on top of the original layer. Double-click the name of your original layer and name it "Lines." Then click on the new layer, and name it the color of your choice. I'm going to use pink for my new layer, so I name it "Pink." Then, with your mouse, hover between the two layers in the layers panel while holding down the Option key on your keyboard. You'll see an arrow with a white rectangle; when you see it, click. The new layer becomes "clipped" to the lines layer.

Don't lock the transparent pixels yet! Instead, take your brush and color the areas of the drawing that you want to be pink—or the color of your choice. When you're finished, lock the transparent pixels.

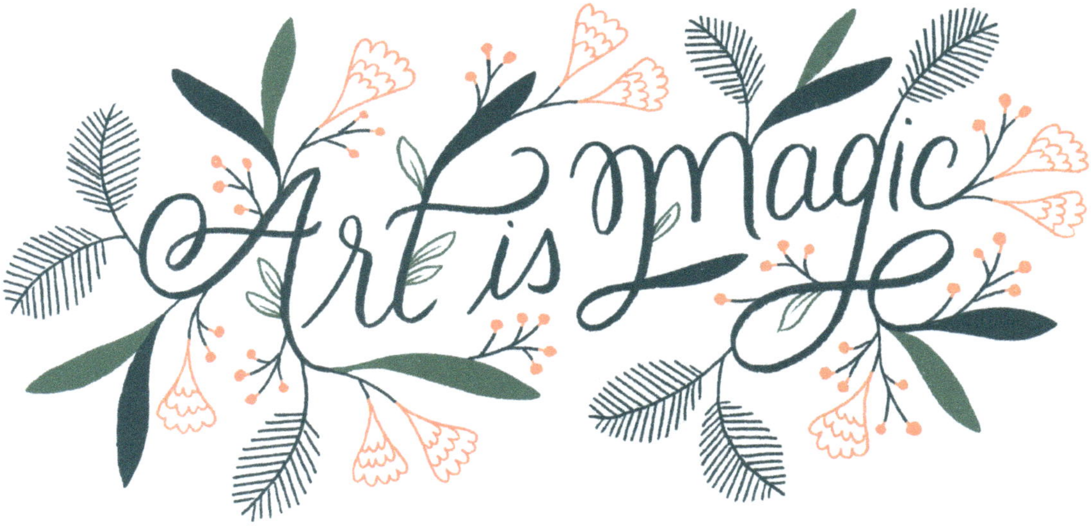

Now repeat this process with another color. Add a new layer, label it with the color name, and paint in those areas of color. I decided to paint some of the long, thin leaves a different color. If you make a mistake, use the eraser tool (or tap E on your keyboard) to erase it. Because the colors are clipped to the illustration, all that erases is the color, not the drawing!

To finish the illustration, add a few color fills underneath the lines layer. To do this, first create a new layer. Now grab that layer in the layer panel and drag it down to the bottom so it is underneath the lines layer. Now everything in this layer will go under the drawing. Select a new color and name the layer that color—in my case, mint!

Then fill in any areas you'd like with the brush. You don't have to clip this to the lines layer—clipping masks can only go in a downward direction. This will be its own layer, sitting below the line drawing.

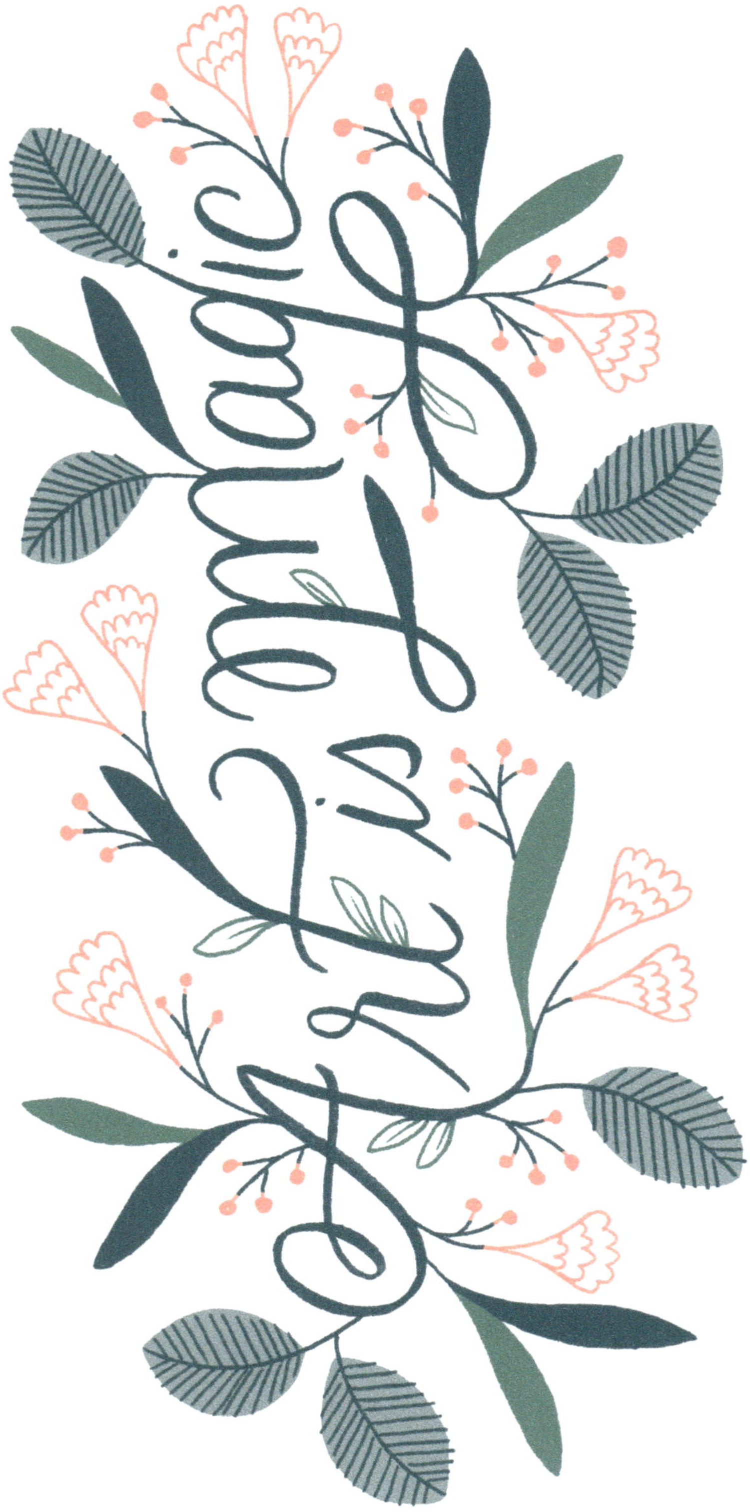

Finish the illustration by adding as many colors as you'd like—either above, clipped to the lines layer, or below as fills. Here's my finished piece. Don't forget to save your work!

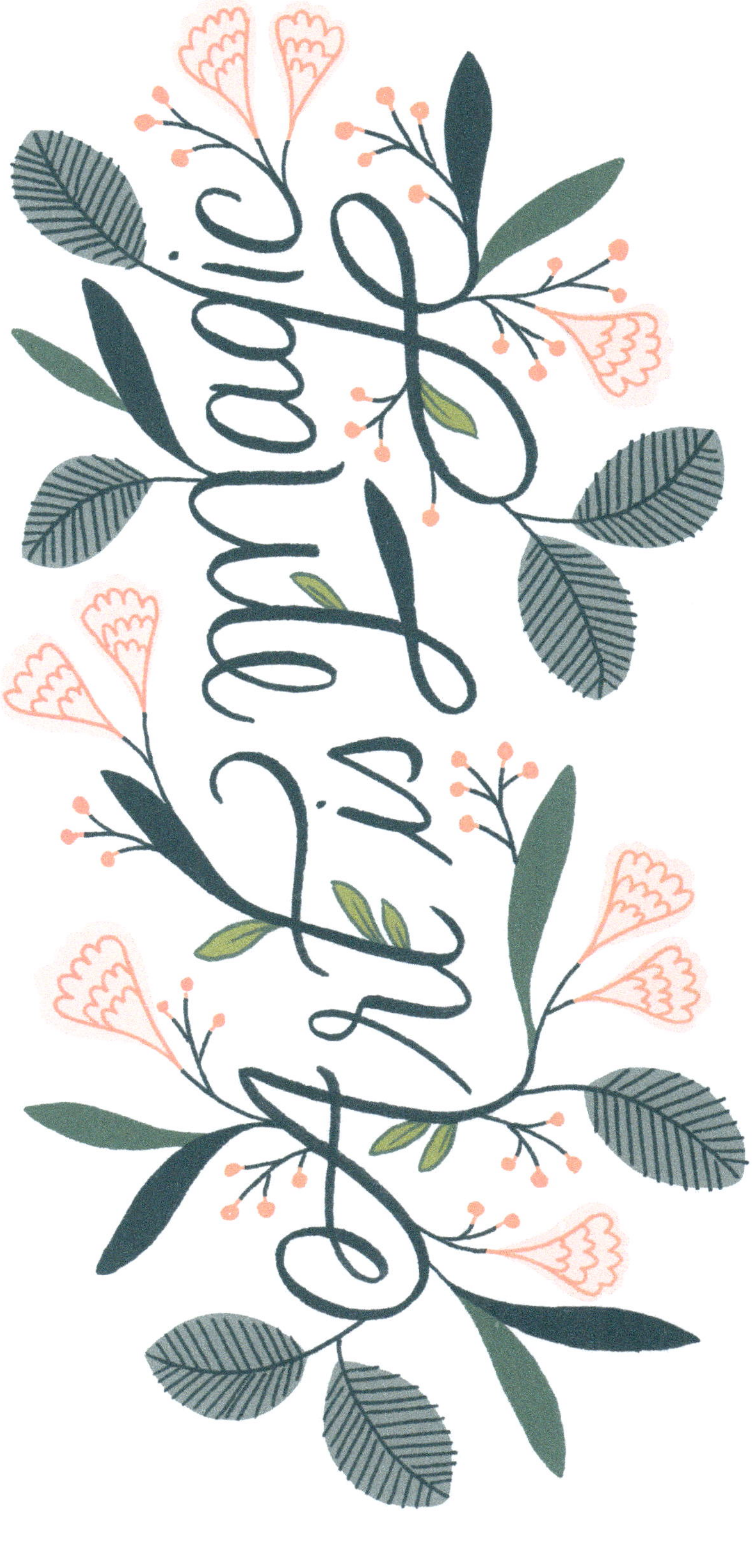

BORDERS, BANNERS

& LETTERS

BORDERS & BANNERS

Borders are a fun way to add interest to your drawings or doodles! Many people use them to embellish bullet journals or planners, and you can add borders to any illustration for instant polish and a framed feel. You can add an entire border, or you can create corner accents. In this section, I will demonstrate how to draw both simple and complex borders and banners, as well as how to approach corner accents. Try this easy step-by-step tutorial to warm up!

1. Use a ruler to draw a straight line with your pencil.

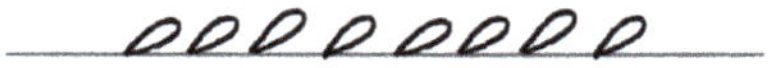

2. With your pen of choice, draw teardrop shapes along the top of the line. For best results, try to make them the same size, angle, and width apart.

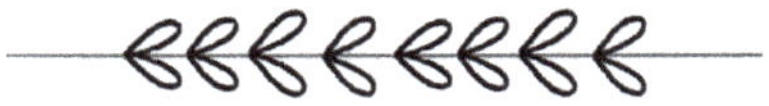

3. Then mirror the teardrop shapes along the bottom of the line.

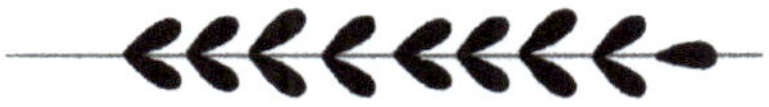

4. Fill in the teardrop shapes with your pen. When you're happy with the length of the border, add an end cap—this could be anything: a circle, diamond, triangle, or flower. I added another teardrop.

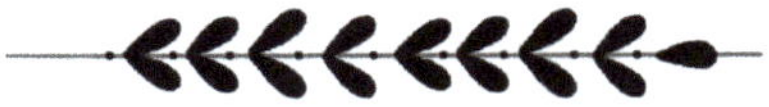

5. For extra interest, add little dots in between the teardrops.

6. After you're satisfied with the border, erase the pencil line and you're done!

SIMPLE BORDERS

Use a ruler to draw a straight line with your pencil. Draw a small semicircle with your pen.

Repeat the semicircle until you reach the end of the line. It's okay if they're not totally uniform—the hand-drawn quality is what makes it special!

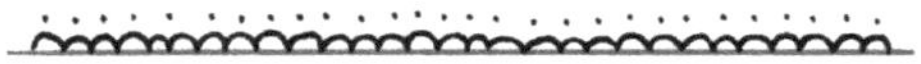

Add dots to the top of each semicircle for added interest.

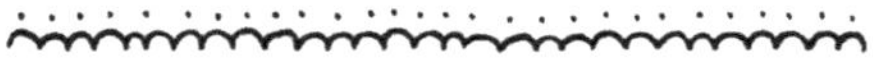

After you're satisfied with your border, erase the pencil line!

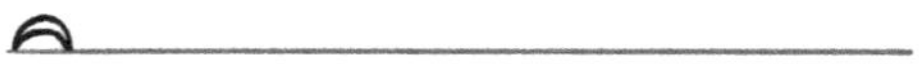

Use a ruler to draw a straight line with your pencil. Draw a small semicircle in pen. Then draw a slightly larger semicircle over the first.

Repeat.

Keep drawing these scaled semicircle sets until you have reached the end of the line.

After you're satisfied with your border, erase the pencil line!

Try doodling some of these other simple borders: small triangles, bunting, crisscrosses, hearts, lace, sunbursts, and feathers. Or make up your own!

PRACTICE HERE

ADVANCED BORDERS

Use a ruler to draw a straight line with your pencil.

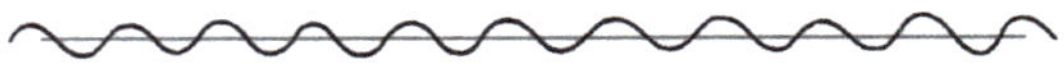

Draw a wavy line over the pencil line with your pen. Try to evenly space the peaks and valleys.

Draw a little leaf on each peak and valley.

Add extra leaves randomly to create interest.

Add a dot between each peak and valley along the center line.

After you're satisfied with your border, erase the pencil line!

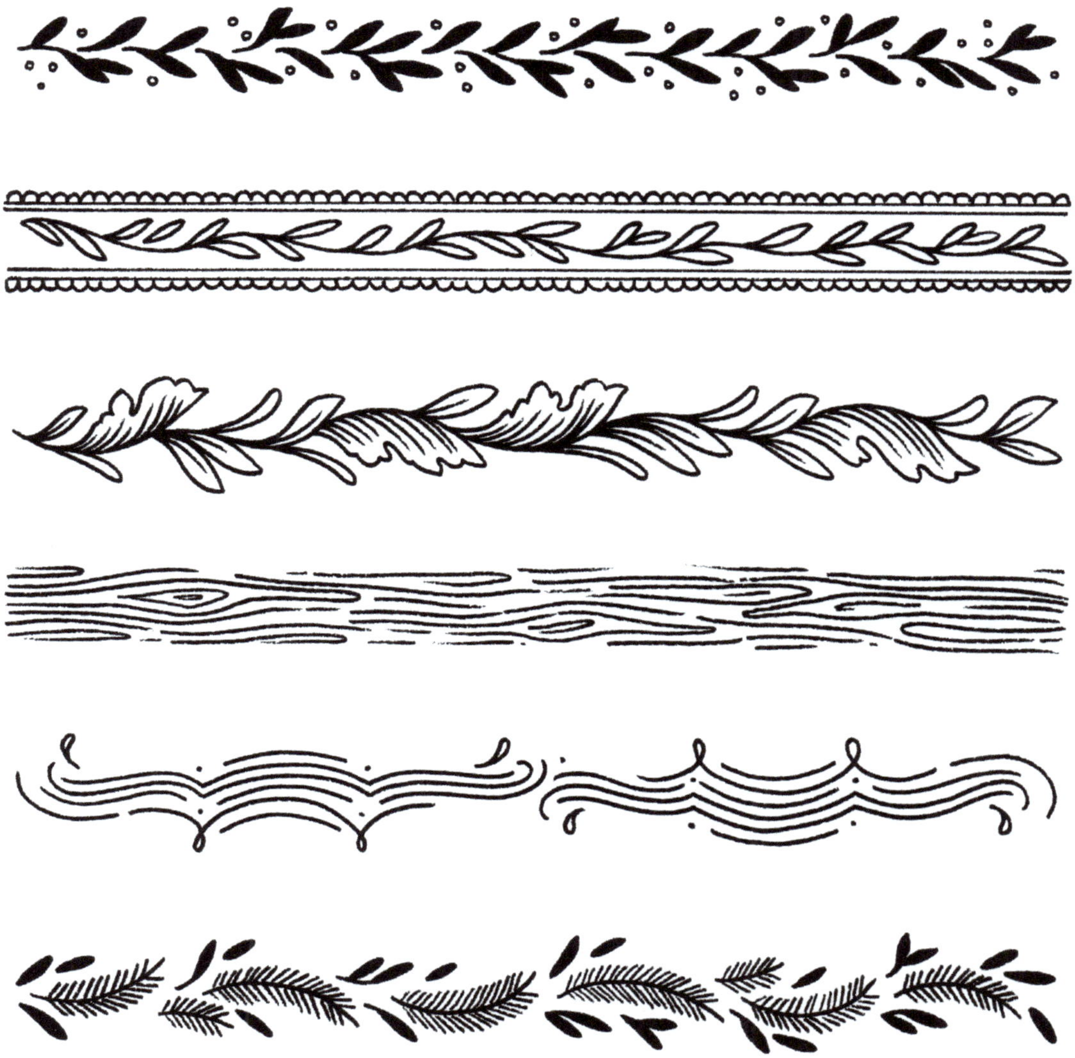

Using the techniques you've learned, try practicing the more advanced borders above, which include the following: wreath, leaves and lace, garland, woodgrain, filigree, and foliage.

CORNER BORDER ACCENTS

Use a ruler to draw a 90-degree corner with your pencil. I find corners are easiest to work with when I have a guide! With your pen, draw two sets of arched lines, keeping them about the same size and parallel to the guide.

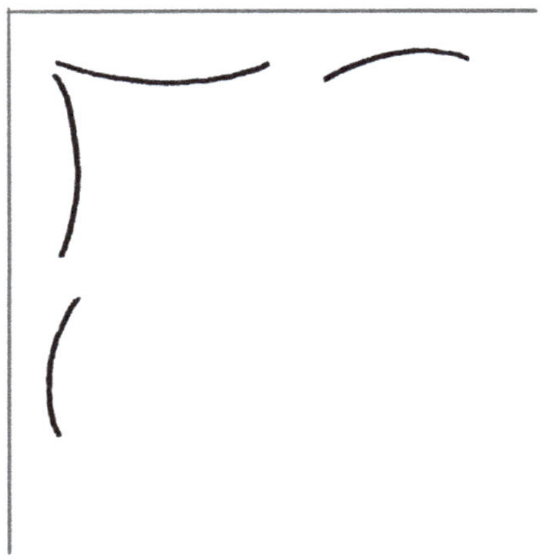

Add leaves and pen strokes to the lines to create the look of vines and foliage.

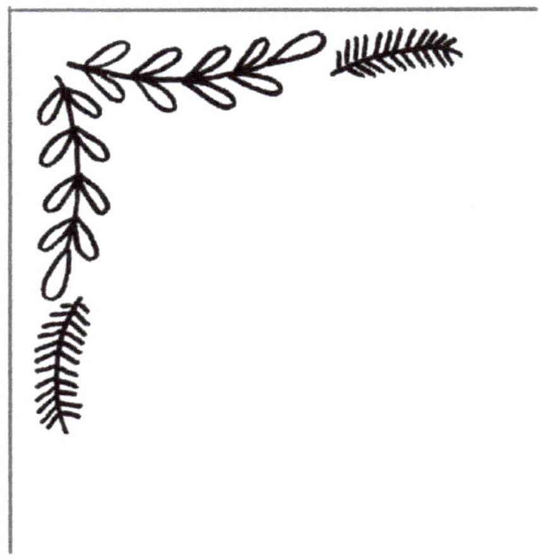

Add even more leaves to fill out blank areas.

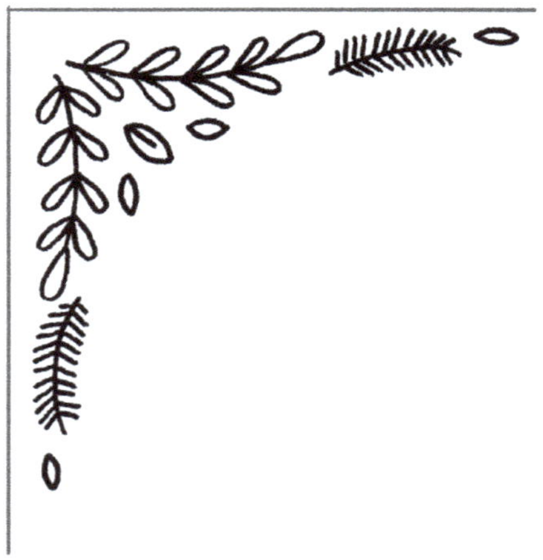

Keep an eye out for little open areas where you can add interest—add small circles or dots in those places. After you're satisfied with your corner, erase the pencil lines!

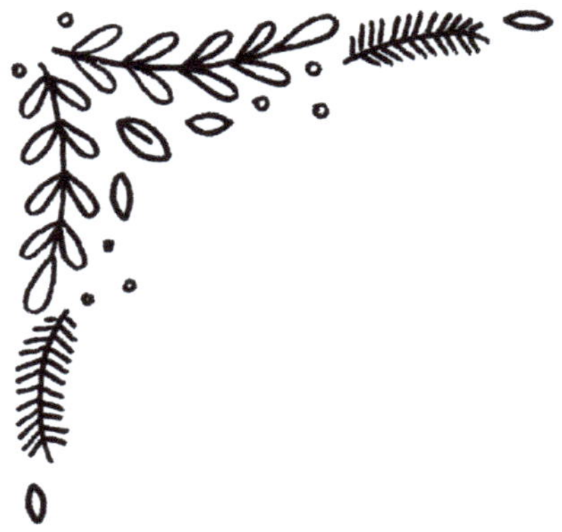

These corner accents are all different, but they follow the same principles of mirroring each element on a 90-degree angle. You can combine elegant corners with straight borders to create a whole, unique border. You can even mix and match—it's all about experimentation and having fun!

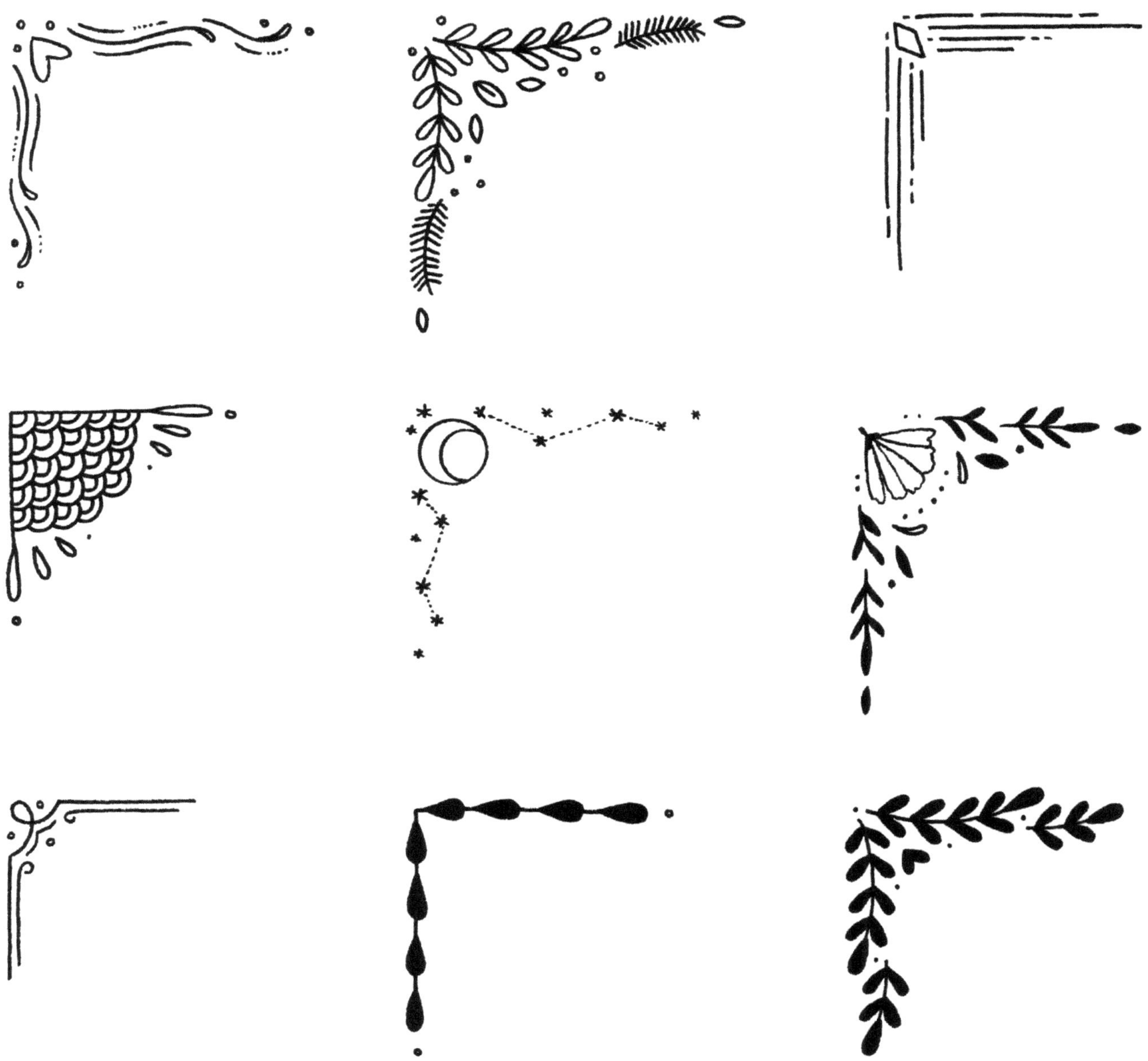

SIMPLE BANNERS

Banners are a great way to add interest to your illustrations, especially when paired with lettering. Once you learn the basic principles of how to create simple banners, you can extrapolate from there and create complex banners for your artwork.

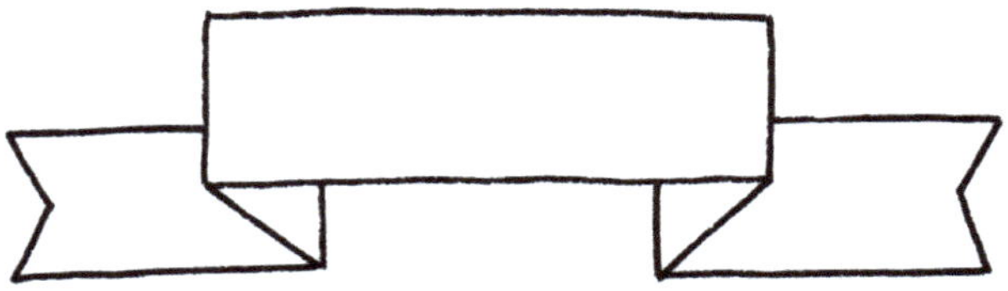

1. Draw a small, thin rectangle. Move halfway down the height of the rectangle and draw a rectangle on each side, making the ends into a flag shape, as shown. They should be about the same width as the original rectangle.

2. Connect the top rectangle to the bottom rectangles with two 45-degree lines, as shown. Voilà—a very simple but elegant banner!

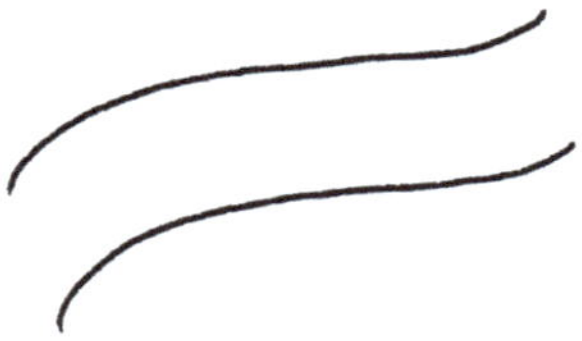

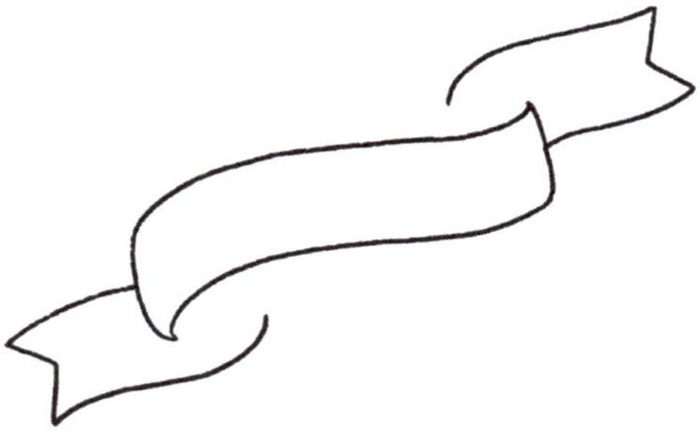

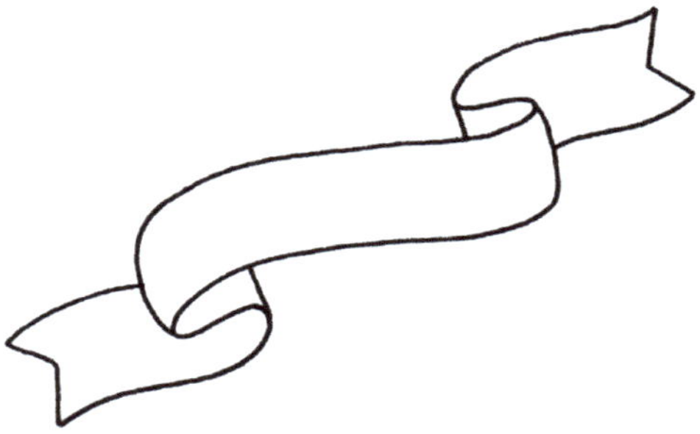

1. Draw two curved, parallel lines.

2. Using the same technique as the straight banner, draw the ends of the curved banner. The left side should be halfway down the original banner, and the right side should be halfway up the original banner. The ends should close like flags.

3. Finally, finish the curve connecting the banners. Don't forget to add parallel lines to the backs of the curves.

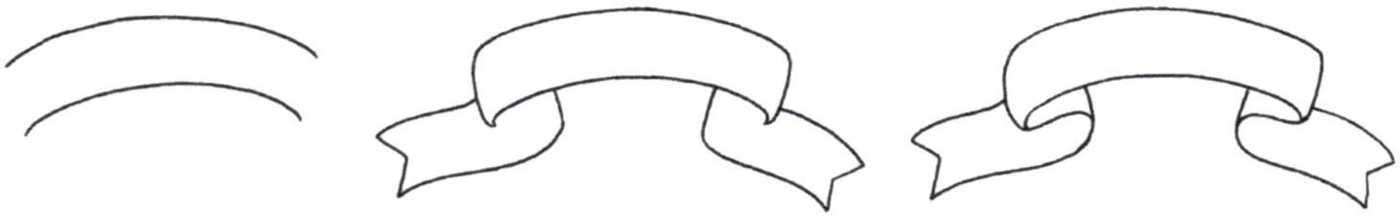

You can use these same techniques to create an arched banner, with both ends of the banner floating below.

PRACTICE HERE

• ARTIST'S TIP •

THE TRICK IS TO ENVISION THE BANNER AS A THIN STRIP OF PAPER IN ACTUAL SPACE—IT ALWAYS REMAINS THE SAME WIDTH, AND IT ALWAYS CURVES CONSISTENTLY.

ADVANCED BANNERS

1.

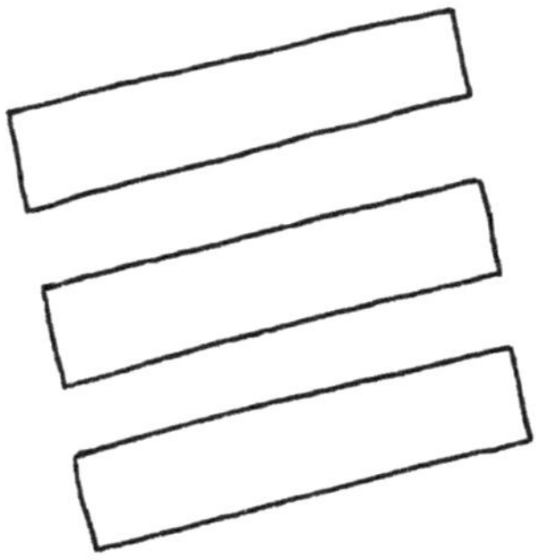

Draw three evenly spaced rectangles on a slant. It helps to keep the space between each banner the same as the width of the banners.

2.

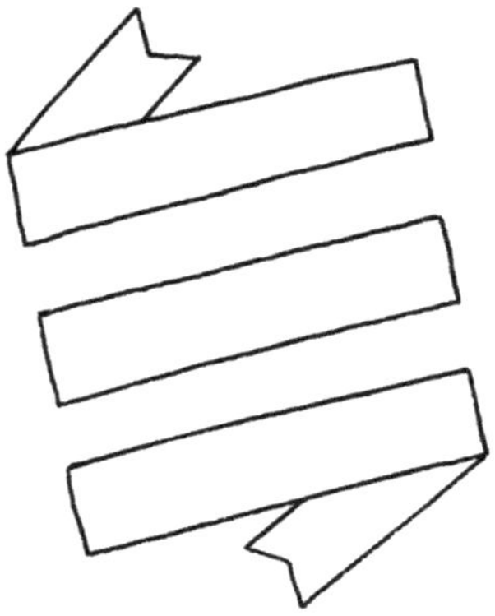

Add a flagged end to the top and bottom banners, as shown.

3.

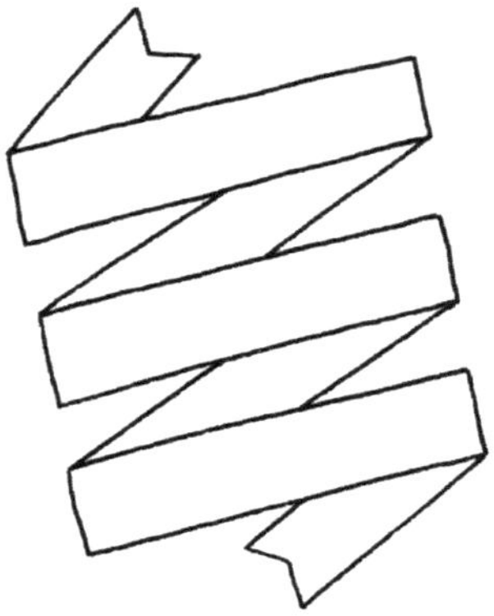

Finally, using parallel lines, connect each rectangle to the opposite side of the next rectangle, moving right to left.

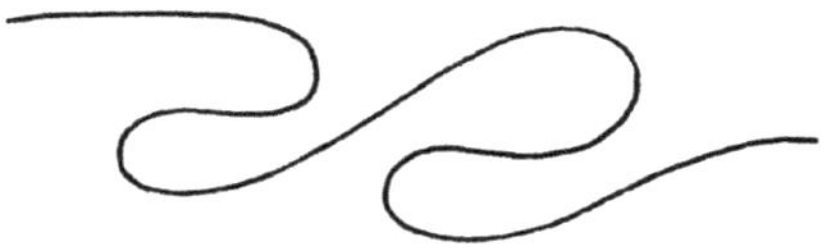

1. Draw a long, wavy line. Try to evenly space the loops of the line, while mentally planning out your banner.

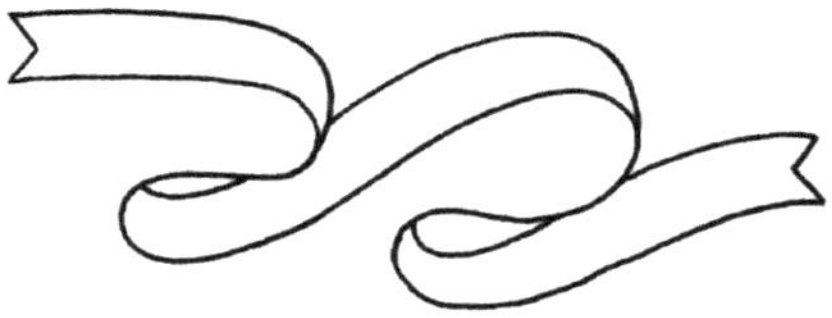

2. Draw parallel wavy lines matching the curves, as shown. Close the ends of the banner with flags.

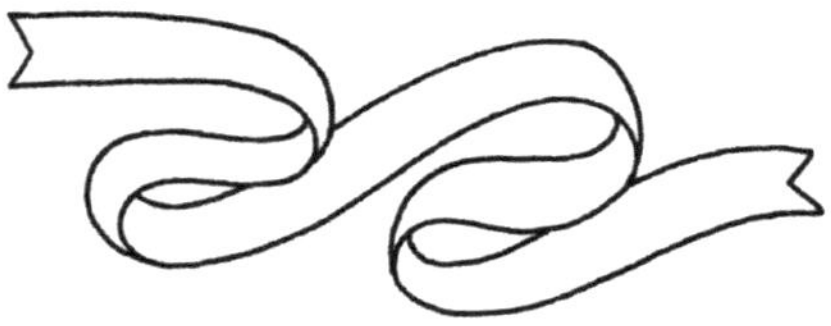

3. Then, using curved parallel lines again, connect the bottom sections of the banner to finish.

Here are some examples of more complex banners. Notice how all the sections of the banners are consistent in width, and all connecting lines are parallel to one another. Experiment with drawing some fancy banners to build your skills.

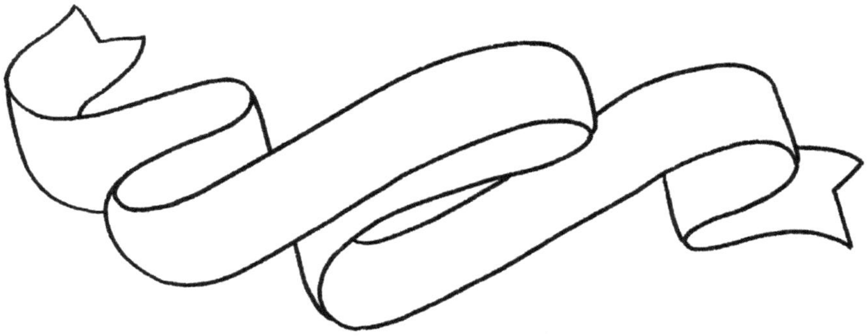

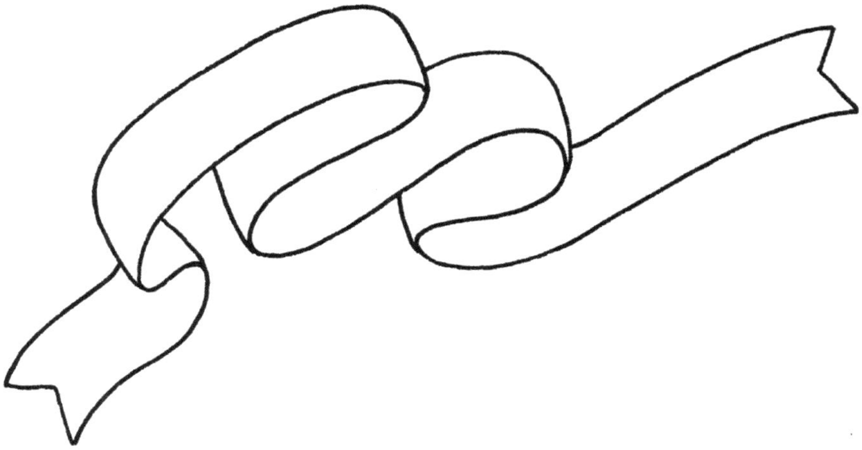

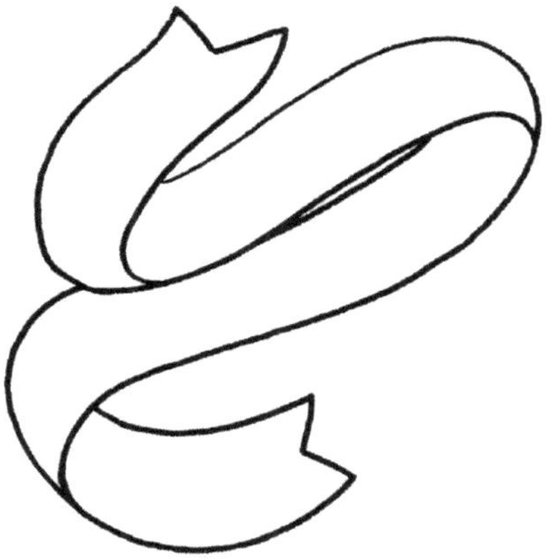

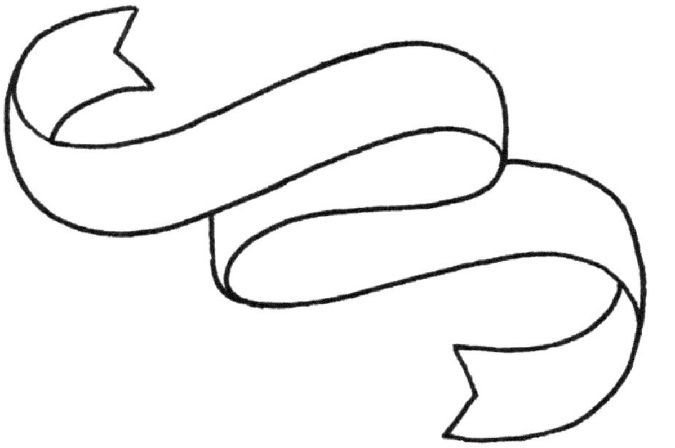

LETTERING

Lettering can make a wonderful addition to your artwork. You can use it as an accent to your illustrations, to create inspirational artwork with quotes, or as beautiful art on its own.

Here are the basic parts of letterforms.

1. Spine: the vertical backbone of the letter
2. Flourish: a fancy swirl or loop that connects seamlessly to the letterform
3. Ligature: when two letterforms are connected
4. Crossbar: a horizontal part of a letterform
5. Ascender: a part of the letterform that extends upward
6. Tail: an accent on a letterform, usually occurring at the end of a word
7. Descender: a part of the letterform that extends downward

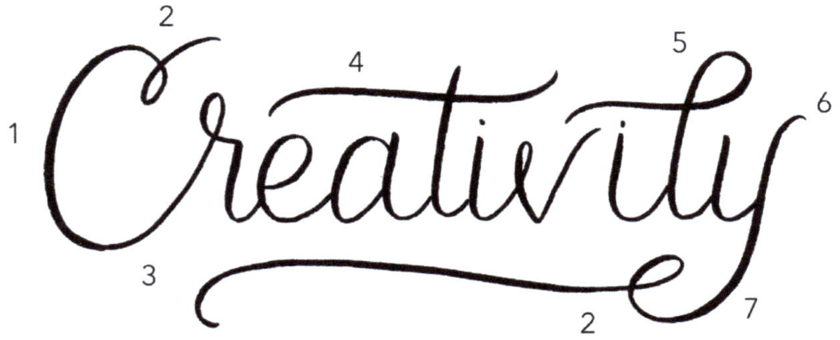

A flourish is a fancy loop or swirl the calligrapher creates—typically on capital letters—by drawing extra lines that circle around the letterform or other letterforms in the word. Making flourishes is fun and experimental and utilizes the same principles of light upstrokes and heavy downstrokes to achieve balance. Trace over the letterforms below, and then try it freehand to see what flourishes you can come up with!

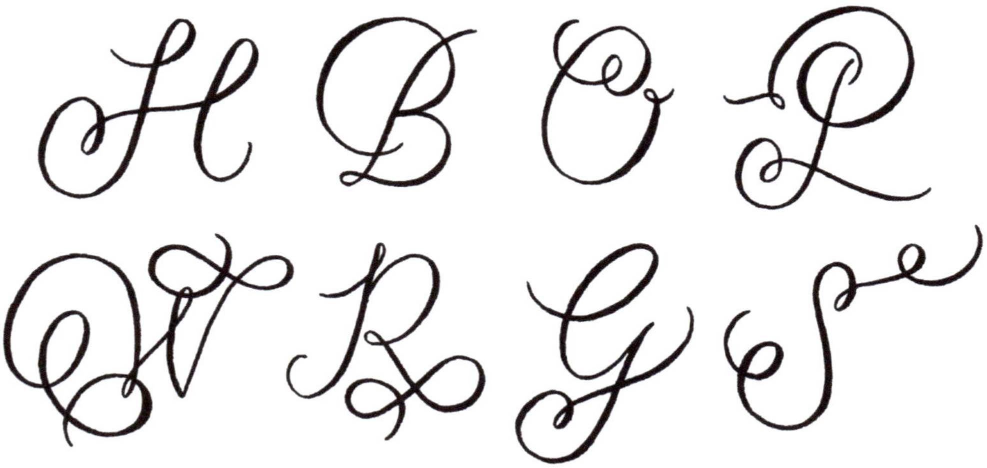

Script can be achieved either with a mono-weight pen (like a ballpoint pen) or a calligraphy pen. Here, I have used my Tombow Fudenosuke Calligraphy Pen to achieve varying weight within each letterform. When working with a mono-weight pen, draw the thick downstrokes with two lines, and fill in the space between. Try placing a piece of tracing paper over the alphabets below and trace the letters. Then recreate them in your sketchbook. Notice that the capital letters tend to have more swooshes or variations.

Remember: when moving up with your pen, you want to create a light, thin stroke. When moving down the letterform, apply more pressure for a thicker stroke. This creates a wonderful, elegant look in your lettering.

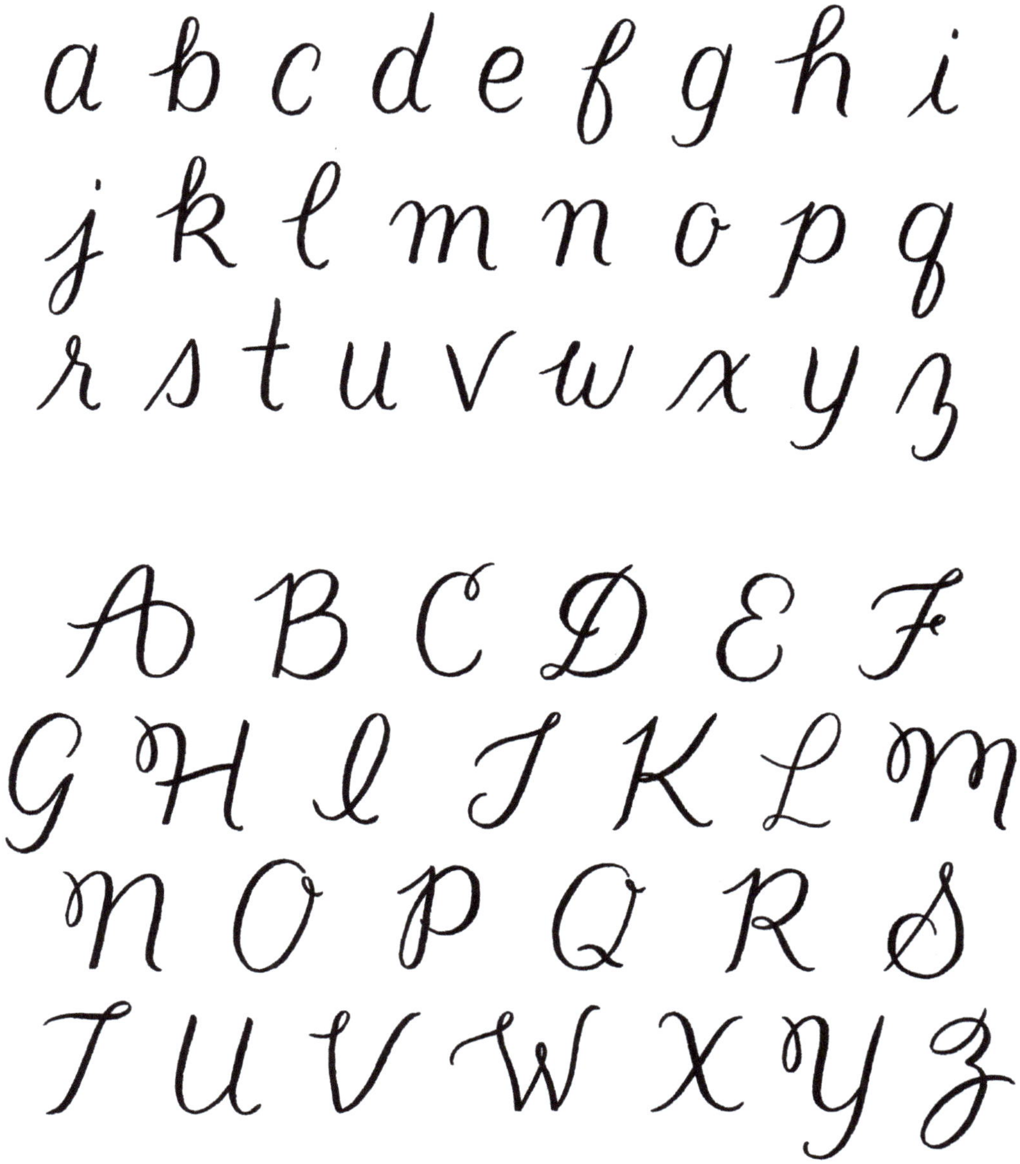

Ligatures occur when the calligrapher connects two letters in the same word in a unique and special way. Ligatures give a word extra personality and interest. They take some practice, but once you start to consider adding ligatures in your lettering, the possibilities are endless. Take a look at the ligatures below and see how they connect naturally—then try your own!

Letter coffee

fine fleek the

Hi or type

HAND-LETTERED DROP CAPS

A drop cap is a decorative element that appears as a special marker, usually in a novel or book. A drop cap can take many forms. In this example, the drop cap has decorative elements on the outside of the letter.

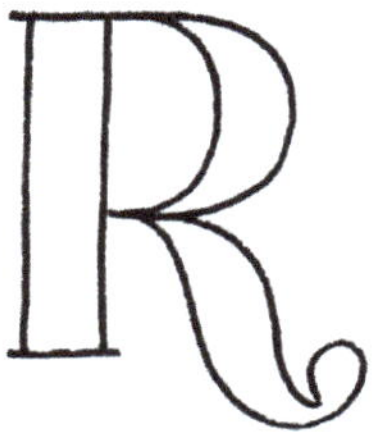

1. Start by sketching your letterform with a pencil. Then carefully ink the lines with pen.

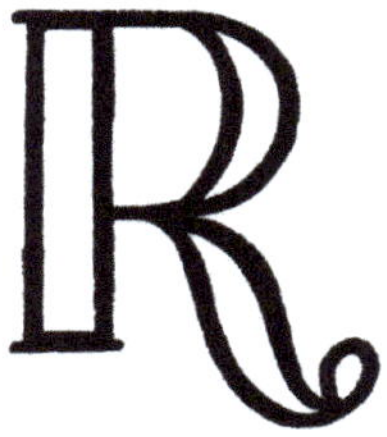

2. Thicken the inside of the letterform to give it some weight.

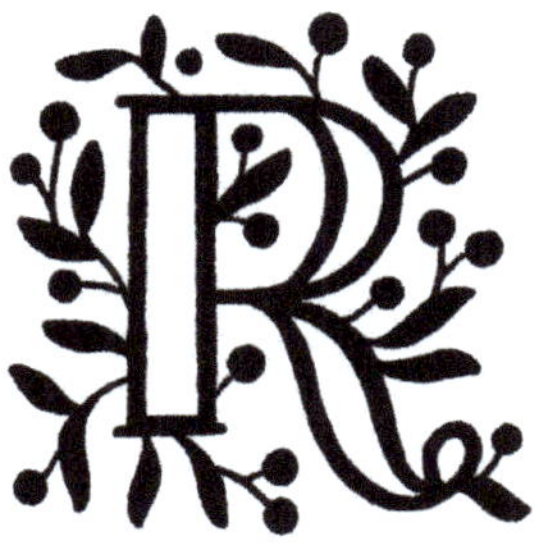

3. Add little leaves and berries to create a unique look. I usually stay in a circular or square shape around the letter.

4. To finish, consider adding dots in any blank areas. Add color, if you'd like! You could also ink the whole letter in color.

In this example, we'll explore customizing the inside of a letterform.

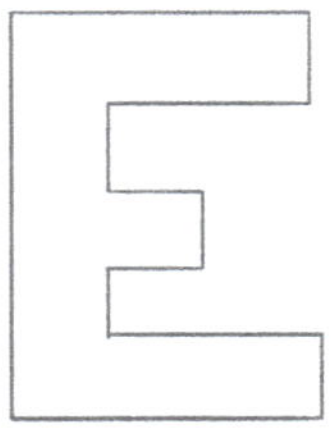

1. Start by sketching the letterform in pencil, but this time, don't ink the outline! We'll erase this later.

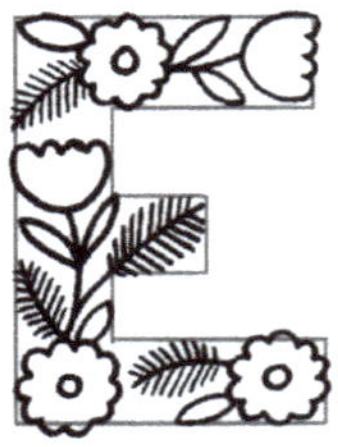

2. Switch to pen and start filling the space within the letter. I usually choose little clusters of flowers and leaves. Start by evenly spacing the flowers, and then add leaves, leaving some areas open for details. Make sure the design elements reach the guide outline to ensure that the final result still looks like the letter!

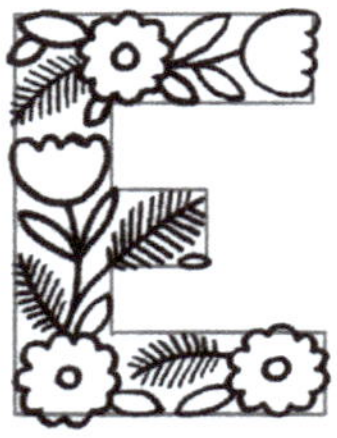

3. Add smaller leaves (or other elements) to fill out the blank areas, bringing them right up to the pencil guide.

4. Fill in the leaves, if you'd like, and add in little dots along any blank spaces of the guide outline. Finally, erase the pencil when the ink is dry. Presto—you have a really cool letterform!

As you can see, there are lots of different ways to explore hand lettering with drop caps. You can swirl lines around a bold letterform, create an elegant crest for a flourished capital, or do a more modern take with a bold, thick letterform. You could overlay a cluster of flowers for a cute initial or intertwine leaves and branches in the front and back of the letter—or even give your letter a theme!

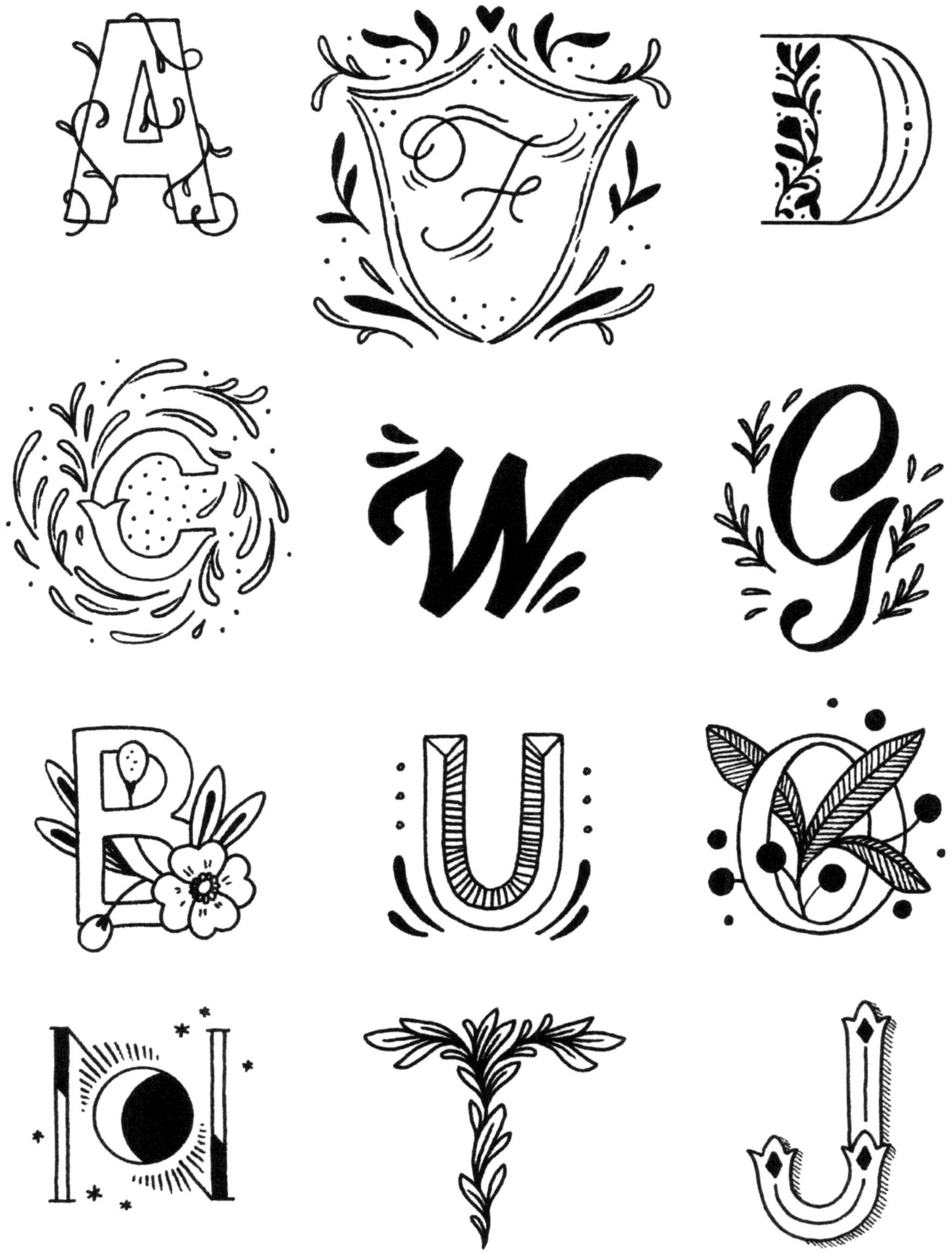

CREATIVE EXERCISE

LETTERED QUOTE & BANNER

Create a hand-lettered quote that includes at least one banner and some elements from the drop cap section. For my illustration, I created a fancy banner for part of the quote and then used techniques from the drop cap section to create the main word: Magic.

Try a quote of your own on page 47. Don't worry about perfection—this is an opportunity to practice and explore some of the new techniques you've learned!

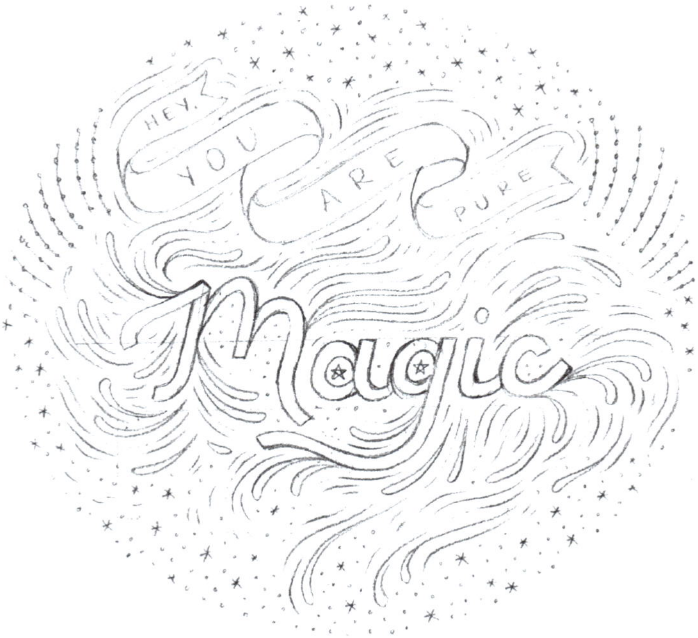

Here is my initial sketch. You can see how I mapped out the main word, sketched in the banner, and added all of the flourishes. This is the fun part!

I worked on inking the main elements first: the banner and the main word. On the main word, I drew the outlines first; then added the fill later.

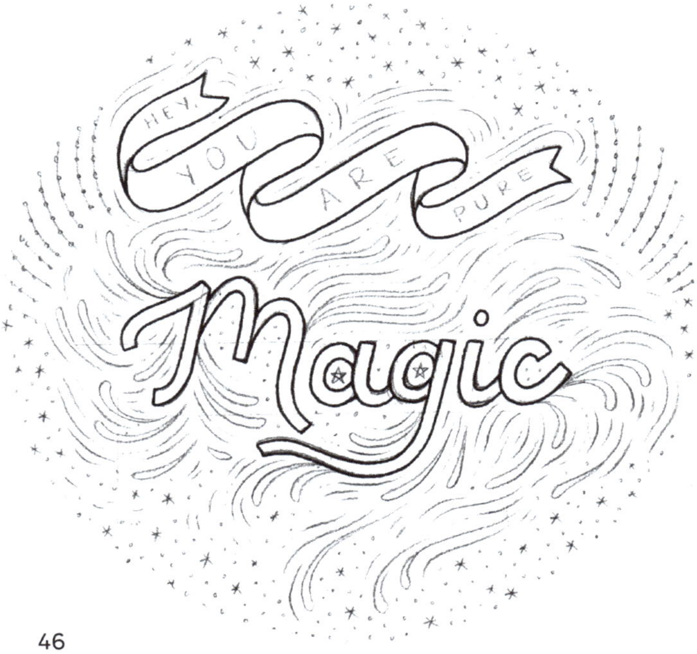

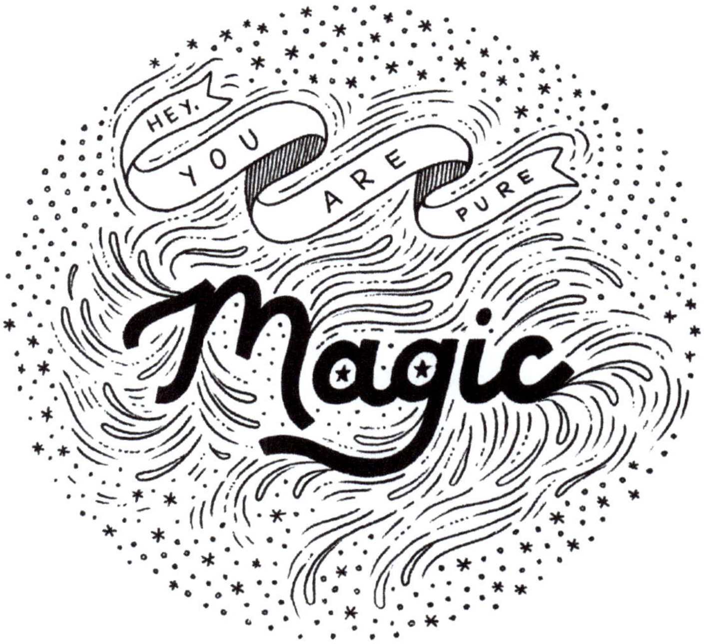

3. Here is the entire illustration finished in ink.

CREATE YOUR OWN LETTERED QUOTE HERE!

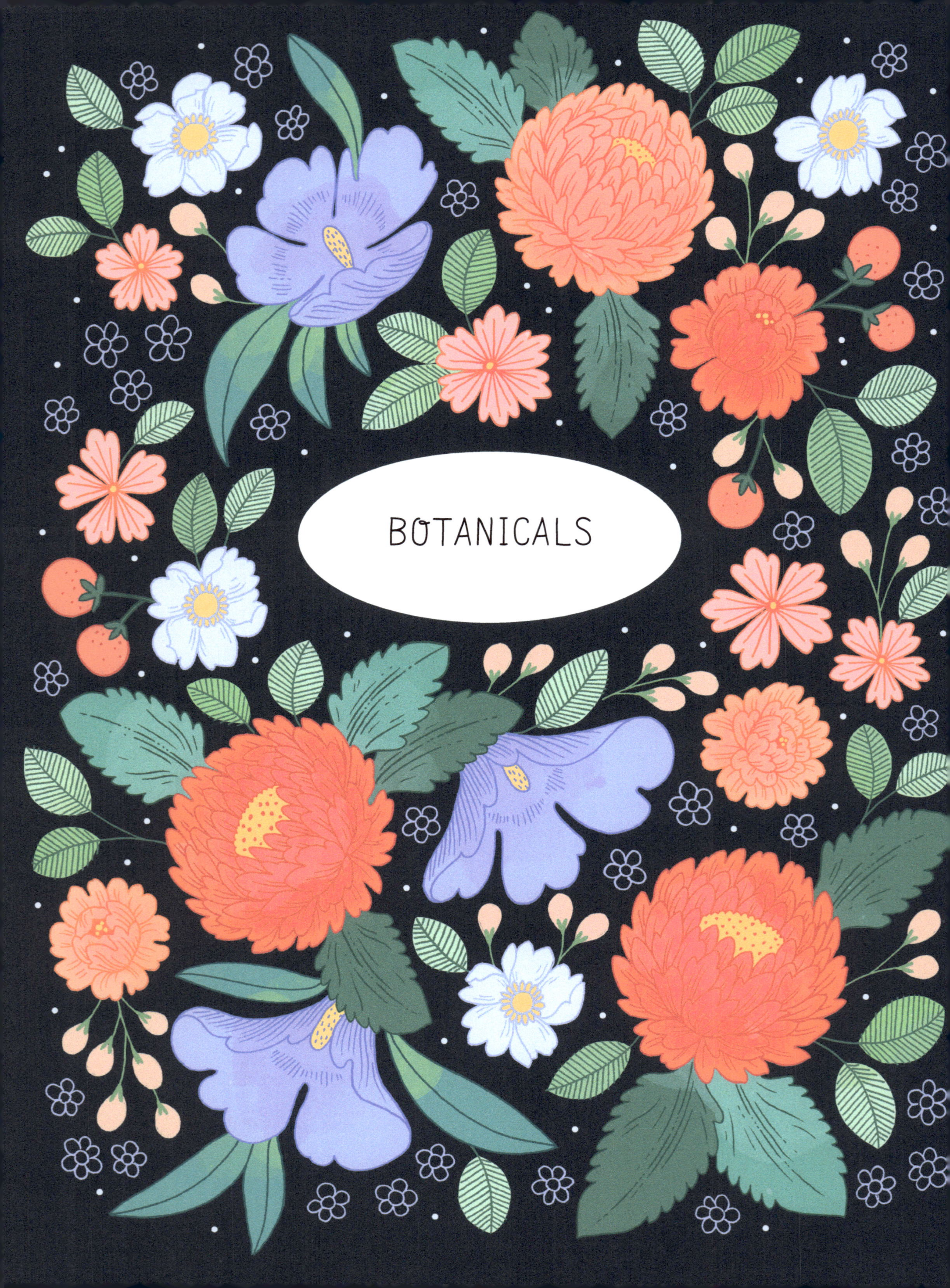
BOTANICALS

LEAVES & FLOWERS

In this section, we'll break down different types of flowers, plants, and leaves to their basic shapes; then we'll discuss how to visually organize them to create stunning floral compositions and illustrative accents. For practice, I highly suggest looking up reference photos to study different petal and leaf shapes—better yet, go out into your neighborhood or park for some life observation! Try the exercises below to warm up.

1.

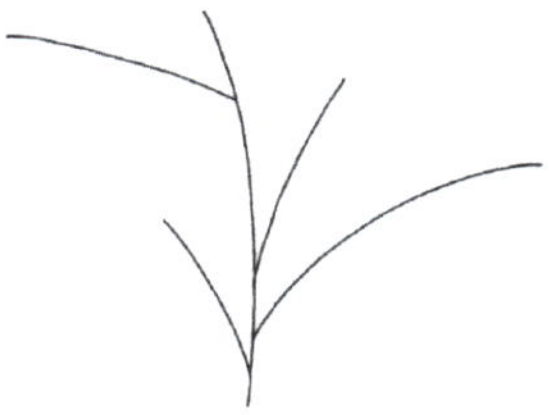

First draw the stem of the cluster with several offshoots for interest. Keep plenty of space for leaves and flowers.

2.

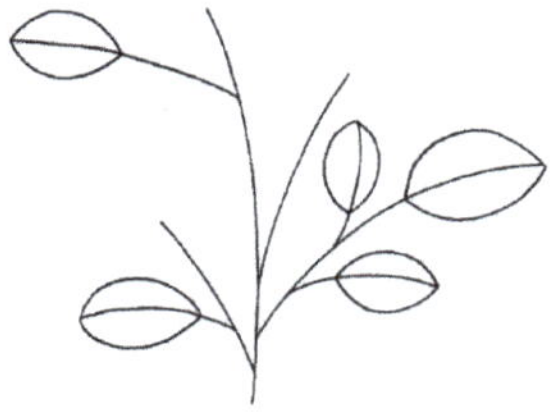

Add leaves to several stems. I draw these by drawing an arched line on each side of the end of a stem. Remember to leave room for the flowers! I like to draw floral clusters with three blooms—the odd number helps with visual balance and interest.

3.

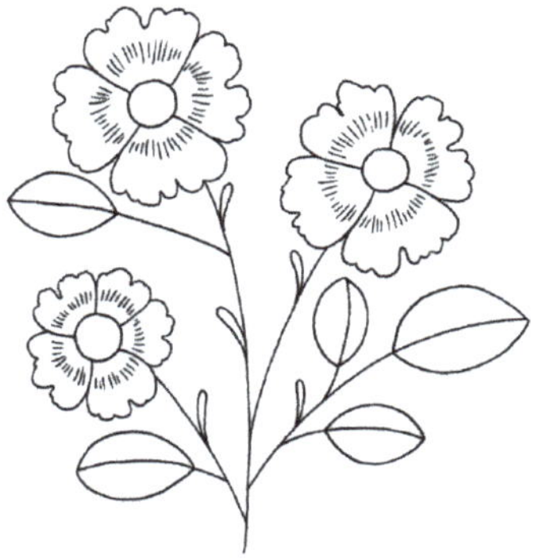

Draw the petals. We'll be exploring lots of different ways to draw petals and flowers! For added interest, I finish the cluster with little buds sprouting from the stems.

1.

Start with a straight vertical line for the center of the leaf.

2.

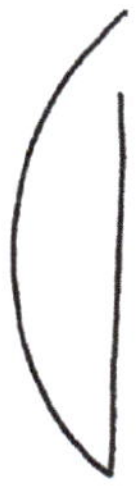

Draw a curved line on one side of the straight line. You can connect it to the top of the line or leave some space.

3.

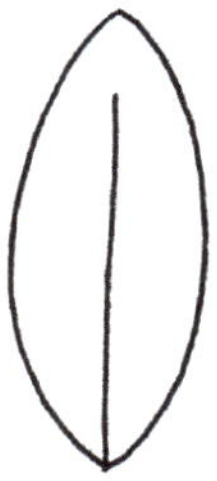

Mirror the curved line on the other side of the straight line. Connect it at the bottom.

4.

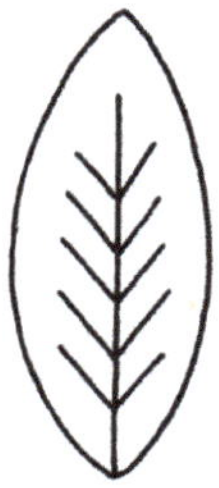

Add diagonal lines for the veins of the leaf.

SIMPLE LEAF VARIATIONS

Now try a different leaf shape, using the same principles! This time begin with a slightly curved line. On one side of the line, draw a dipping line. Keep the top pointed and the bottom rounded out. Then mirror that line on the other side.

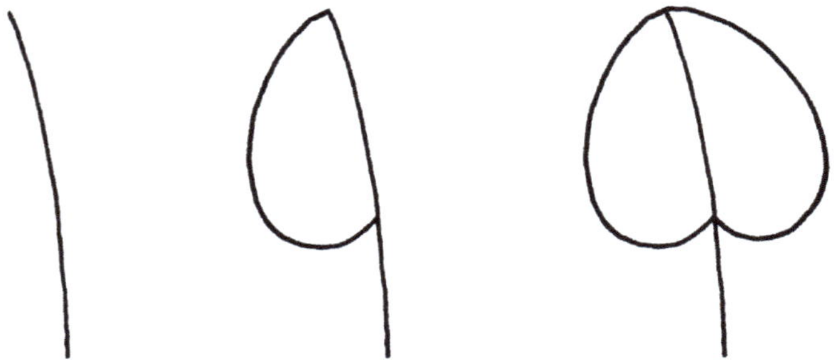

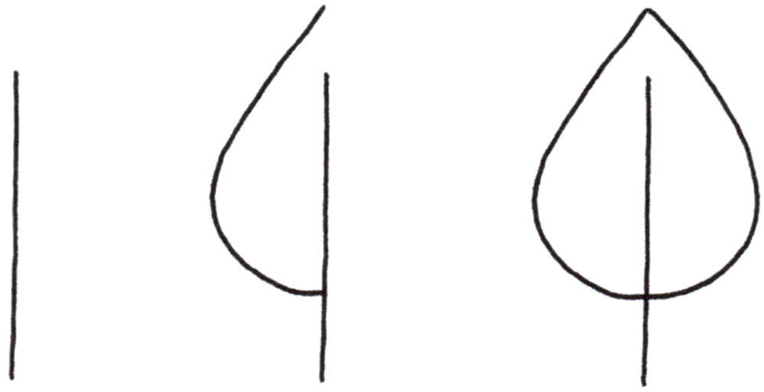

One more! Start with another straight line. Let's make this leaf a spade shape. Draw a rounded bottom and a pointed top on one side of the straight line. Mirror the same curve on the other side. You can even use this simple process to create complex leaf shapes. Many shapes in nature are symmetrical!

Leaf Shapes

Here are some examples of different leaf shapes found in nature. Notice how some are rounded, some are pointed, some are skinny, and some have many arms. There are infinite varieties!

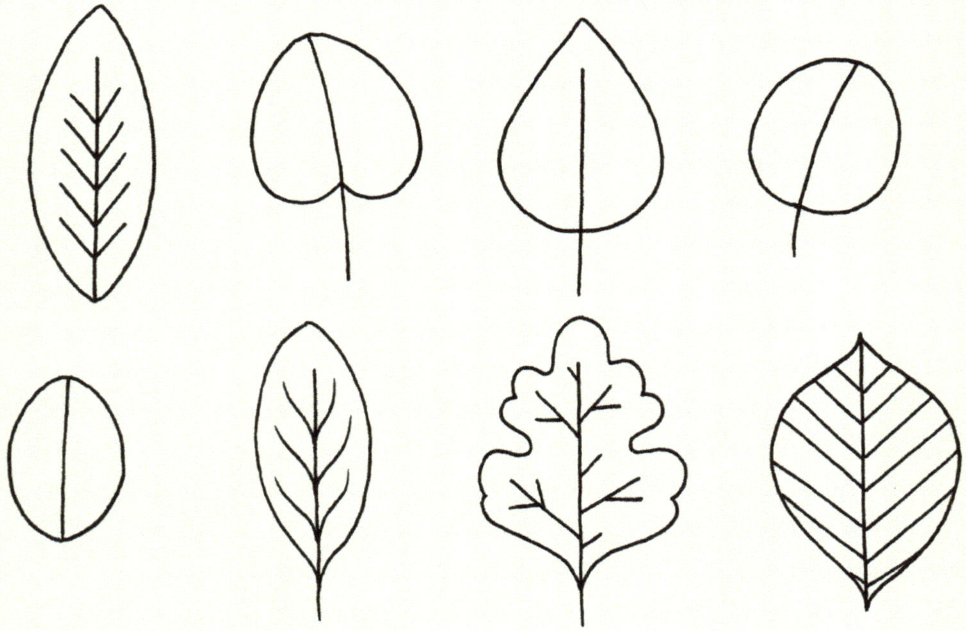

COMPLEX LEAF VARIATIONS

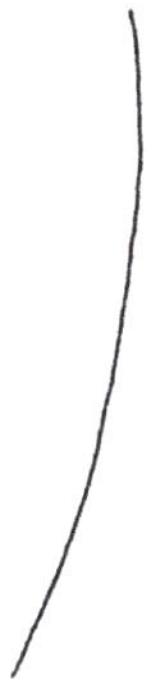

1. Draw a slightly curved line.

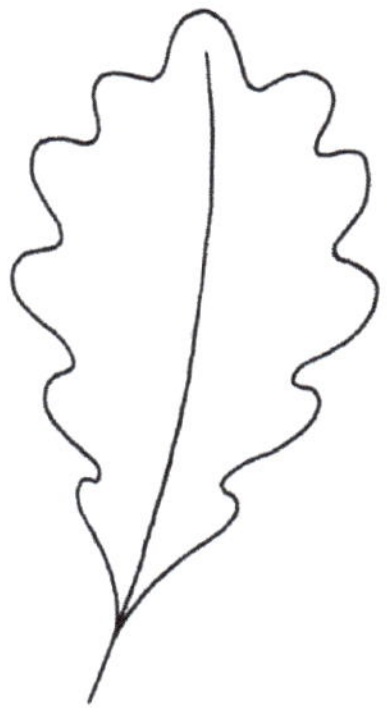

2. Using the same technique as you used for basic leaf shapes, draw a wavy line in an arc along one side of the center line. Mirror it on the other side.

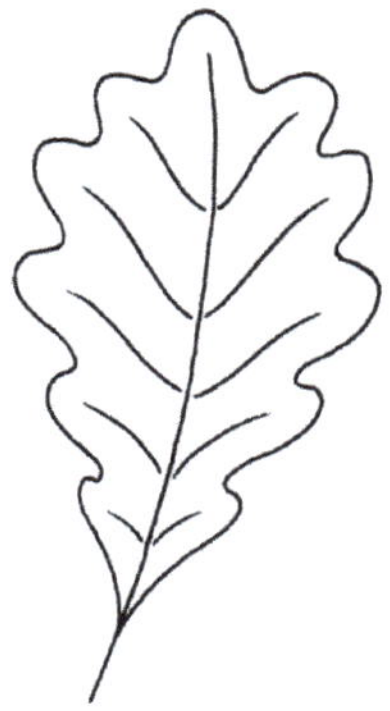

3. Drawing outward from the center line in a wave-like motion, create the veins of the leaf.

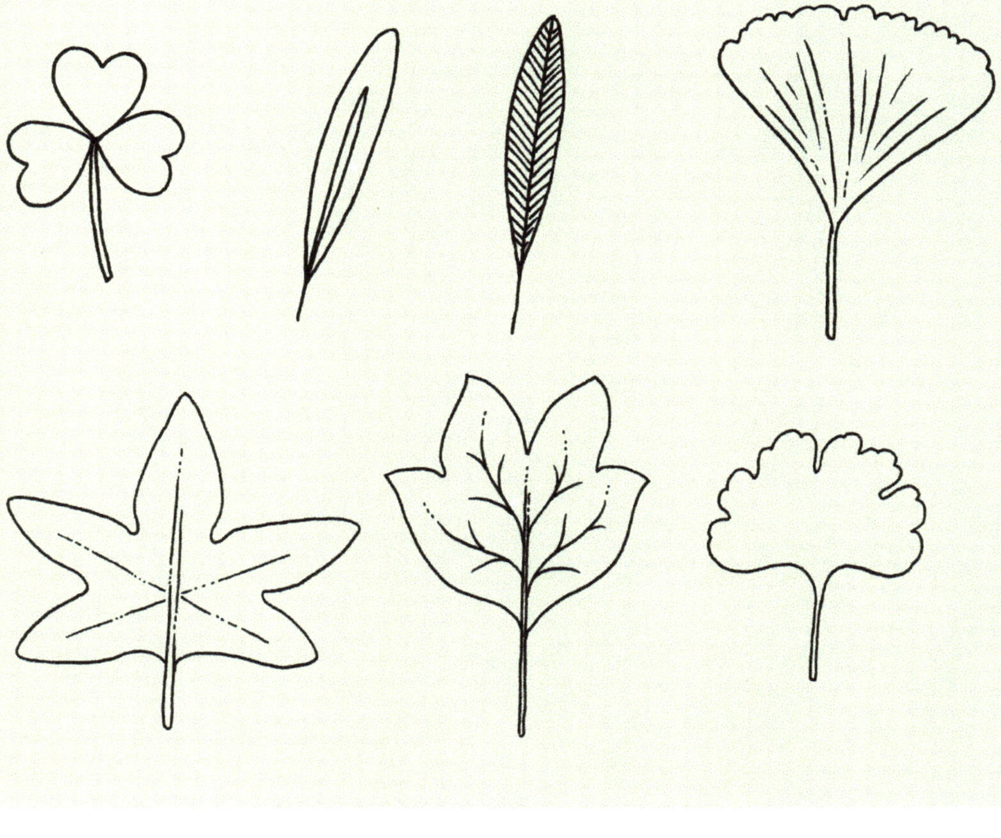

Try drawing a more complex fern. Start with a curved line. In an outward motion, stroke in the blades on one side, tapering as you reach the top. Mirror on the other side. Next add the leaves, starting with a cluster at the top. Add teardrop-shaped leaves on every branch.

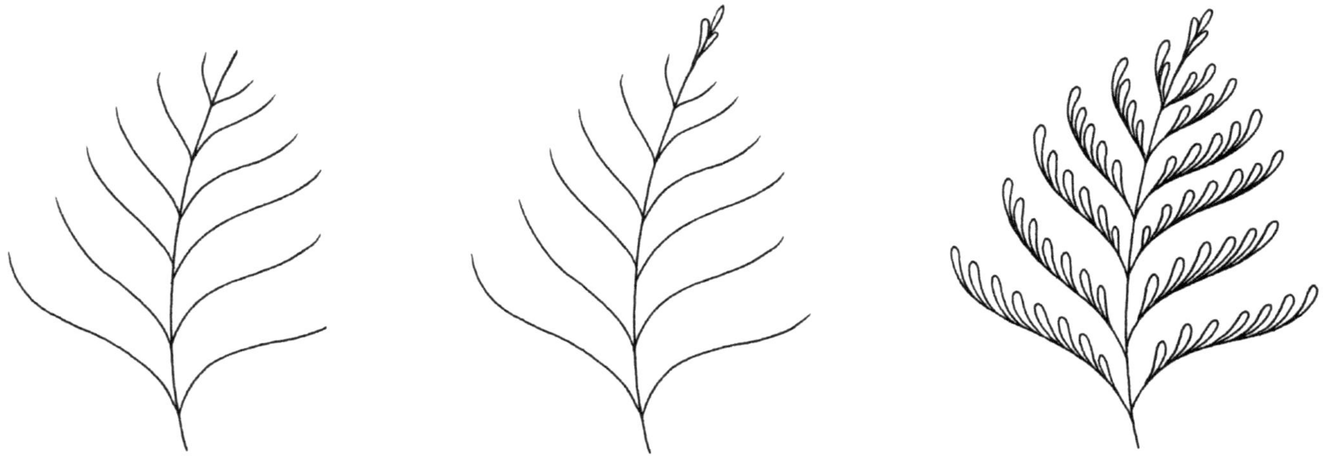

Here are some other variations of complex leaves. You can do a lot by just altering the length of the leaf tips or their formations.

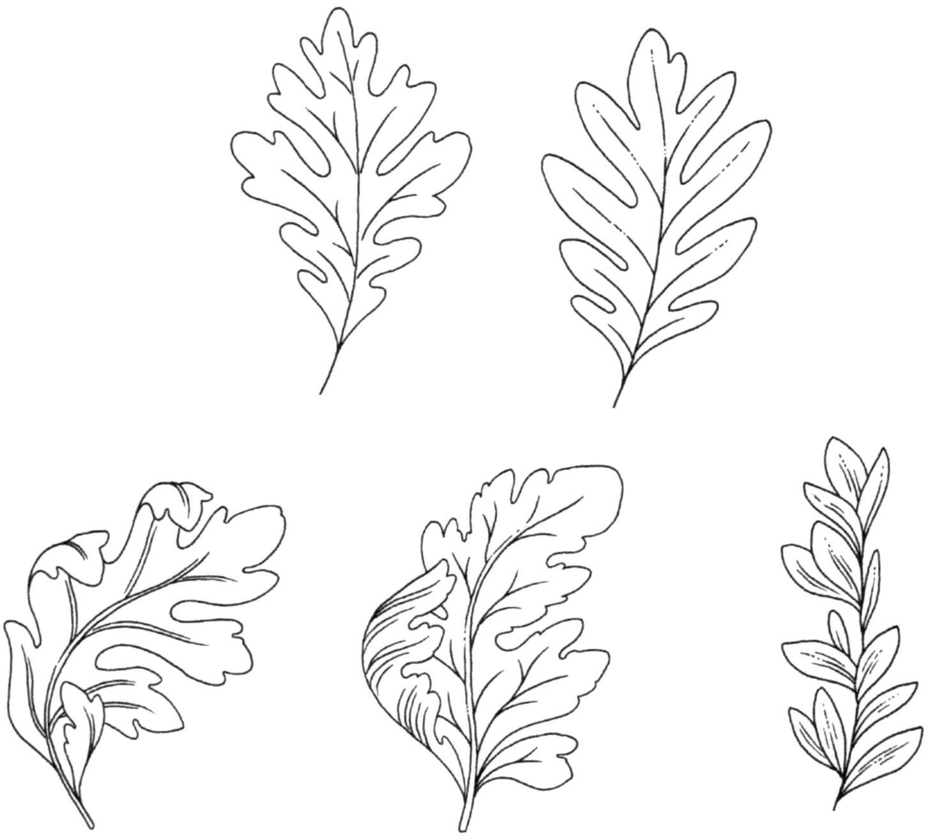

SIMPLE FLOWERS

Draw a small circle for the center. Draw teardrop-shaped petals extending outward from the center. Make sure the petals are about the same size, length, and width. Some flowers have five petals, or six, or even ten—it just depends on how you draw the petals, so don't be afraid to experiment!

For this four-petaled bloom, start with a larger center circle. Draw a wider petal that curves out and pinches to a point at the top. Since this flower has four petals, draw the same petal shape across from the first, rather than next to it. This will help you maintain symmetry. Finish the sides with the same petal shape.

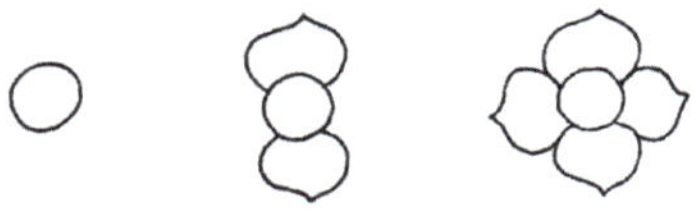

This flower has lots of long petals, like a daisy. Start with a small center circle. Draw a long, skinny petal on the top and bottom. To keep the petals symmetrical, draw the skinny petal shapes on each side of the circle, perpendicular to the first two. Finish by filling in petals around the center.

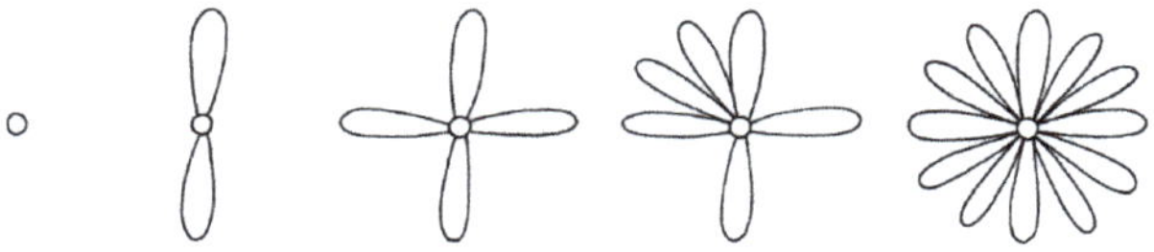

This flower has overlapping petals. Start with a dot to mark the center point. Then draw a C-shaped line from the center dot up and around to the right—don't complete the line! Moving counterclockwise, continue drawing C-shaped petals, connecting each to the "back" of the petal before it.

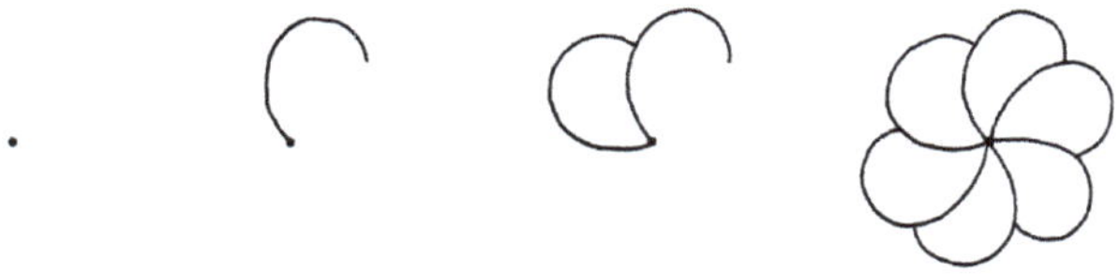

Take a look at these examples and experiment with different petal shapes, quantities, and embellishments!

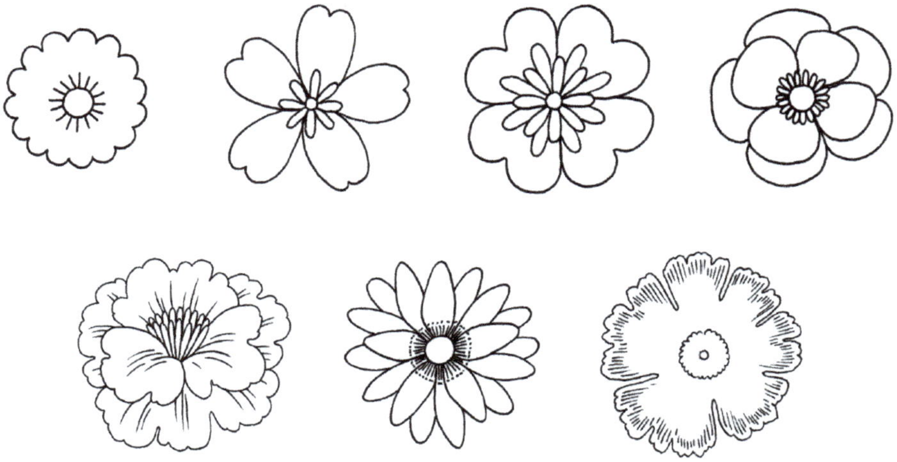

COMPLEX FLORALS

For more complex flowers, I like to start with a very loose pencil sketch. Sketch a large circle to mark the ends of the petals and a smaller, inner circle for the center.

1. Over the sketch, use pen to draw a small center. Here, I chose a berry-like shape.

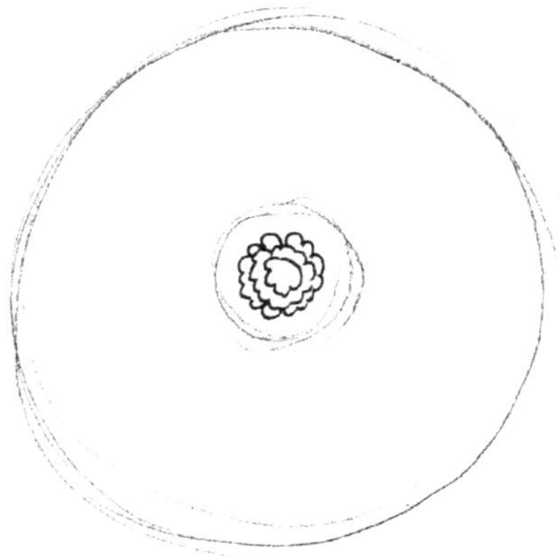

2. Next add clusters of stamen (the part that produces pollen) around the center. I layered rod-like shapes; it's okay if they overlap or go in different directions!

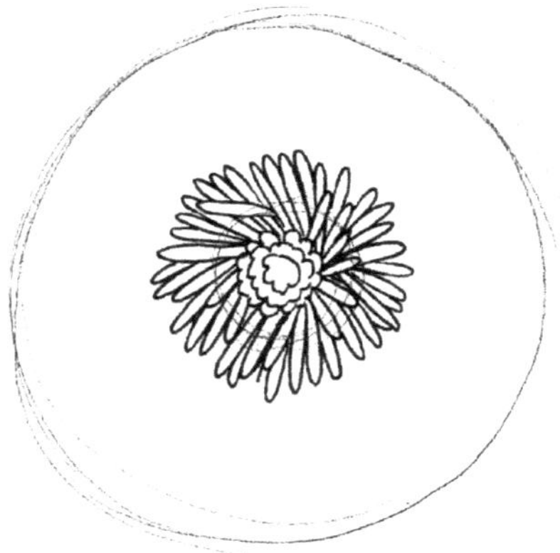

3. Add the petals, creating varied edges and layering them within the outer circle.

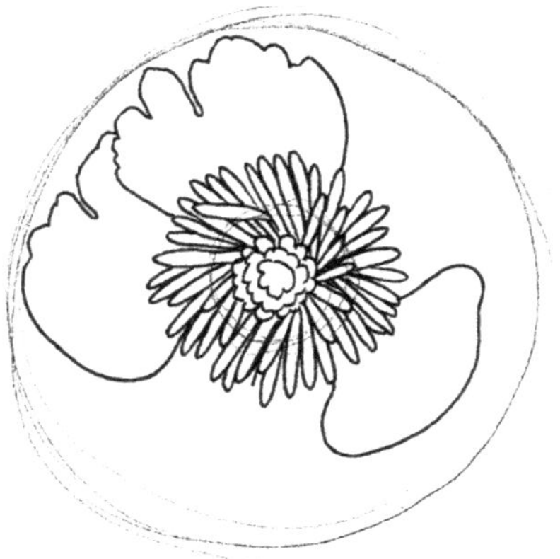

4. Add more petals—overlapping adds interest and dimensionality! The edges should be organic, with ripples and dips.

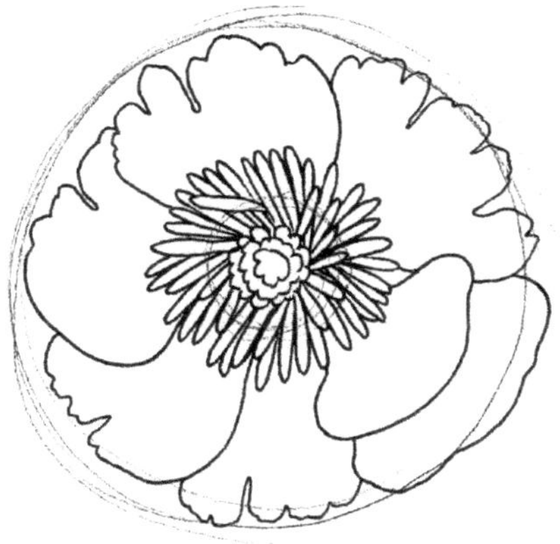

5. Finally, add embellishment lines to create the illusion of cupped petals. Erase the pencil lines, and you're finished.

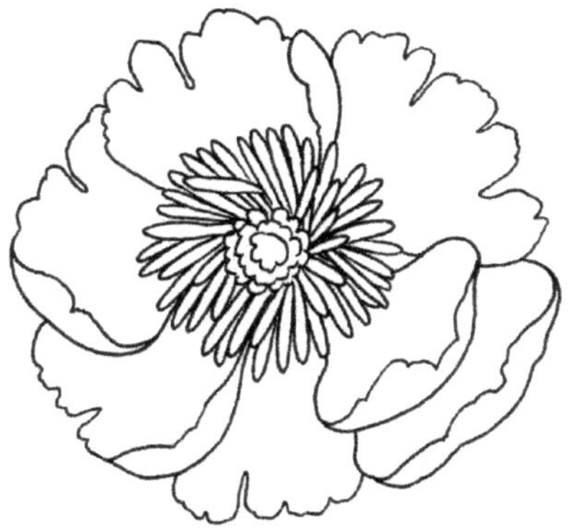

You can use this same technique of building the flower from the inside out with so many different types of flowers. Here are a couple of examples.

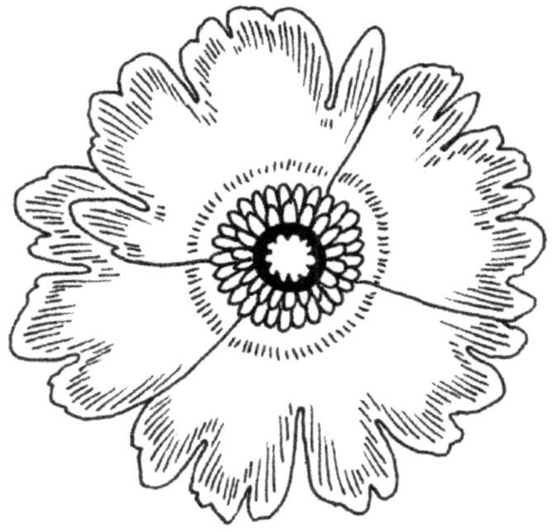

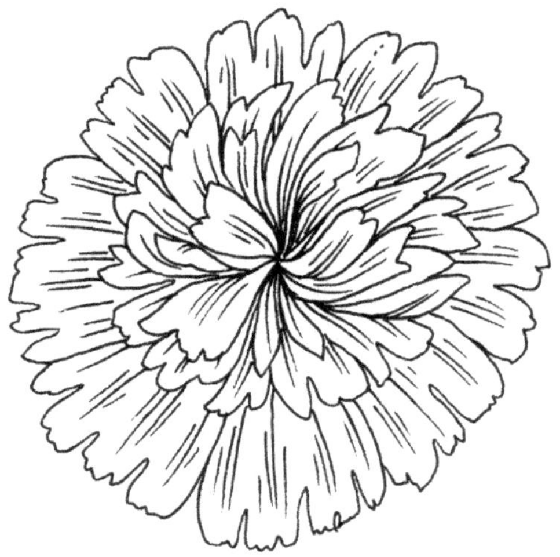

1. Start with loose pencil guidelines. With pen, draw small petals that point into the center. Start on the outer rim, and work your way in to achieve proper layering.

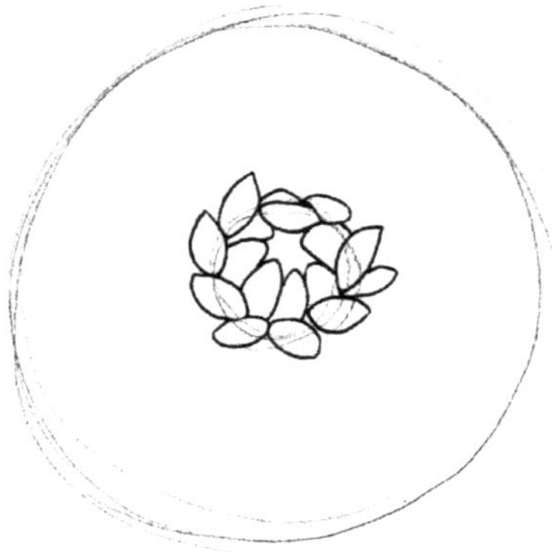

2. Then draw larger petals around the center. These don't have to be perfectly symmetrical—have fun with it!

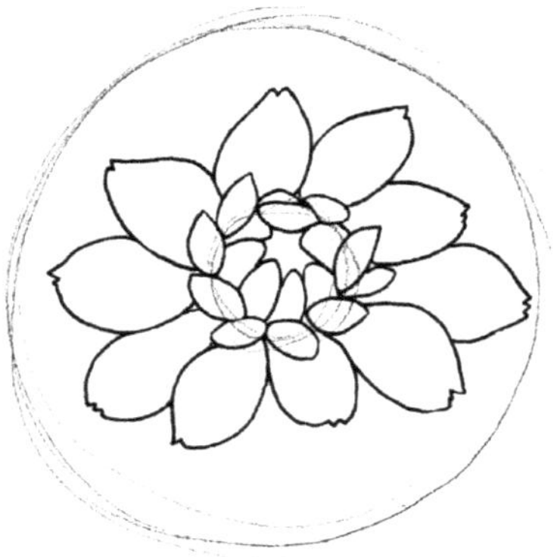

3. Keep filling in petals until you reach the outer circle of your pencil sketch.

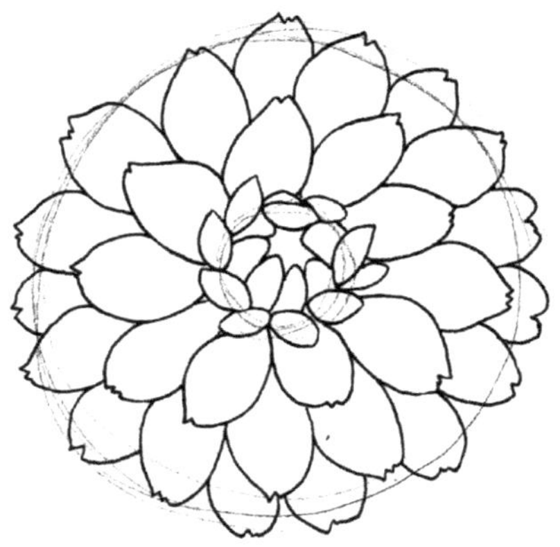

4. Then add leaves. I like to add them in clusters of three for visual balance.

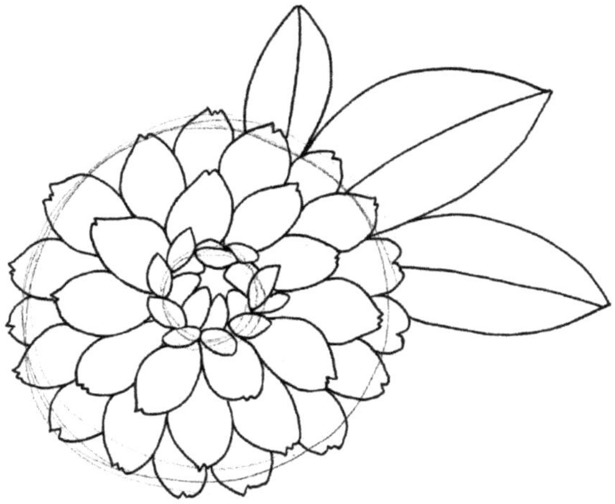

5. Finally, add little embellishment marks to the petals. You can hatch the petals down the centers or along the edges. Erase the pencil lines.

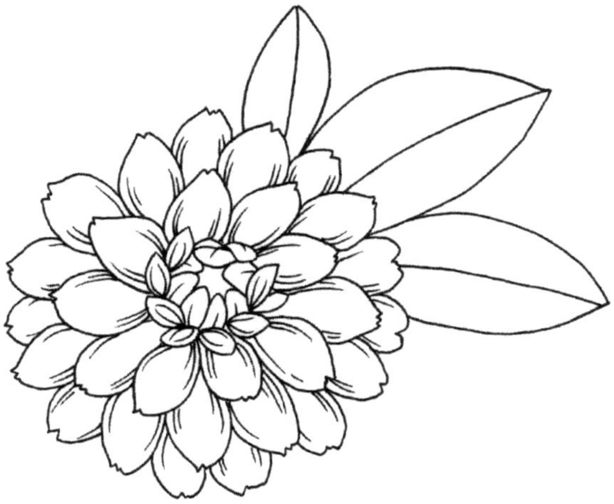

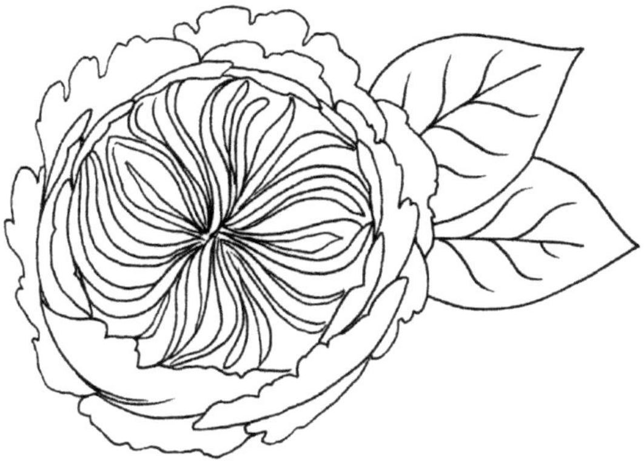

Use the same technique to draw this peony. The center should be much larger, since the ruffled petals make the central focus. The outer petals are smaller. Taper and point the leaves, making sure to include the veins. This is where a photo reference comes in handy!

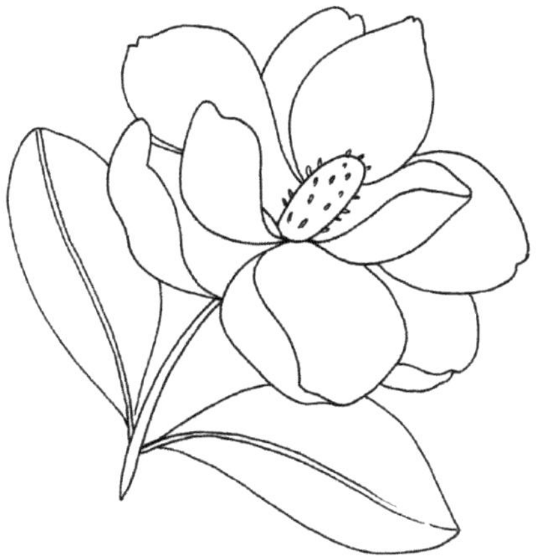

Another beautiful flower is the magnolia. The center is a cylinder rather than a circle. This flower has few petals, but they are large. Its smooth, broad leaves are even larger than its petals!

BUILDING COMPLEX FLORAL CLUSTERS & BOUQUETS

For complex clusters, with overlapping flowers, leaves, and buds, begin with a pencil sketch. I like to block things in with basic shapes, but you can sketch in more detail if you'd like.

Start with a pencil guide, using general shapes. Then use pen to draw the stems.

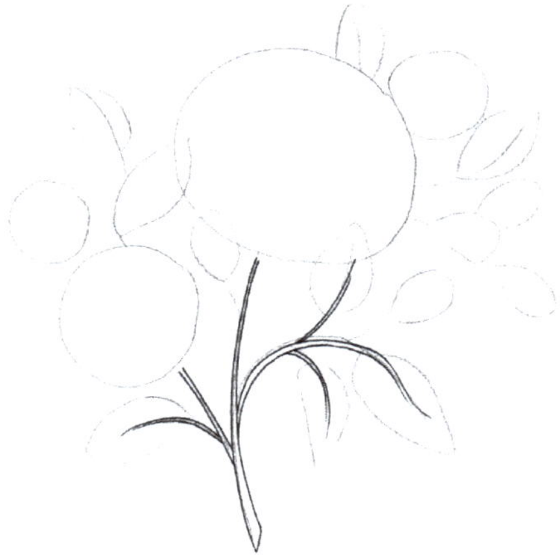

Next draw the flowers, adding stems to fill out the cluster. Keep an eye on where the leaves overlap in your sketch, and leave those areas open.

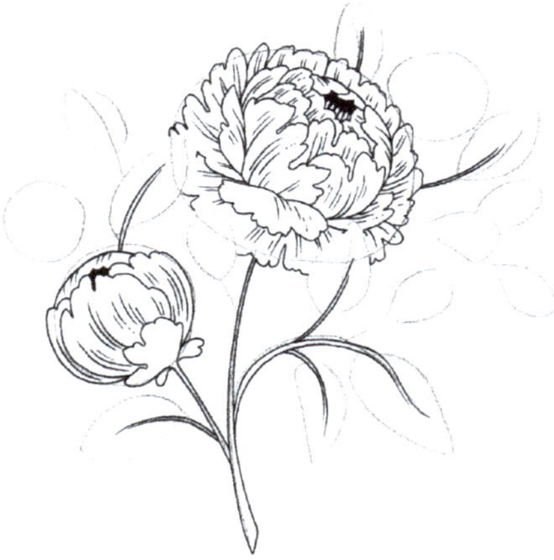

Fill in the leaves, connecting them to the lines you laid down for the flowers.

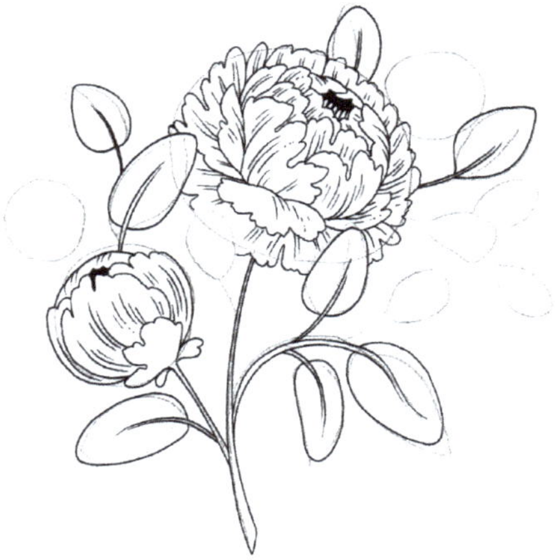

Now develop the smaller flowers.

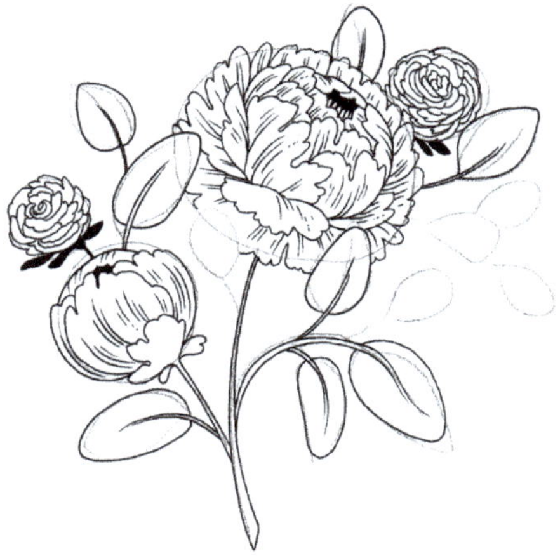

Finally, finish the buds and erase the pencil lines.
Add color, if you'd like, with traditional or digital tools.

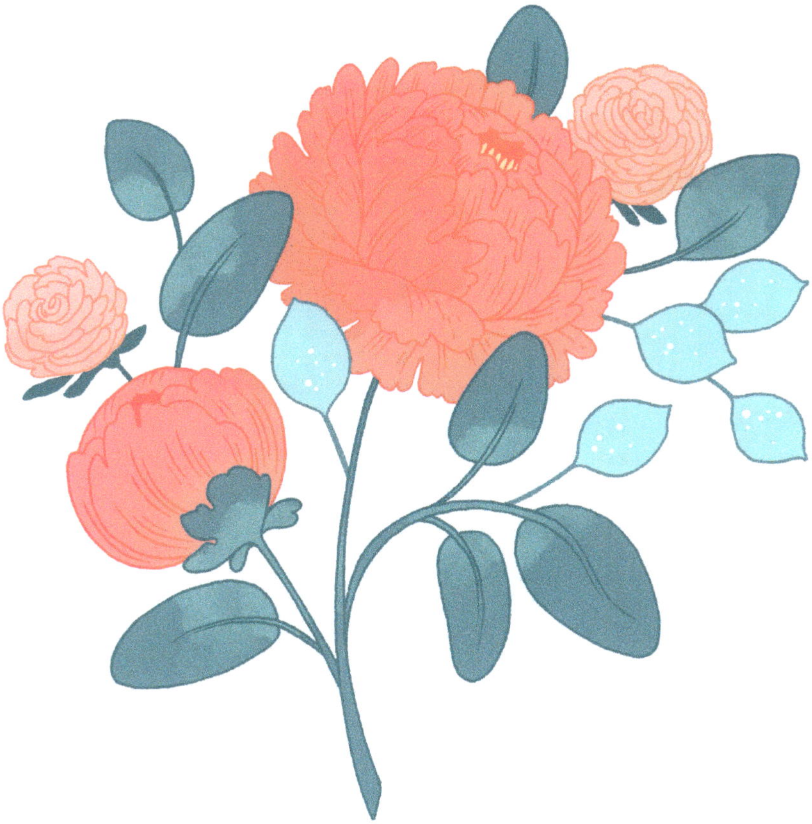

OTHER COMPLEX CLUSTERS

This giant peony cluster is surrounded by tiny berries. It's fun to really push the envelope of size relationships in a cluster.

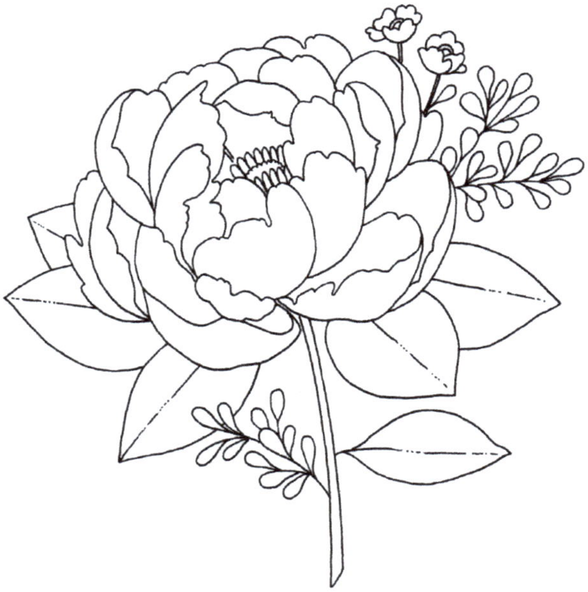

This cluster of wildflowers varies in size, with lots of buds and scalloped leaves.

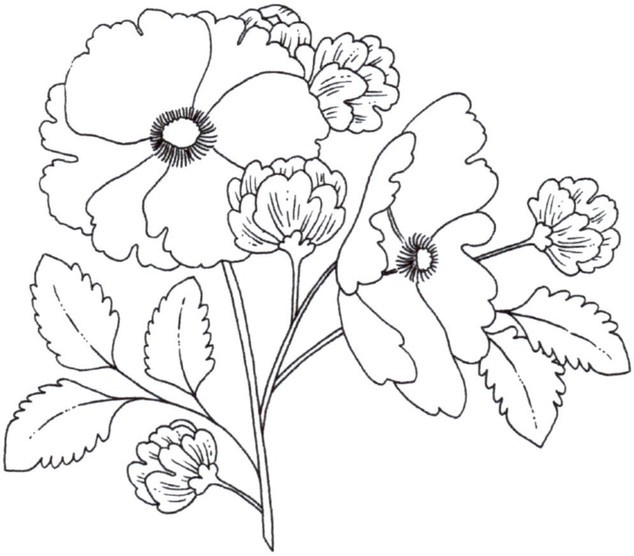

FLOWER BUDS

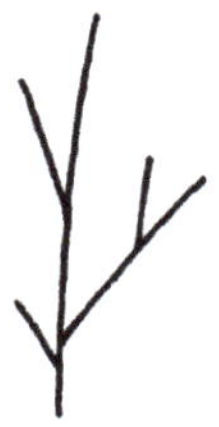

1. Like the floral cluster, start with the stem of the buds and build arms out from the center.

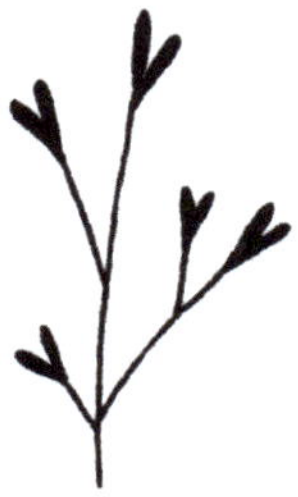

2. Add a little heart shape at the end of each stem.

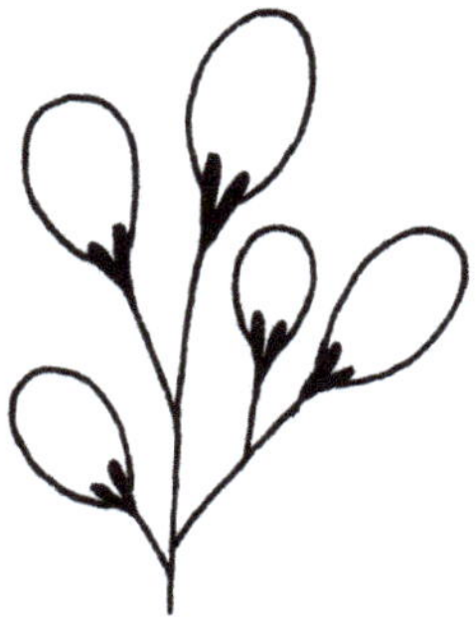

3. Draw an oval around each heart.

Buds are smaller flowers that have not yet bloomed. Here are some examples of different bud shapes and formations. Mix these in with your full florals for more variation in your illustrations!

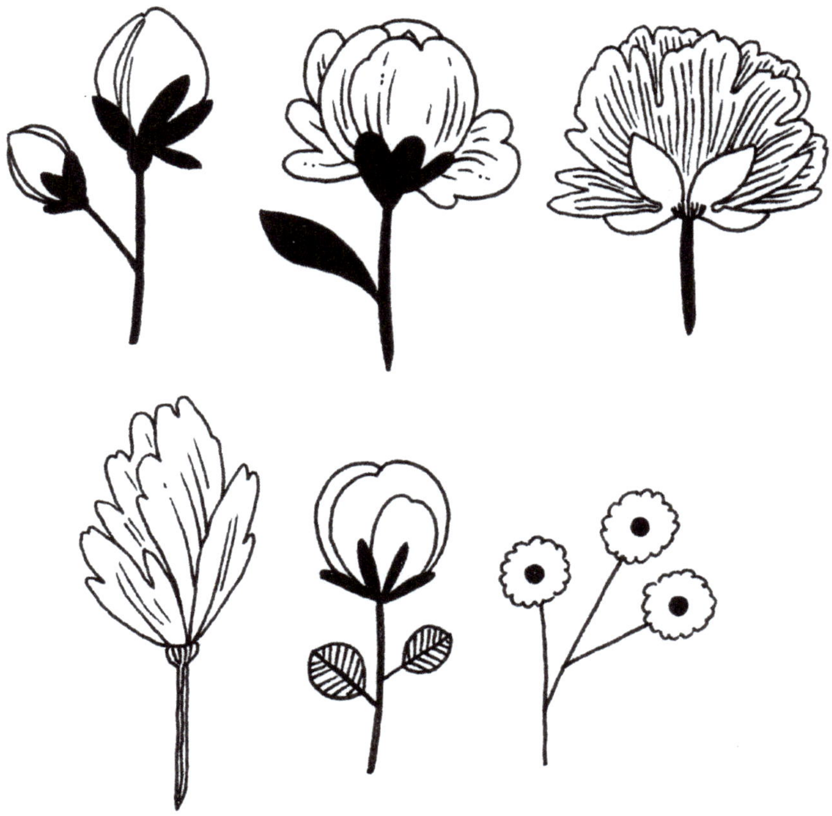

TROPICAL PLANTS

MONSTERA

Working along a curved line, draw one side of the leaf that is pointed toward the top and rounded at the bottom. Monstera has gaps in its leaves, so be sure to add these variations. Draw the other side of the leaf. The gaps on this side should vary from the first—this plant doesn't have symmetrical leaves. Finish by drawing holes in the leaf.

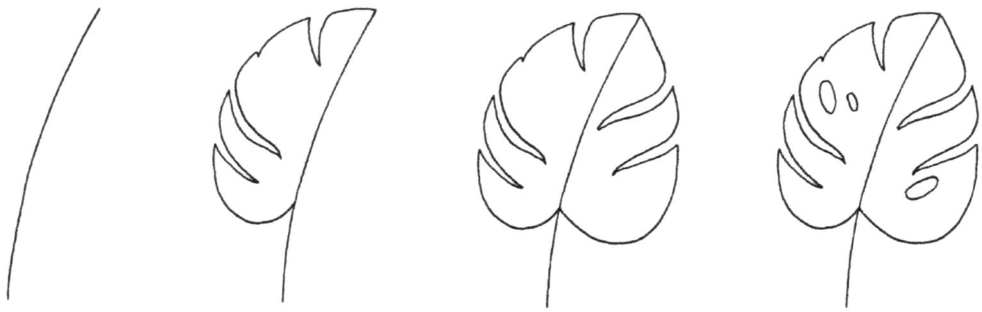

PALM

For this palm, start with a curved line. Draw the top few long, thin leaves. Fill in one side of the center line with thin leaves that angle upward. Fill in the other side the same way, with the leaves facing the opposite direction.

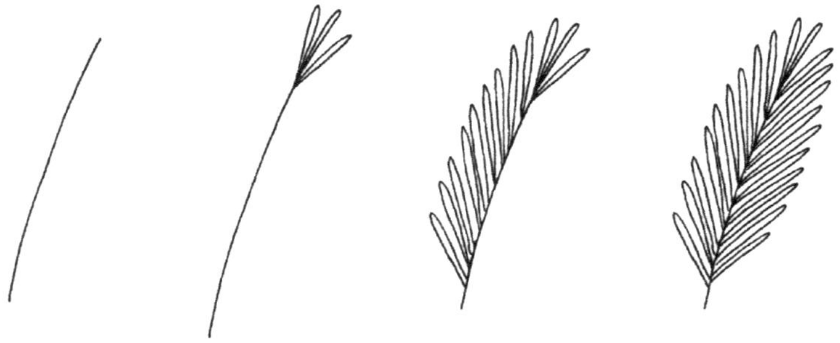

BANANA LEAF

Start with a curved line. Draw one side of the leaf with a long, wavy line. Don't forget to add sharp notches where the leaf splits. Draw the other side of the leaf. The notches don't have to be symmetrical, and you can vary them in size and length. Add straight, angled lines from the center outward to complete the leaf's vein structure.

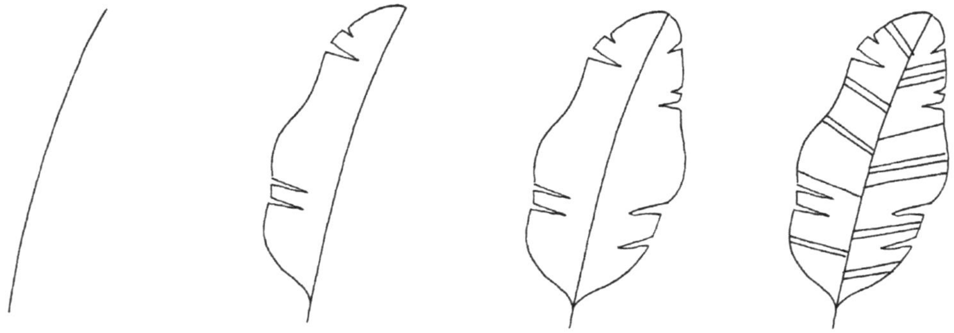

FAN PALM

To draw a fan palm, start with a small line. Add a circular top with a dot in the center. Finish the leaf with lines that radiate out from the center to suggest the leaf's vein structure.

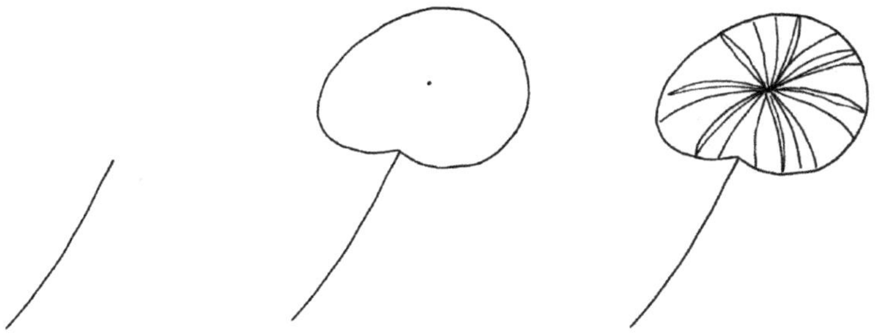

DRAGON LEAF

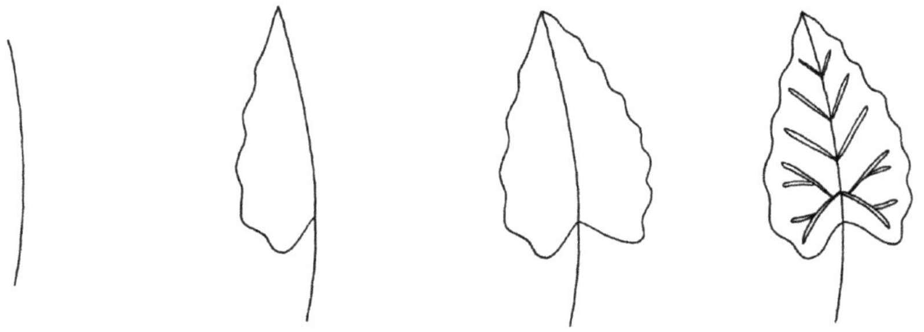

Start with a curved line. Draw one side of the leaf with a wavy line. Mirror the other side of the leaf with another wavy line. Try to make this one as symmetrical as possible! Add the vein network, drawing angled lines out from the center.

SPIKY PALM

For this spiky palm, draw a small, straight stem with a long, thin, pointed leaf shape on top. Add two more leaves to the side, one pointing up and one pointing down. Mirror the leaves on the other side. Fill in extra leaves to create a fan-like appearance.

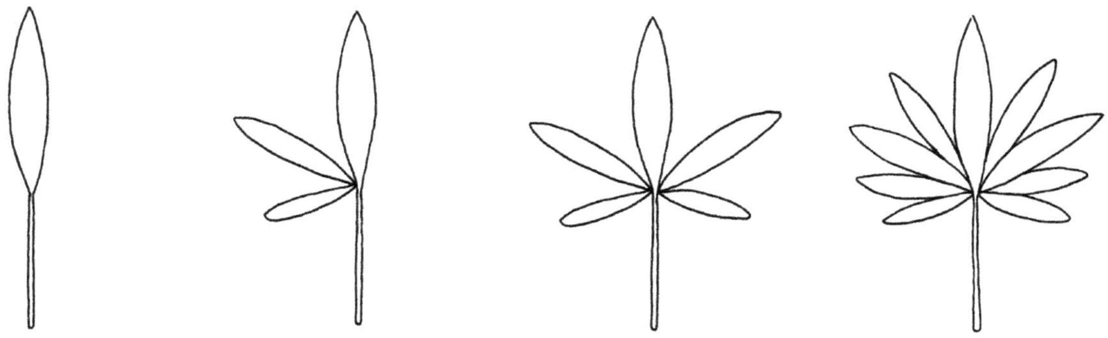

WINTER PLANTS

PINE BRANCH

Start with a curved line and a small stem on each side. Fill in the top of one stem with long, thin pine needles. Fill the other stems in, from the top down, with needles. Finish the stem with needles all the way to the bottom.

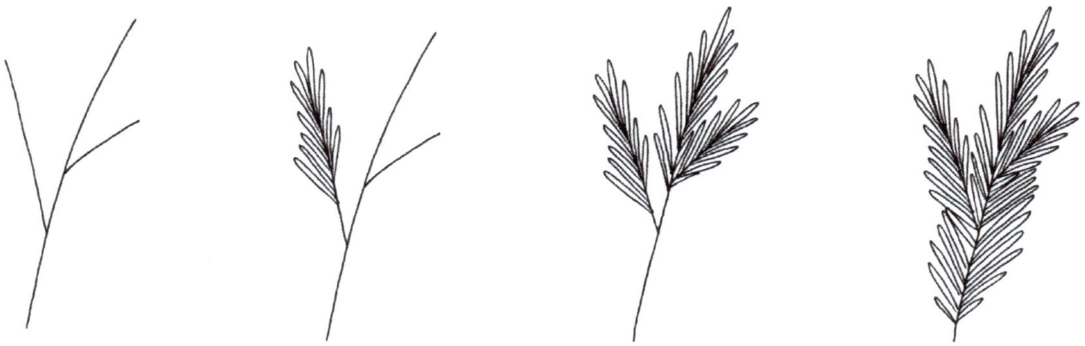

HOLLY BERRIES

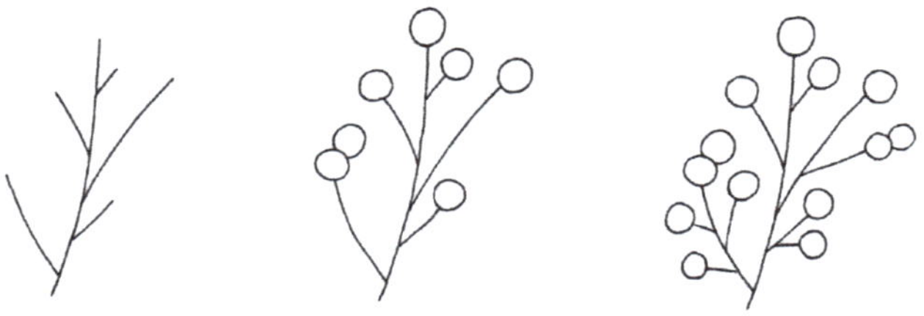

Draw a curved line with lots of stems coming off in all directions, but leave space for the berries! Draw small circles at the ends of the stems for berries. It's okay if berries touch or overlap. If the branch looks thin, fill in negative space with more stems and berries.

HOLLY LEAF

Start with a short, curved line. Draw one side of the leaf, with curved sides that create two points. Connect the side at the top and bottom of the stem. Mirror on the other side. Add lines coming from the center of the stem for the veins.

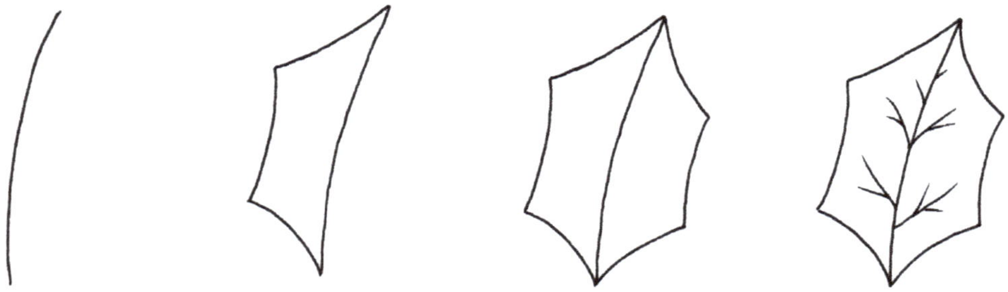

MISTLETOE

Draw two long stems, with two shorter stems coming from the base. Finish the end of each stem with a long, pointed leaf. Add berries in the negative space. If it looks thin, add more leaves—they can overlap!

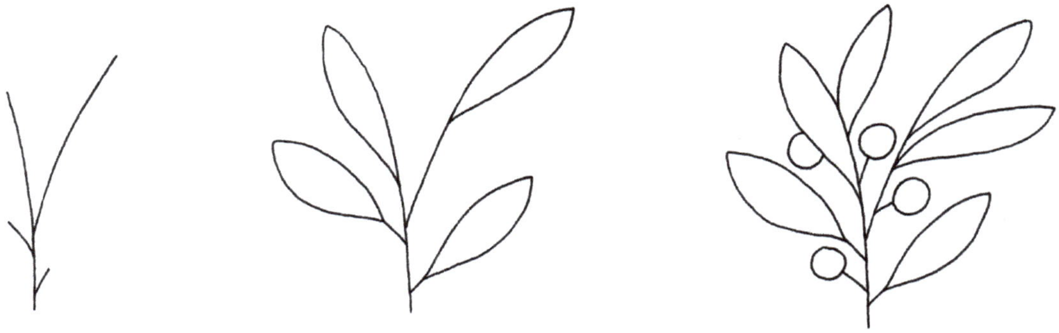

POINSETTIA

Draw a cluster of berry-like shapes for the center. Then draw six pointed petals around the center. Poinsettia petals usually vary slightly in size and shape. Draw six more larger petals. Add details to the centers of the petals to show the vein structure.

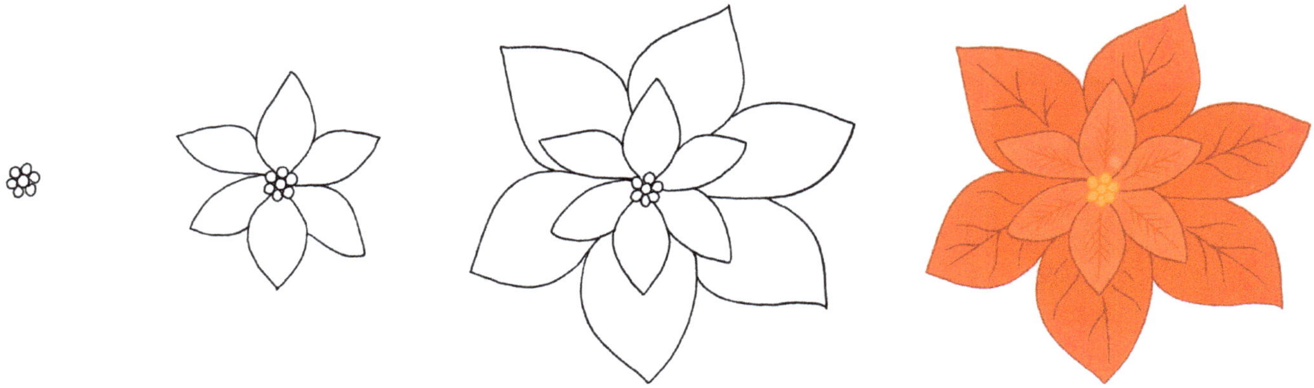

• ARTIST'S TIP •

USE REFERENCE PHOTOS OF FAVORITE PLANTS AND FLOWERS TO HELP YOU RENDER THE DETAILS.

SUCCULENTS, CACTI & DESERT PLANTS

PRICKLY PEAR

Start with a large teardrop shape. Add a few smaller shapes to the top and sides of the cactus—they can be different shapes and sizes! Add a few cactus buds to fill some of the negative space. Accent the cactus with little lines for the needles.

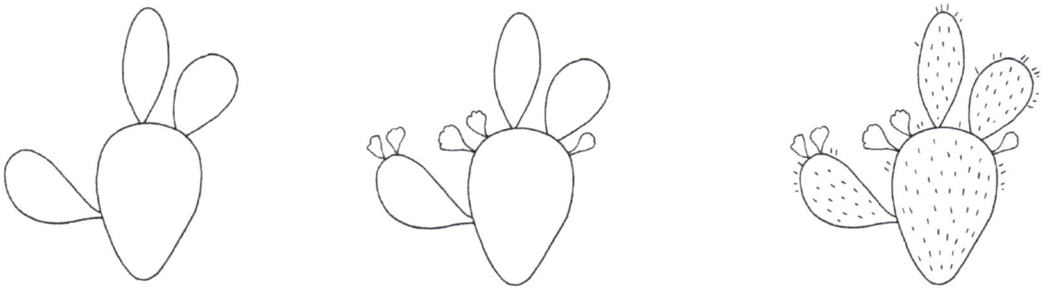

SUCCULENT

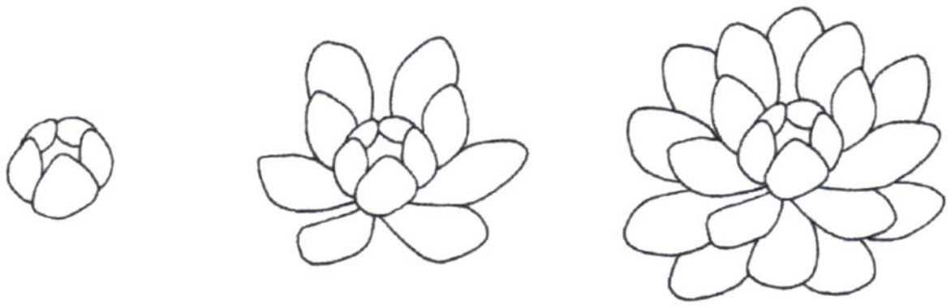

Draw a cluster of succulent petals facing inward. It's okay to overlap! Draw more, larger succulent petals facing outward around the center. Fill the rest of the gaps with more petals until it is full.

SNAKE PLANT

Draw a long, thin leaf shape. Add different-sized leaves on either side. Fill the gaps with more leaves until it is full. Draw a line up the center of each leaf, and add hatching details.

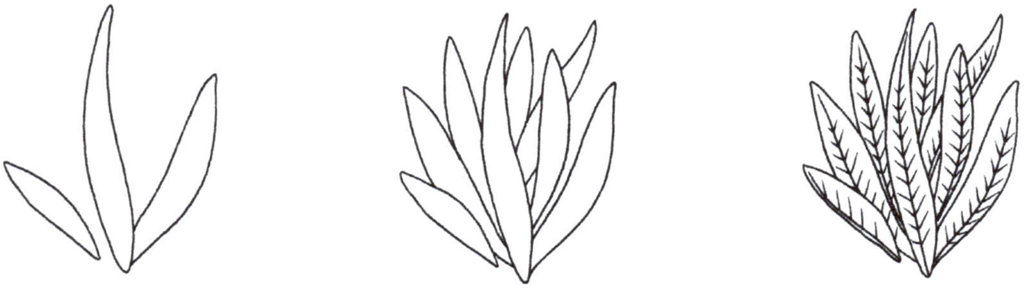

SAGUARO

Draw a tall cylinder with several indentations. Add two small cylinders to the top. Keep adding the arms of the cactus until it is full. Draw lines down each arm of the cactus, and finish with little lines for the needles.

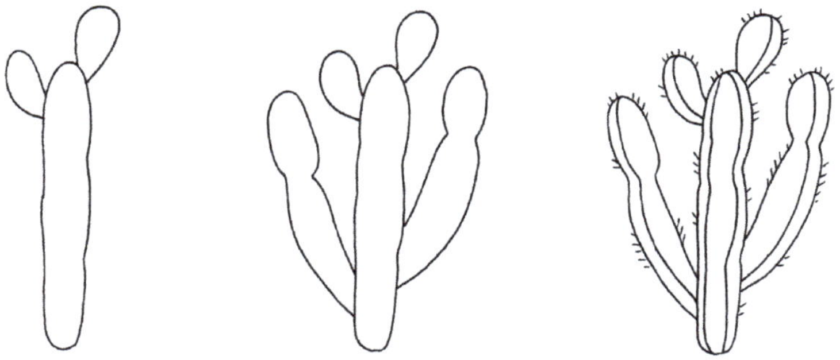

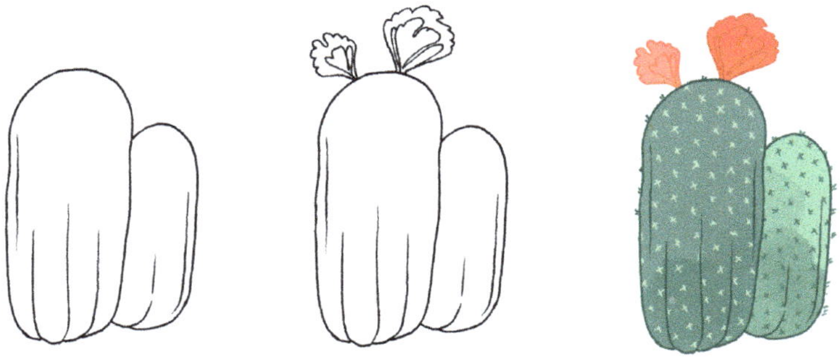

CACTUS

Draw two large, wide cylinders that vary in size. Add small cactus flowers to the top of one of the cacti. Add x-marks in a pattern across the cacti for the needles.

ALOE VERA

Aloe vera is very similar to snake plant! Follow the same steps, but let the tips come to a rounded point, and make the leaves longer and thinner.

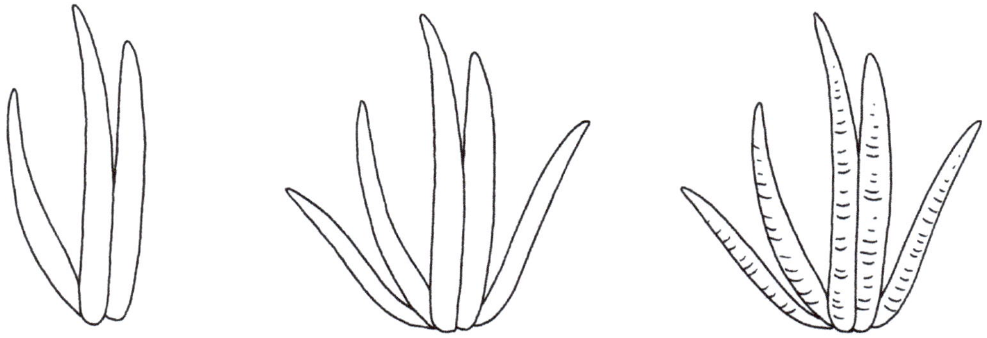

TREES

PALM

Draw a long, thin curved trunk, and add two circles for coconuts. Then add palm leaves around the center of the tree and coconuts. Finish by adding lines to the palm leaves that angle from the center outward. Add banding to the trunk.

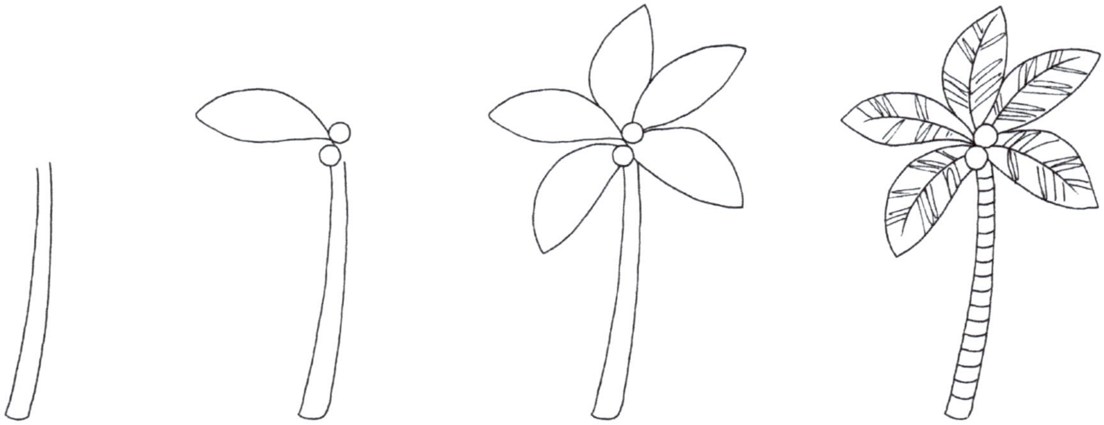

OAK

Draw a large bell shape; the edges should be almost "scraggly" to indicate lots of leaves. Move your pen in and out in quick strokes to achieve this look. Add a wide-set, sturdy, and short trunk. Draw hatching lines to create bark texture. Add dipping lines, similar to those you drew on the outside of the tree, on the inside to indicate the shapes of the leaves in the tree.

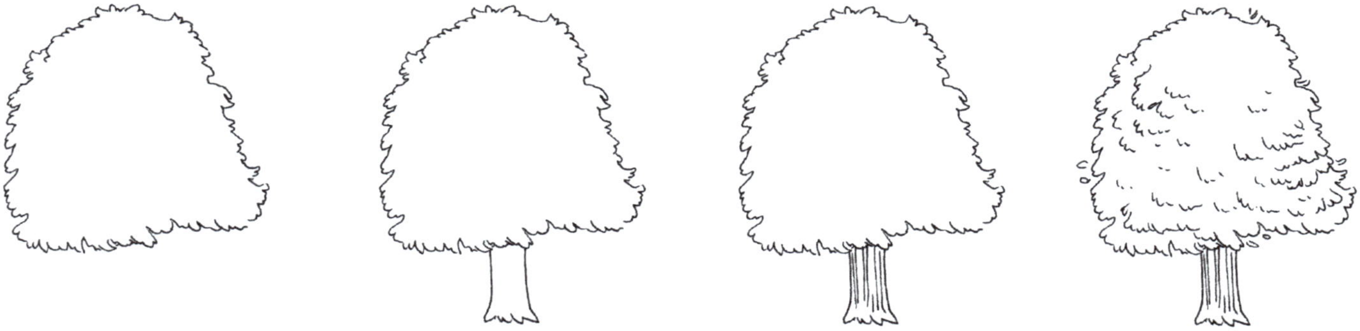

Here are some other tree examples: apple, birch, redwood, and pine. Give it a whirl and try your hand at drawing these trees.

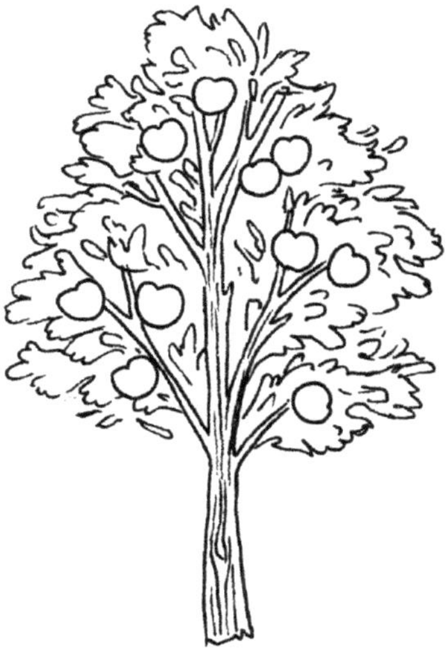

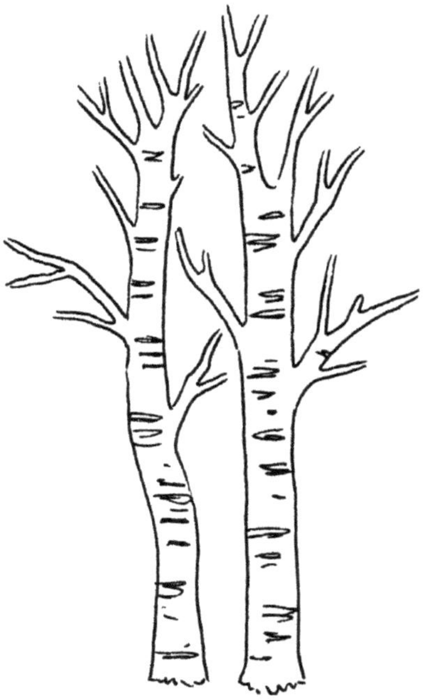

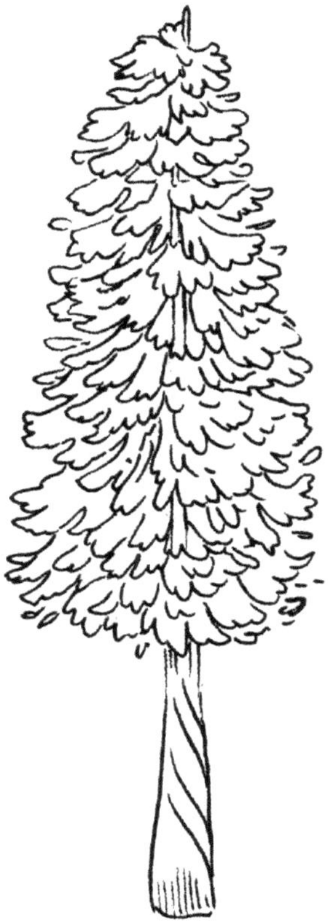

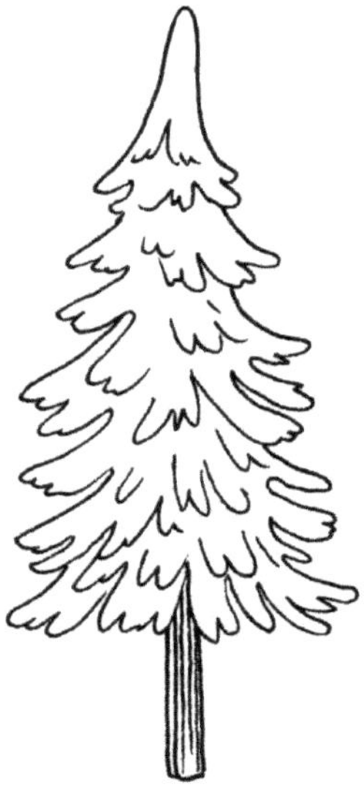

MODERN, STYLIZED FLORALS

Taking what you've learned in this section, here are just a few ways you can take the shapes you've learned to draw and simplify them into modern, stylized floral illustrations. The trick is to have fun and think outside the box—no shape is incorrect!

Start by drawing a small, vertical straight line with a large tulip shape at the end: a wide, domed center with two points on each side and a bell-curve down to the bottom. Draw a simple leaf on each side of the stem.

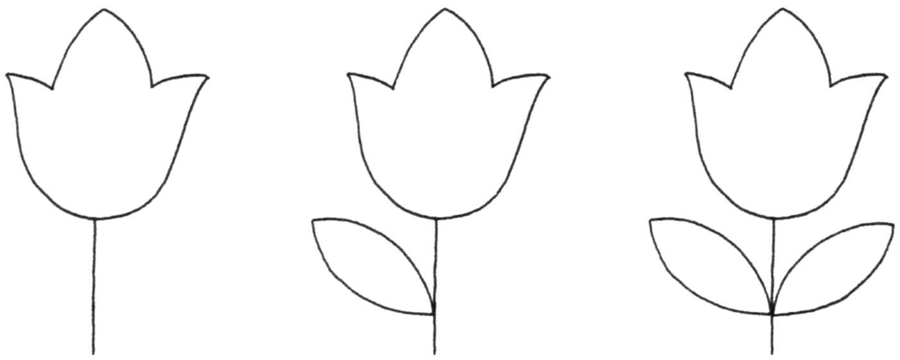

Here are some examples of stylized flowers and buds. They range from lilies, to dandelions and daisies. I encourage you to pull out your sketchbook and practice drawing some stylized florals that begin with traditional shapes.

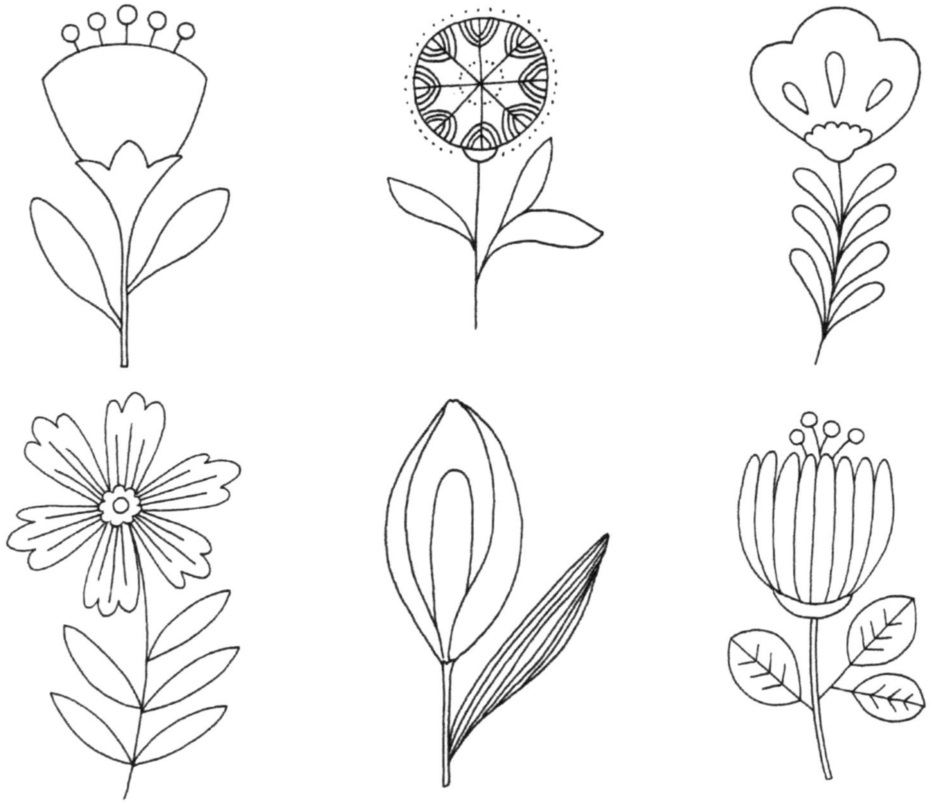

TERRARIUM

Fill the terrarium with your own beautiful garden! Reflect on your favorite plants or flowers to draw, and combine them here. Don't forget to add interesting leaf shapes, buds, and berries! You can even throw in some stylized florals here. Anything goes, so have fun!

ARCHITECTURE & CITY LIFE

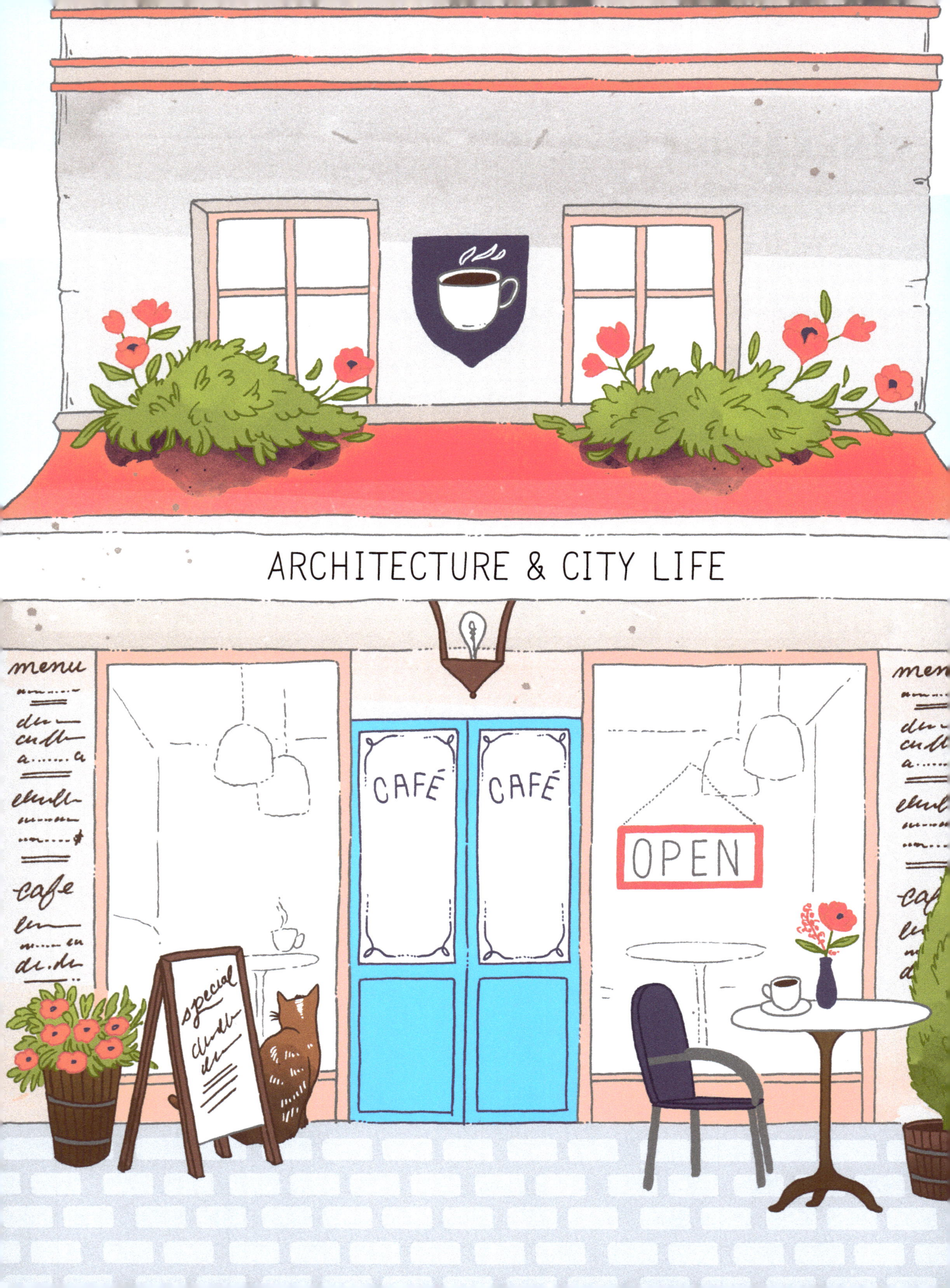

CITY BUILDINGS

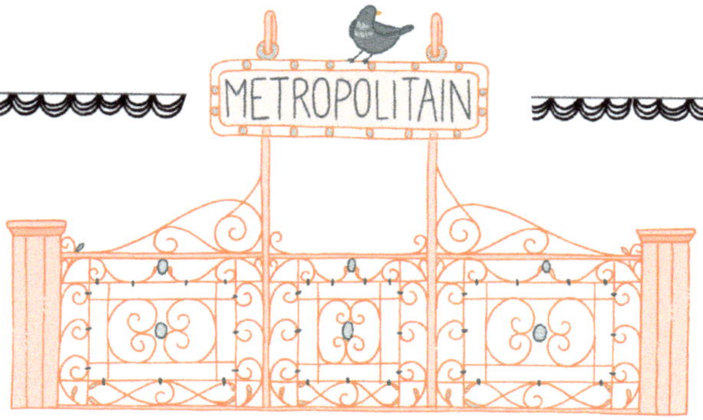

In this section, we'll explore different types of architecture, iconic landmarks, signage, and scenes from city life. For these types of drawings, I recommend gathering good reference photos, as well as a ruler, pencil, and pen. Many of these drawings start with a penciled geometric base, to which we'll add details. As you practice these examples, remember that the keys to drawing architecture are symmetry, space, and simplification.

CITY SKYLINE

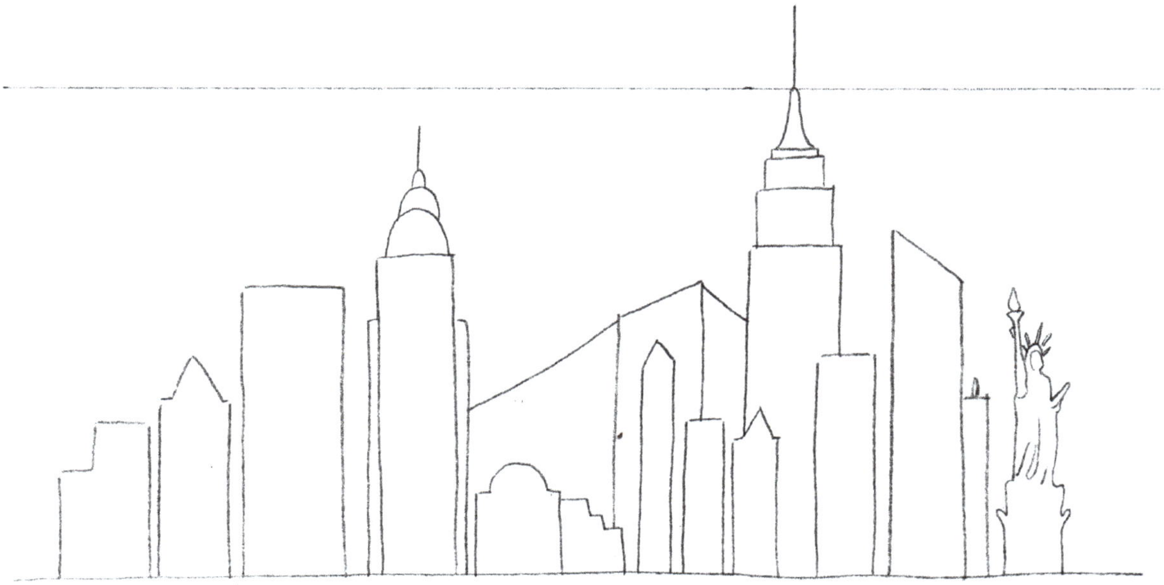

1. Using your pencil and a ruler, draw a straight horizontal line for the groundline. Then draw another horizontal line above it. These parallel lines will help you determine the relative proportions of your skyline. Draw the tallest building first. Using your reference, keep adding buildings from tallest to smallest. Simple pencil lines will work here.

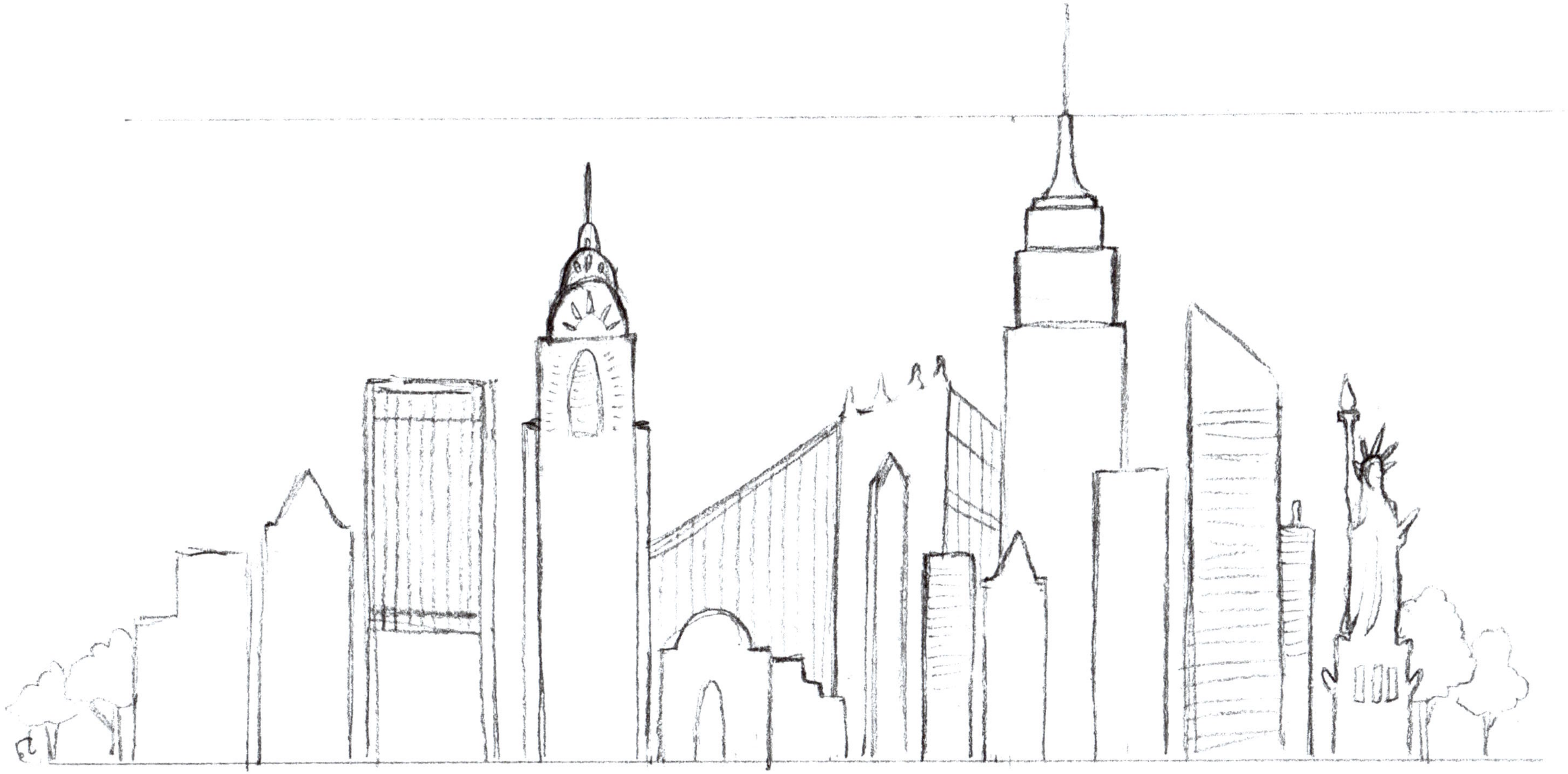

2. Next add details. You can add as many or as few details as you'd like.

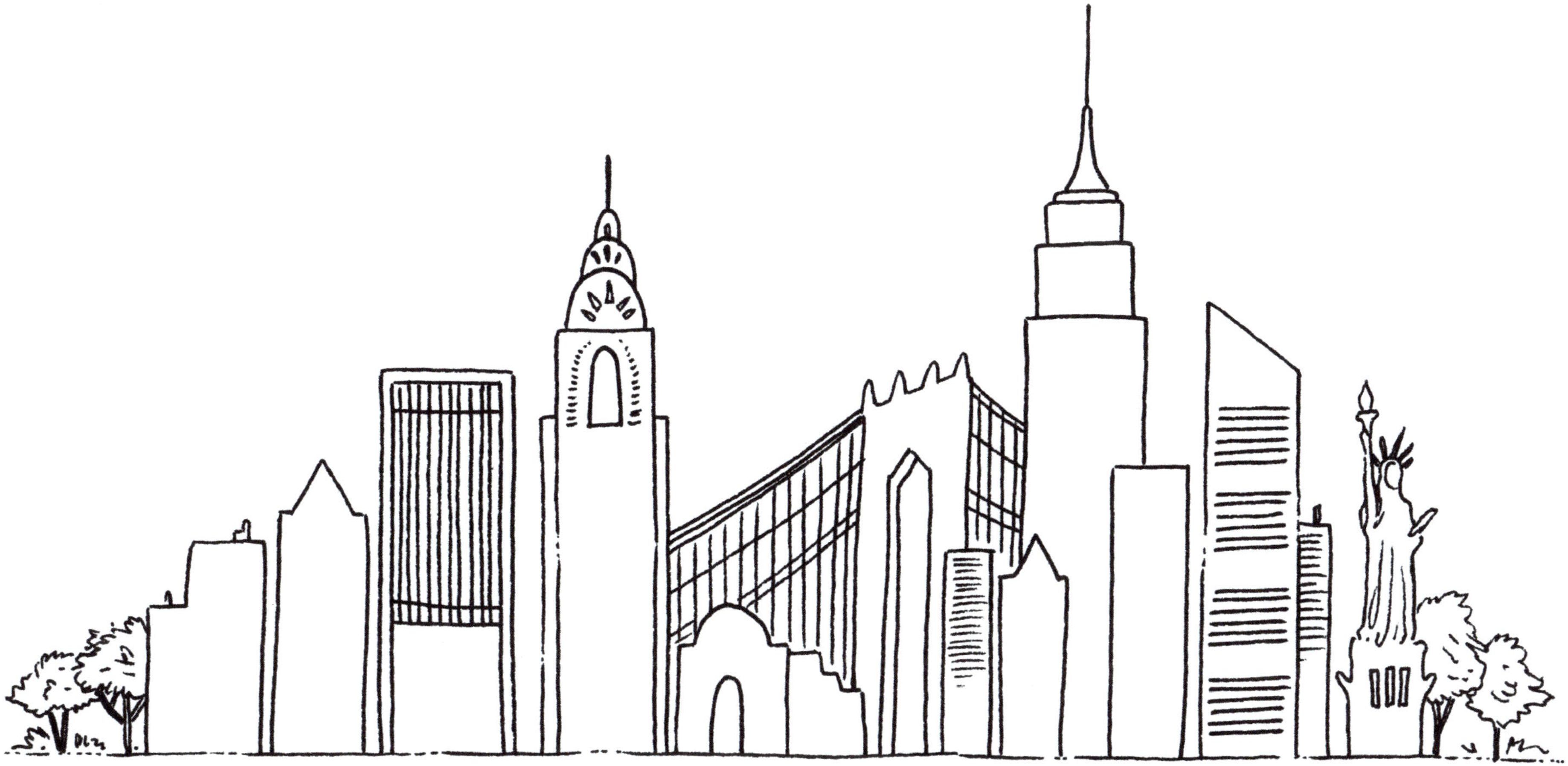

3. Finally, use pen to finish the illustration with more details. When the ink is dry, erase the pencil marks.

BASIC SKYSCRAPER

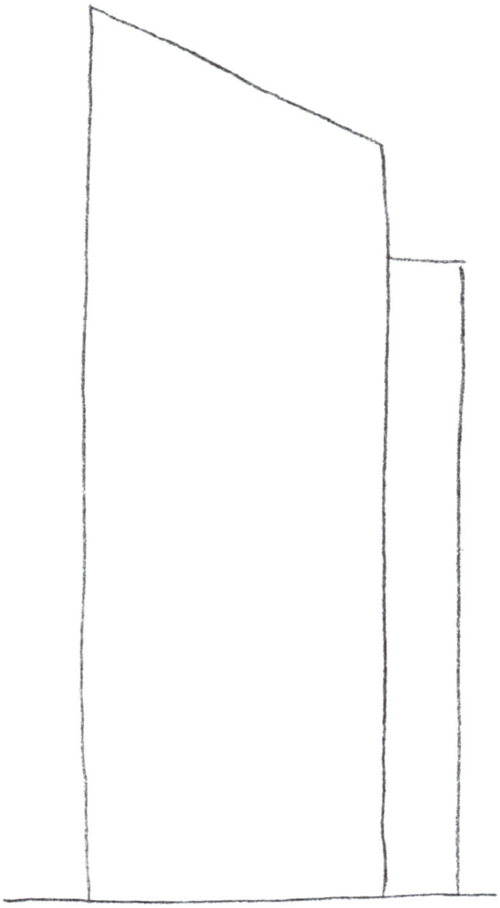

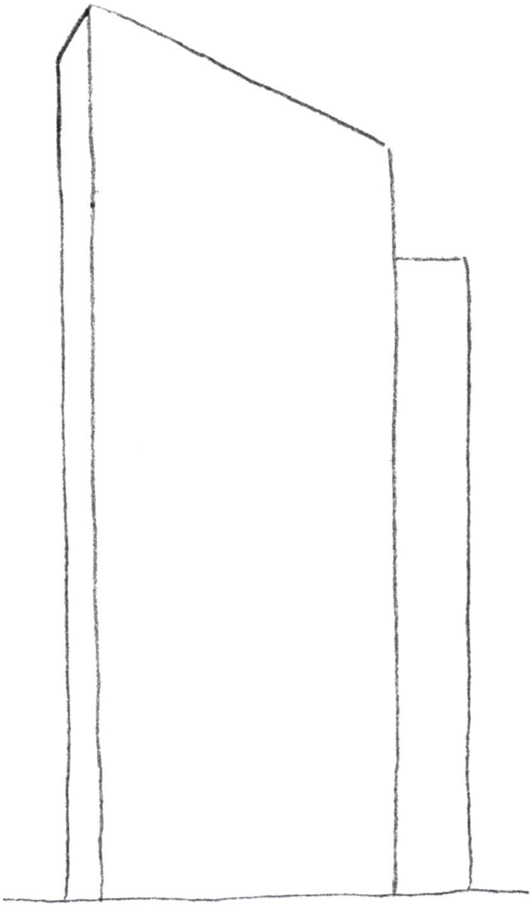

1. Start with a horizontal groundline. Then draw a tall, thin rectangle perpendicular to this line followed by a larger shape to represent the bulk of the building. For interest, I chose a skyscraper with a slanted top.

2. From the top point of the skyscraper, draw a short downward line at a 45-degree angle away from the building and connect it to the groundline with a line that runs parallel to the building. This gives the skyscraper some depth and perspective.

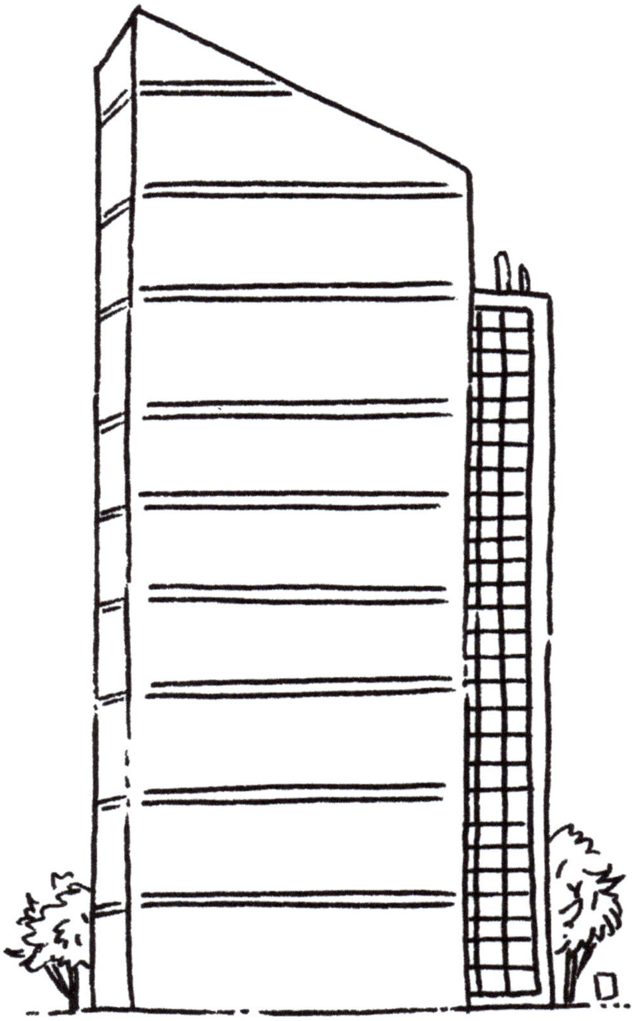

3. Refine the drawing with pen by straightening out rough lines and adding details, such as the lines on the skyscraper, windows, and a little tree.

CITY HOME

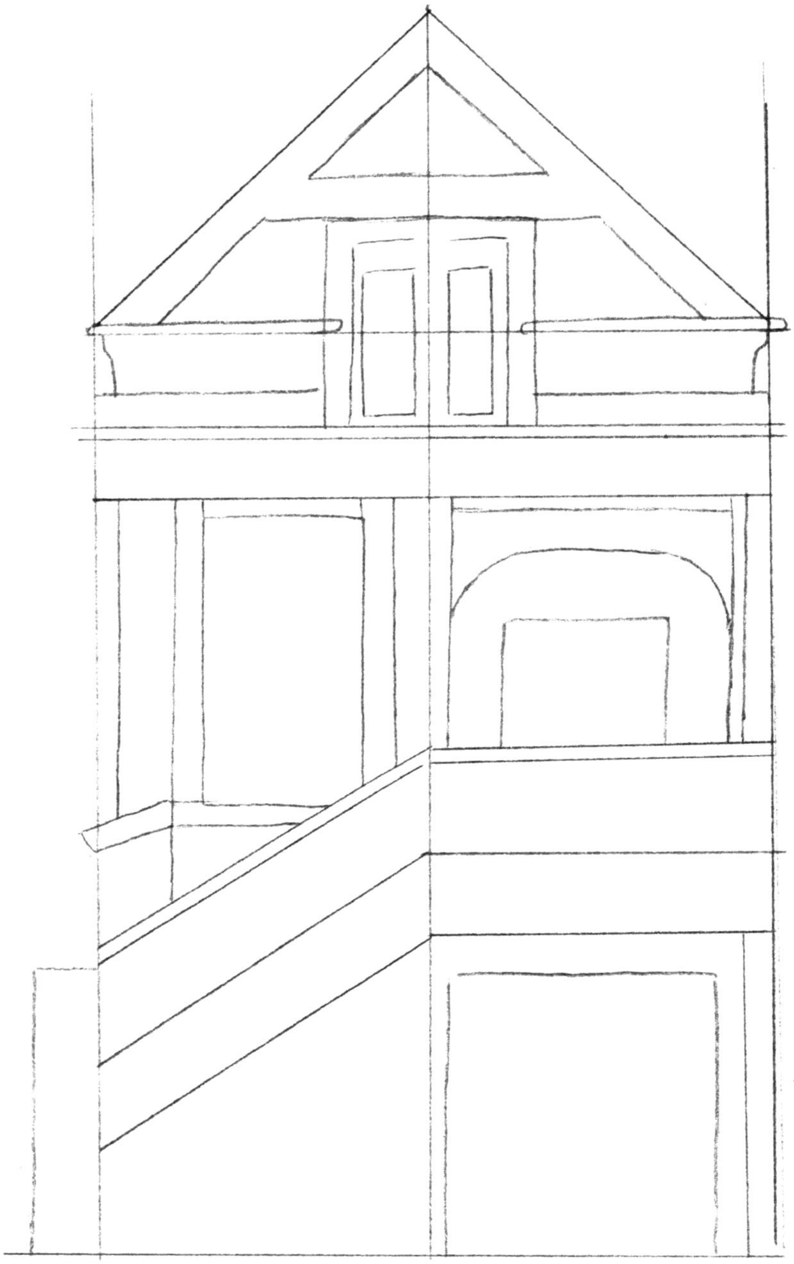

Now let's draw a San Francisco "Painted Lady" home. Use your reference photo and a ruler to plot out the groundline, a parallel top line, and the sides of the home. In my reference, the upper most elements of the home are symmetrical along the center of the house, so I also drew a vertical line through the center. Block out the major sections of the house, planning the placement of the doors, windows, stairs, and architectural features.

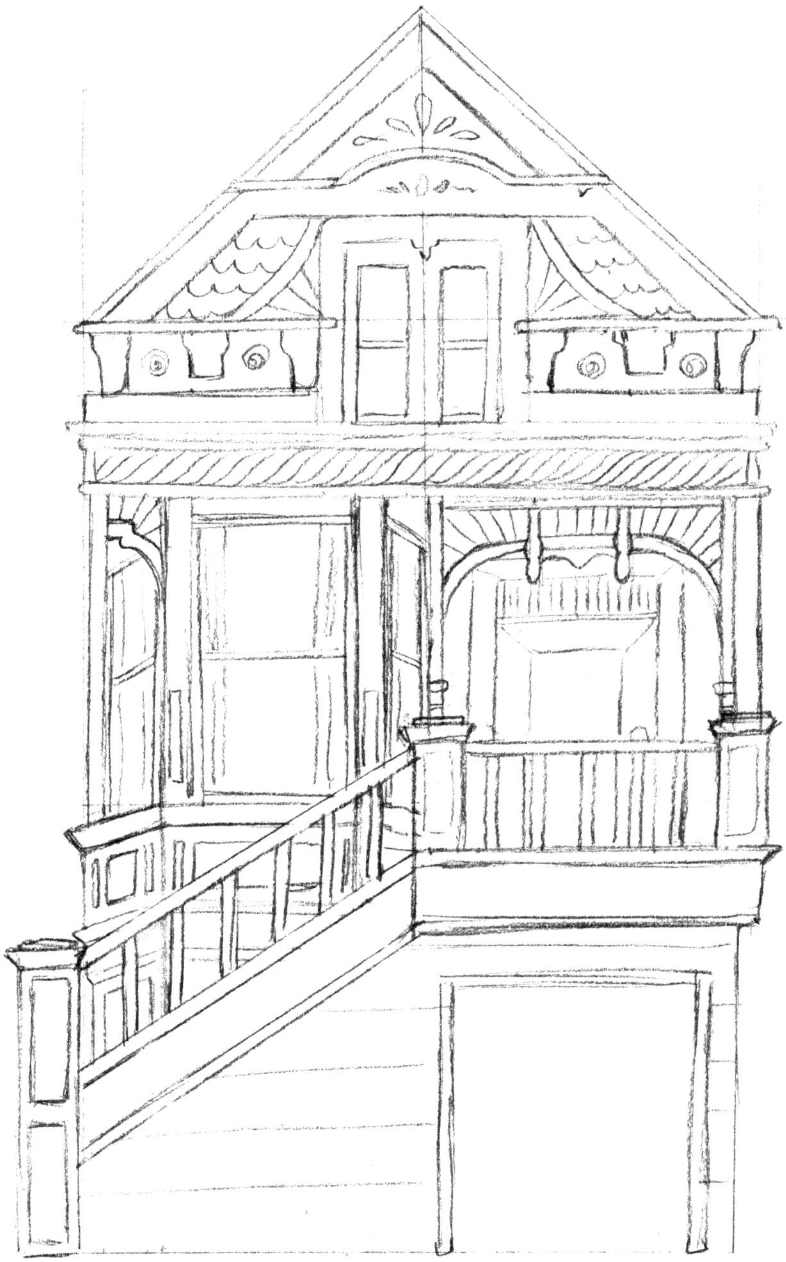

2. Using your guide, study your reference photo and add all the details, including the windowpanes, archway over the door, spindles on the staircase, and some of the decorative elements. At this point, keeping the elements rough is fine.

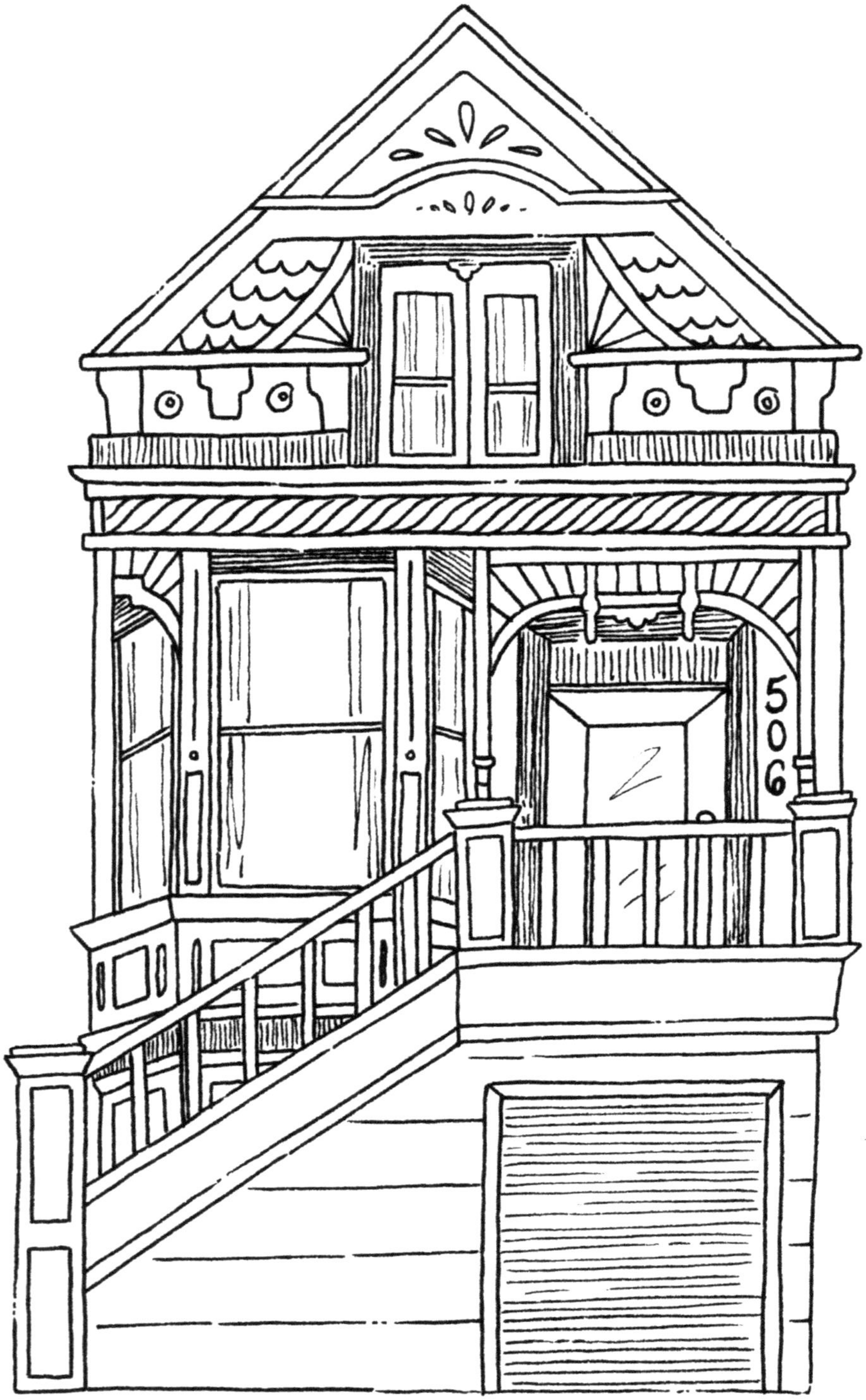

3. With pen, finalize all the details. I start by drawing all the vertical lines first, followed by the horizontal lines; then I finish the finer details.

• ARTIST'S TIP •

USE THIS SAME PROCESS FOR THE DIFFERENT ARCHITECTURE IN THIS SECTION. WITH JUST A LITTLE PRACTICE, YOU CAN TAKE A REFERENCE PHOTO OF ANYTHING AND DRAW ANY STYLE!

CITY CAFE

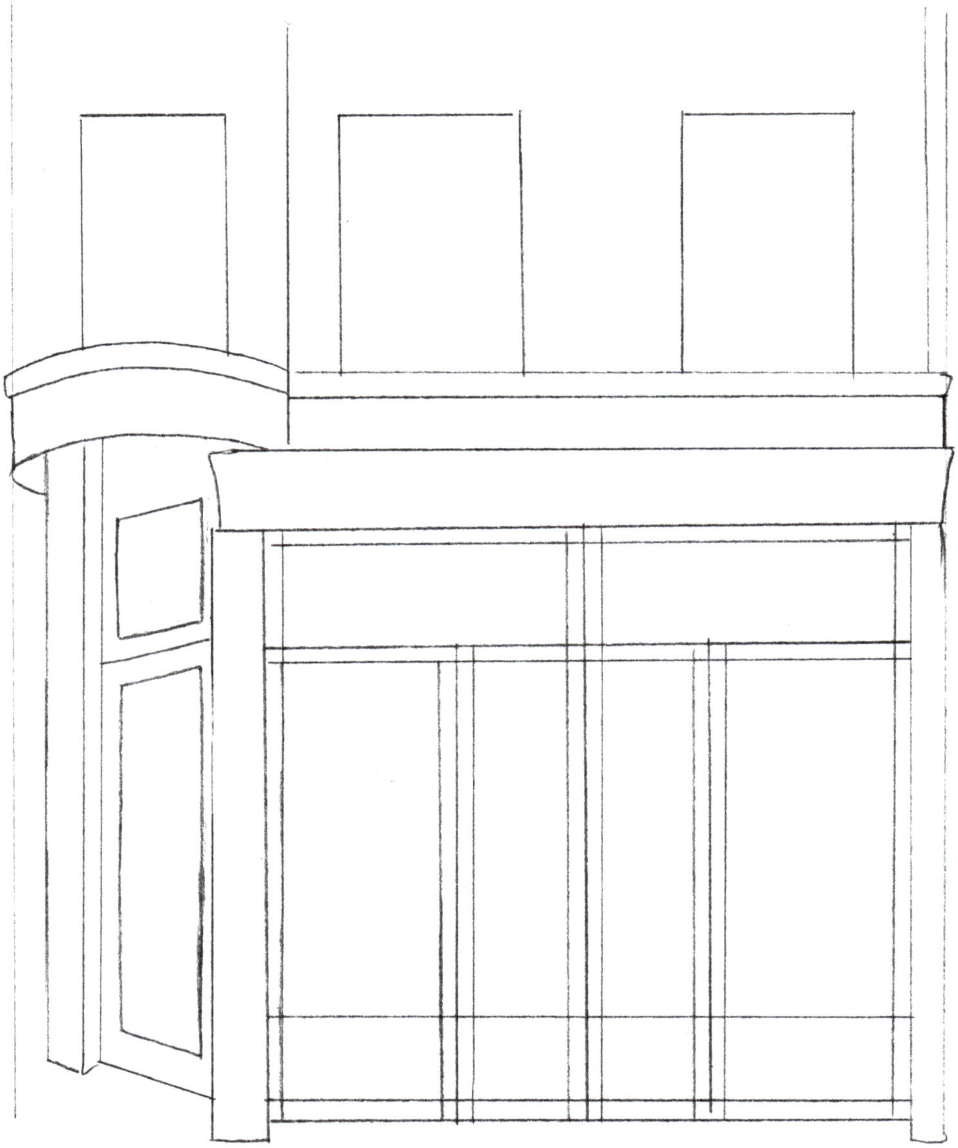

1. Gather your reference and ruler. Block in the building and its windows, signage, and door.

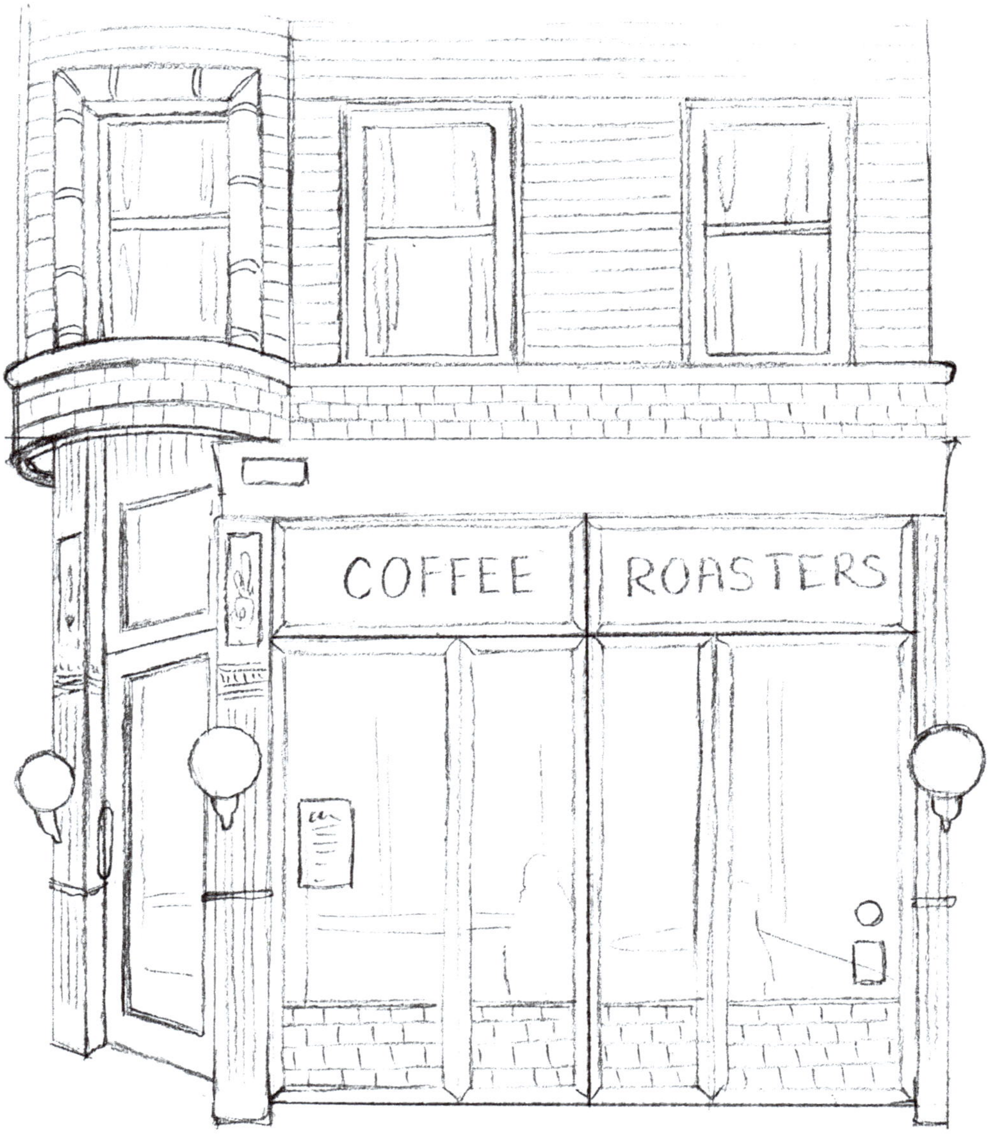

2

Using your guide and reference, add details, such as the windowpanes, brick, lamps, and frames.

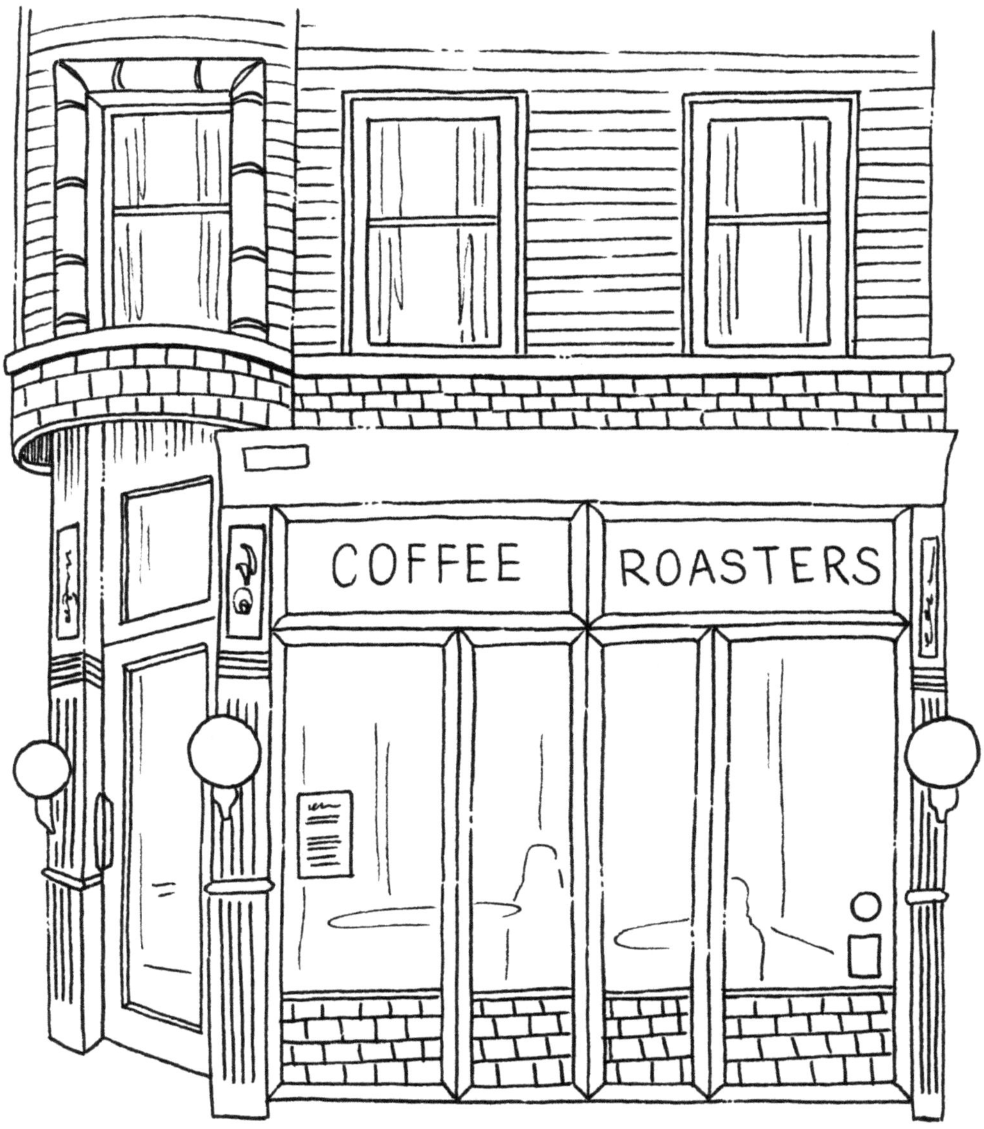

Use pen to ink the lines and finalize all the details. It's okay if your lines aren't perfectly straight. What gives a drawing personality is your own mark-making! To achieve a "through-the-glass" look, I use a lighter, broken touch, suggesting only general, amorphous shapes. This gives the illusion of objects inside the space.

DISTINCTIVE ARCHITECTURE & ICONIC LANDMARKS

On the following pages, we'll look at how to draw different types of distinctive architecture and iconic landmarks. I drew all of these buildings from photographic references, and I highly encourage the use of references when working with architecture in your own illustrations.

EIFFEL TOWER

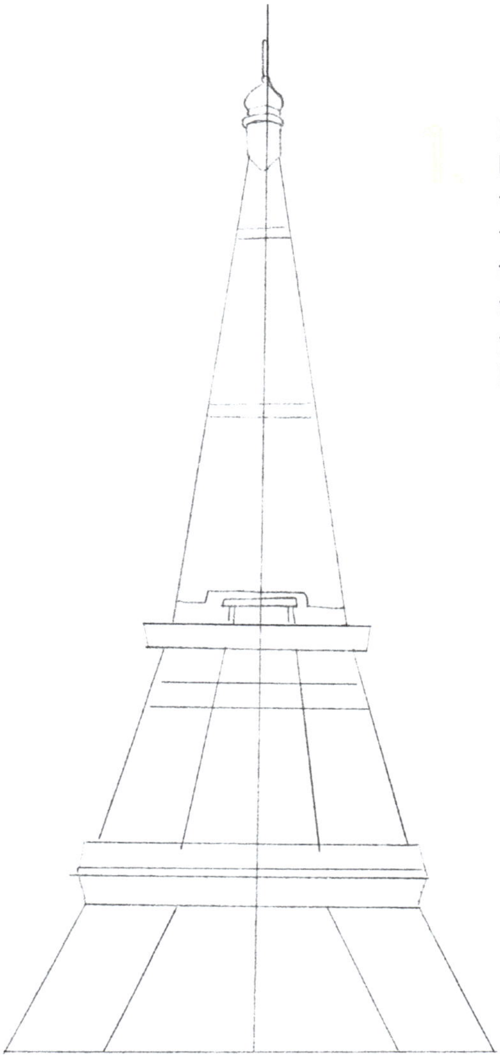

1. Draw the groundline, followed by a vertical line rising from the center. Draw a tall, very thin triangle for the tower's framework. Using your reference, generally plot out the platforms with horizontal lines. Define the angles of the legs.

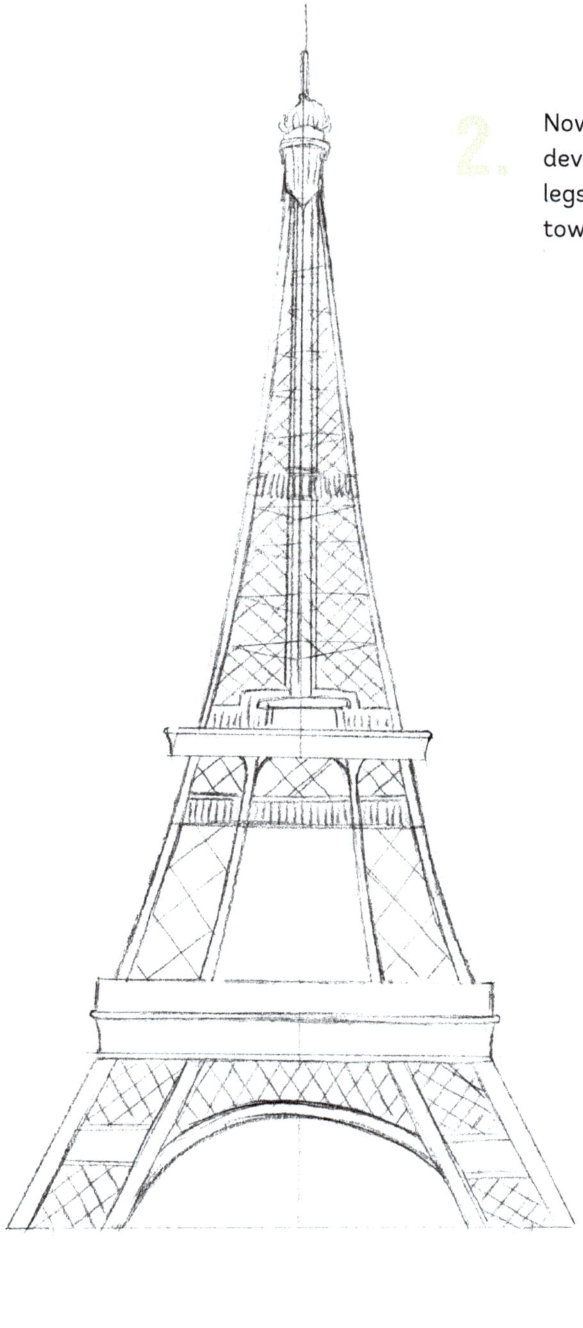

2. Now add rough details. Here, I develop the framework of the legs and sides, the top of the tower, and the center details.

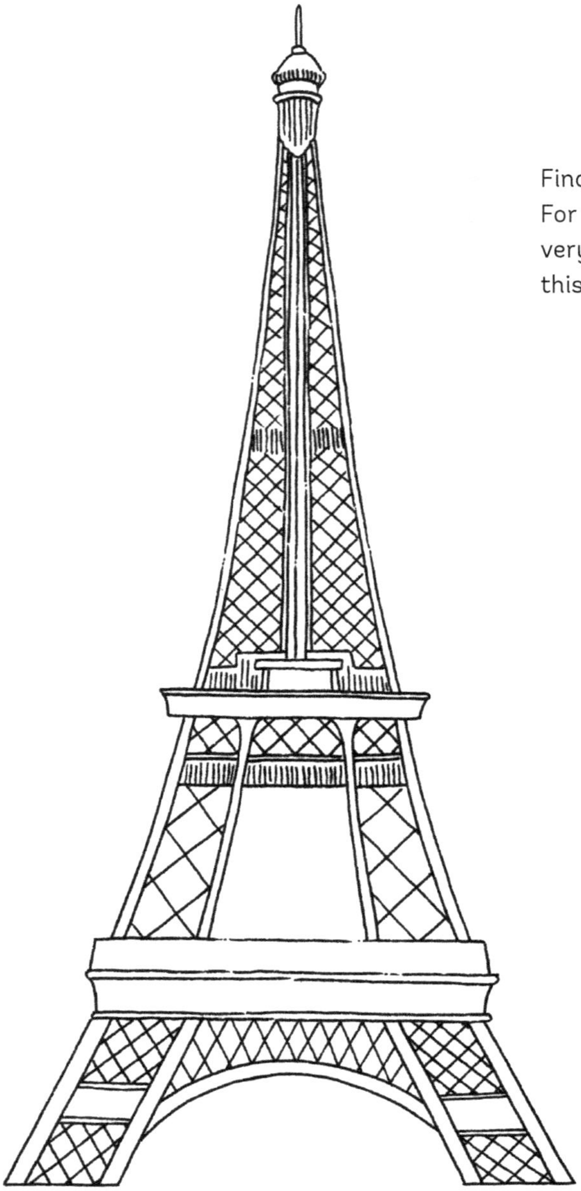

Finalize the details with pen. For the crosshatching, I use very precise lines to simplify this complicated structure.

BIG BEN

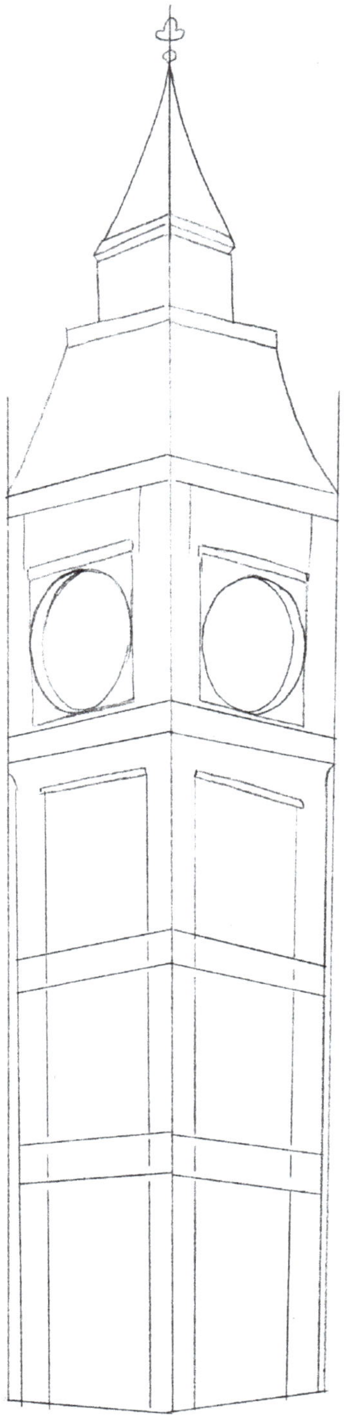

Begin with three vertical lines to block in the general shape; connect them at the bottom. Using your reference and ruler, plot out major architectural features of the tower.

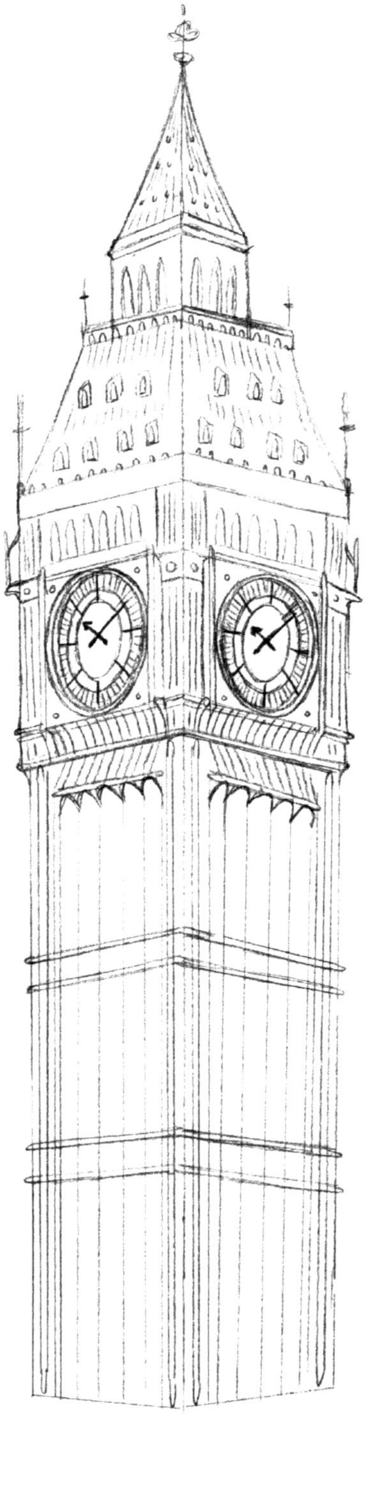

2

Sketch in the details:
windows, clockface,
and decorative lining.

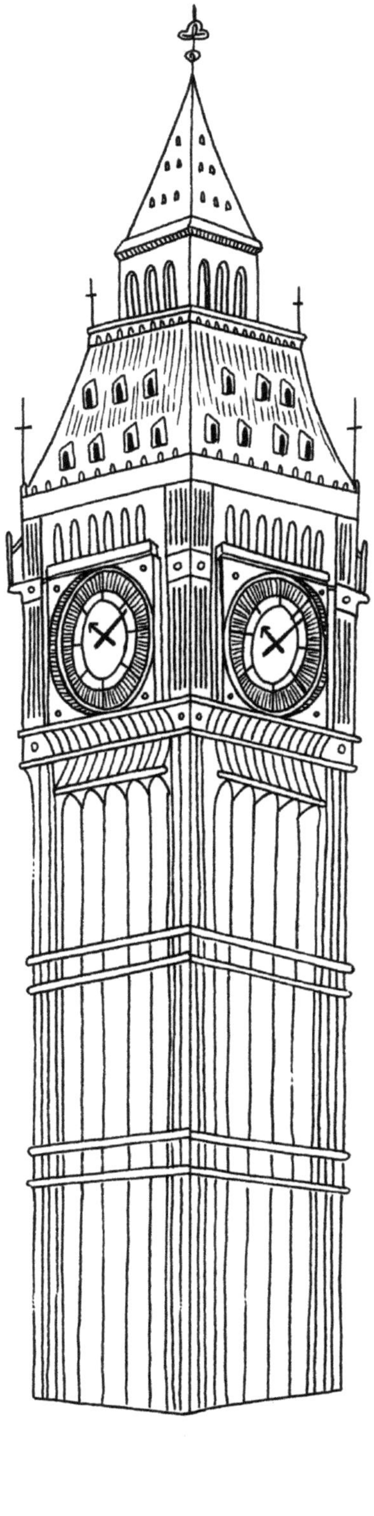

3. With pen, finalize the architectural lines and details.

EMPIRE STATE BUILDING

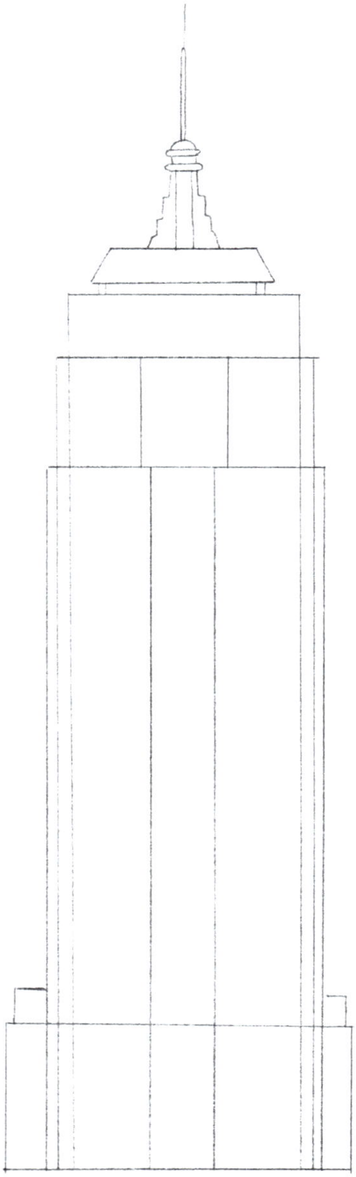

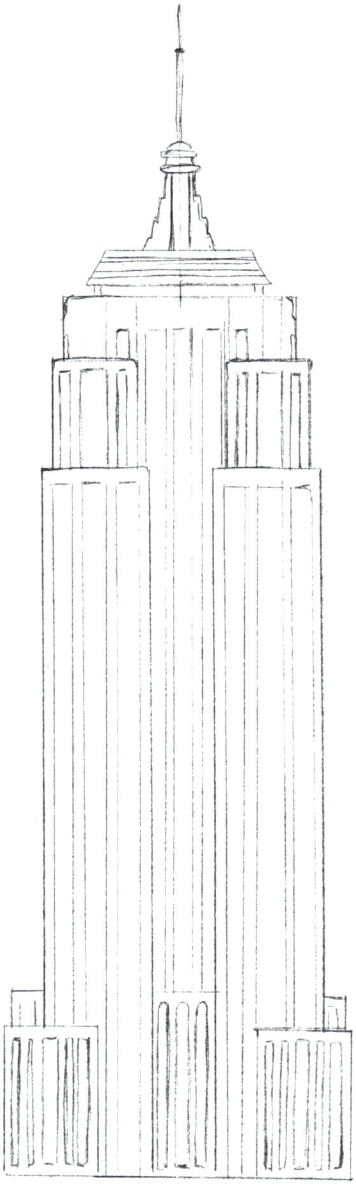

The Empire State Building was created in the Art Deco style and is known for its symmetrical design and layered parallel lines. Lay down the groundline and a tall, thin rectangle. Using your reference, draw overlapping rectangles on top of the original rectangle.

Sketch in the details, adding the top spire and the windows.

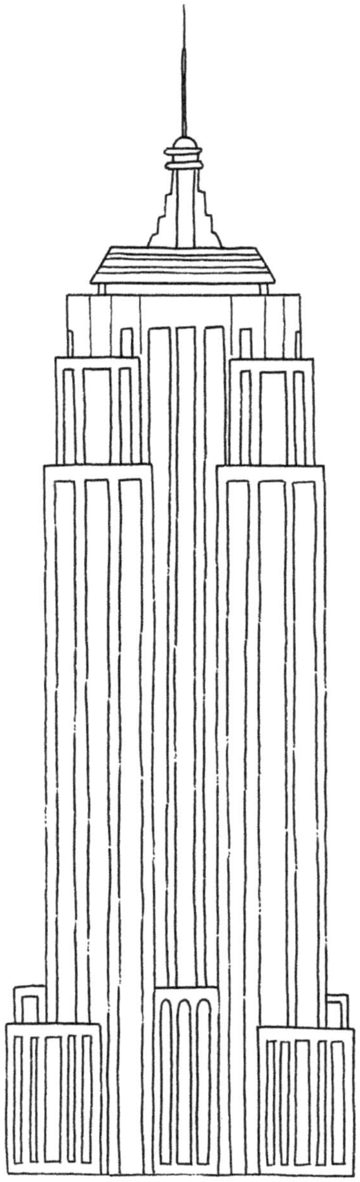

3. Ink all of the details carefully, defining the long lines of the building.

FORBIDDEN CITY

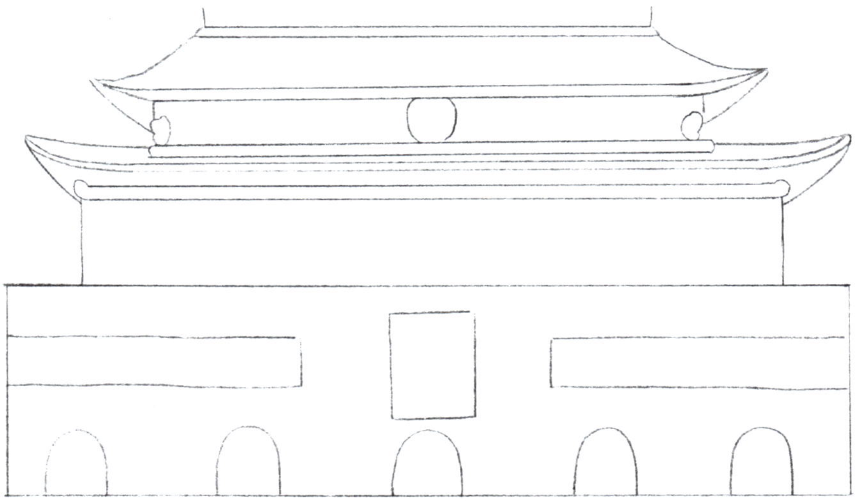

I love architecture like this! The roofs are the most fun to draw, and the ornamental elements are really cool. Draw a long, horizontal rectangle for the base. Then draw a smaller rectangle on top, followed by another—like layering a cake. Block in the roof and arches.

Develop the details, including the lines on the roof, the lanterns, and the portrait.

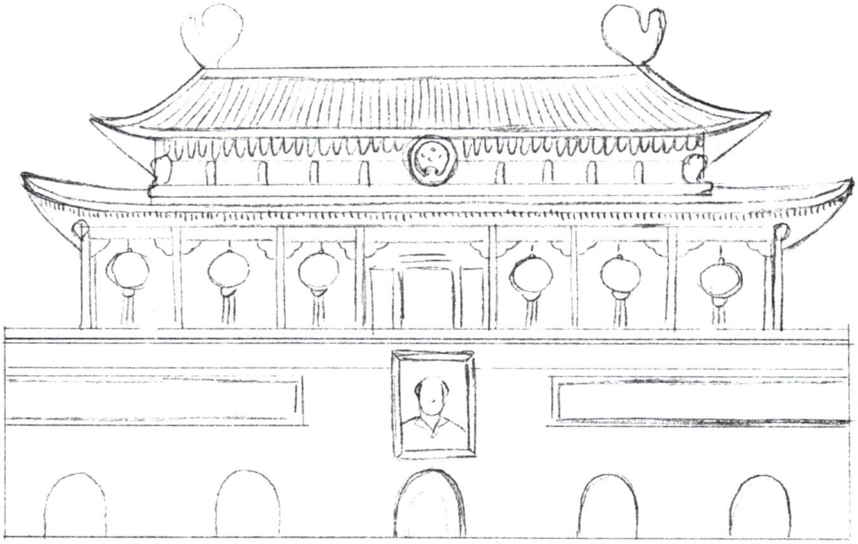

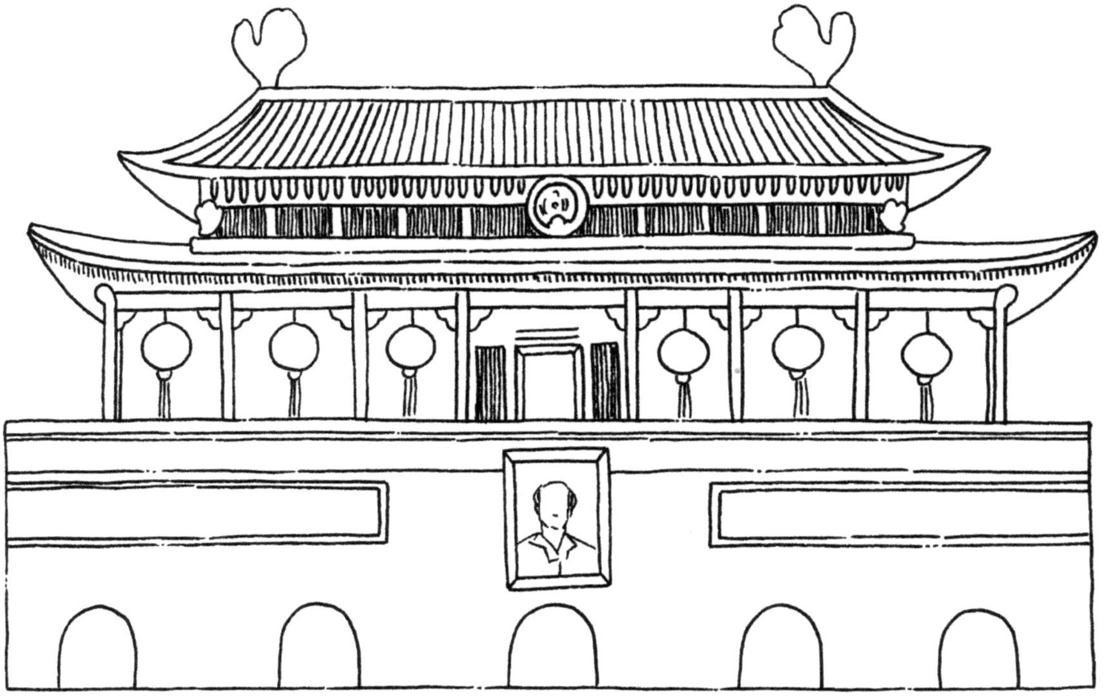

3. With pen, finalize the lines and details, adding hatching and extra marks in places to give the temple personality.

TAJ MAHAL

Draw a groundline followed by five vertical rectangles, making the center rectangle the widest and tallest. Add a thin tower on each side; then block in the domes, openings, and main sections.

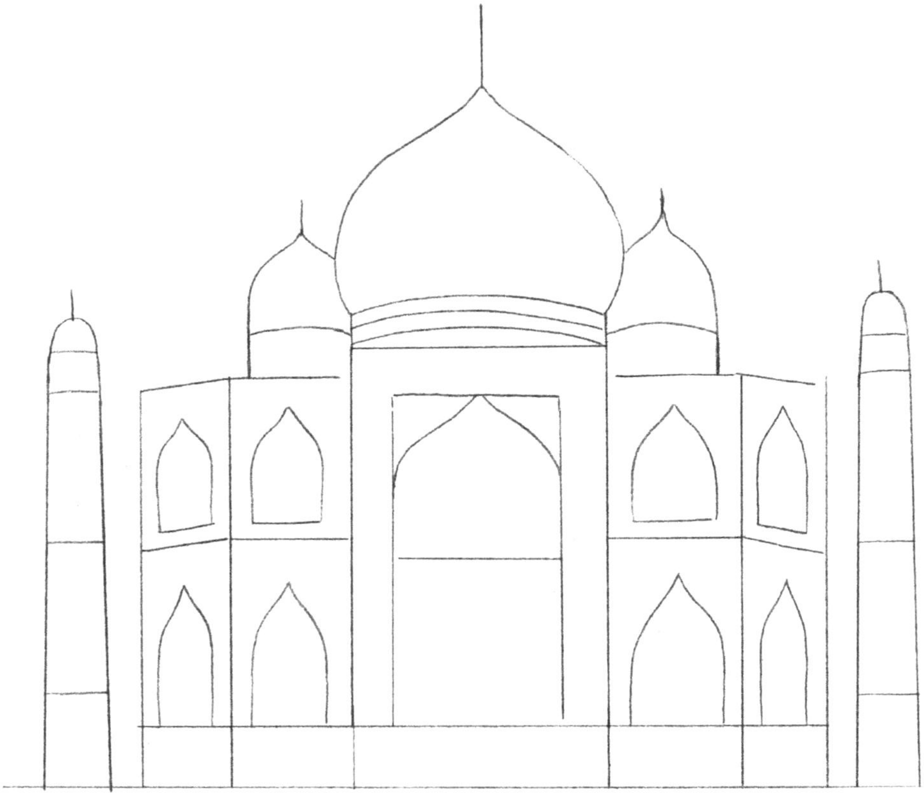

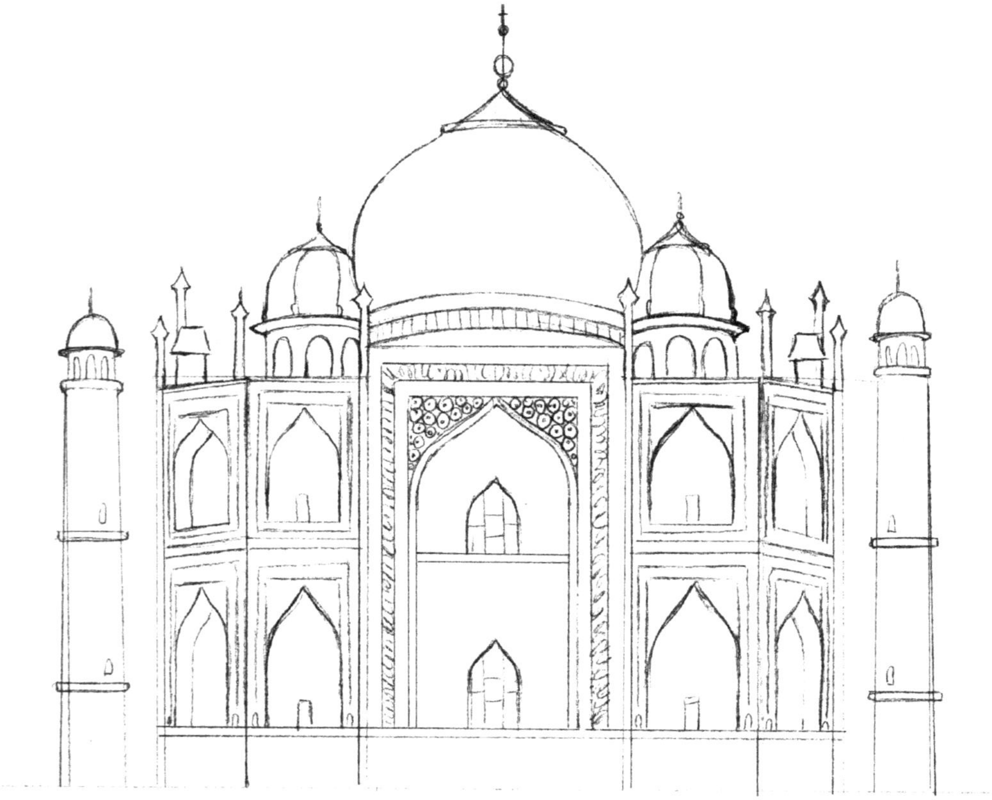

Develop the details, including the archways, ribs of the towers, doorways, and decorations. Make sure the symmetrical elements are the same width and height. Consistency makes the drawing!

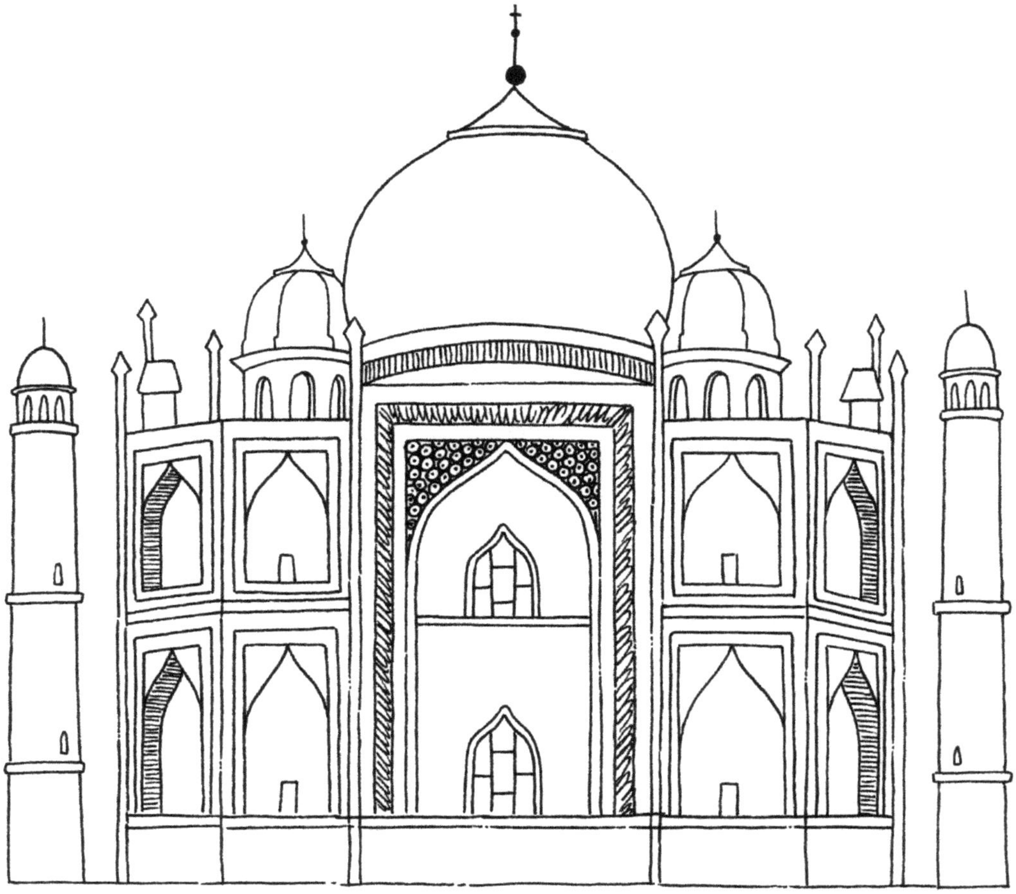

Use your pen to ink the final lines and details.

AMSTERDAM ROW HOMES

1. For these iconic row homes, start with a long, horizontal rectangle. Then break it into five similar sections with vertical lines. Using your reference, draw the basic outlines of the houses. What makes these so wonderful are the varied roof shapes!

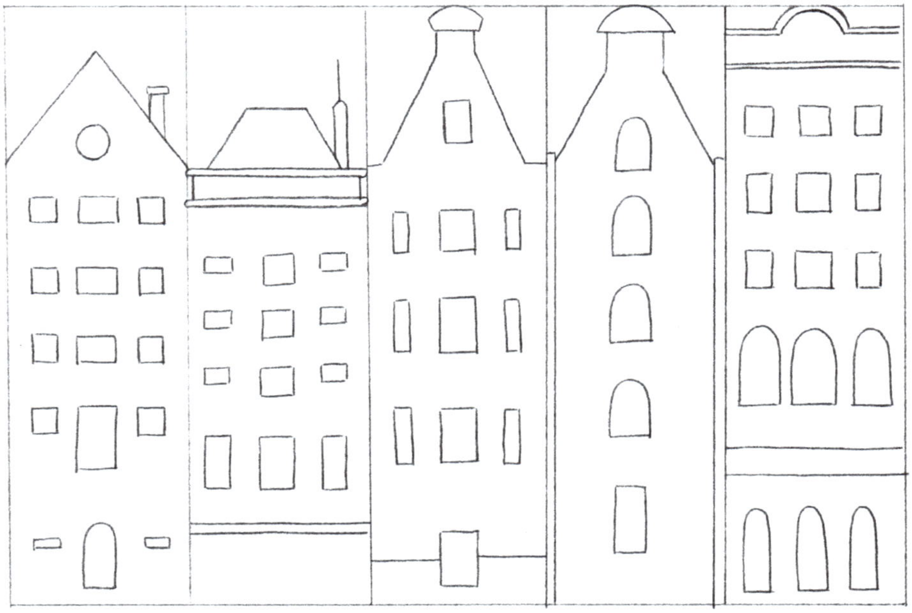

2. Refine the windows, decorative elements, and other details.

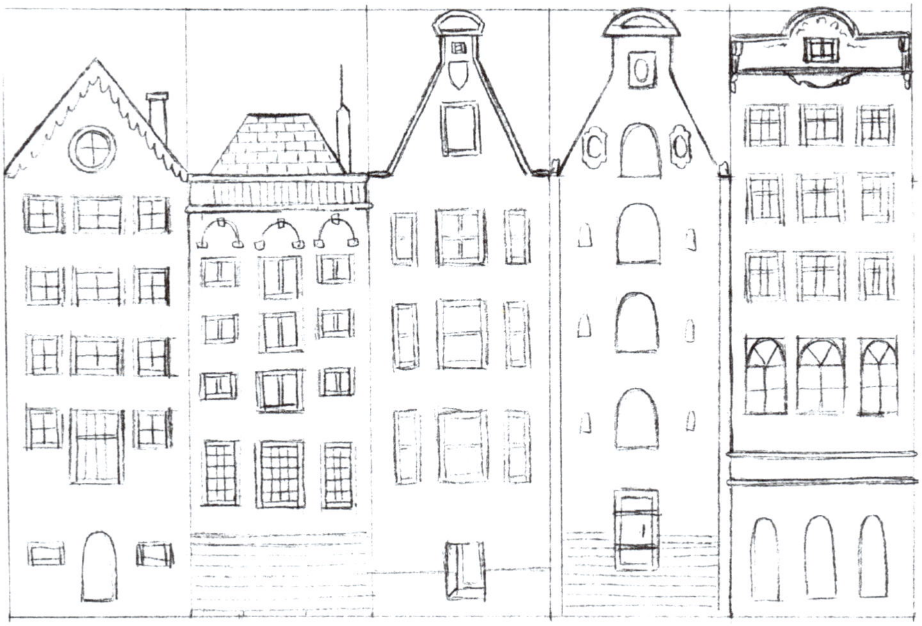

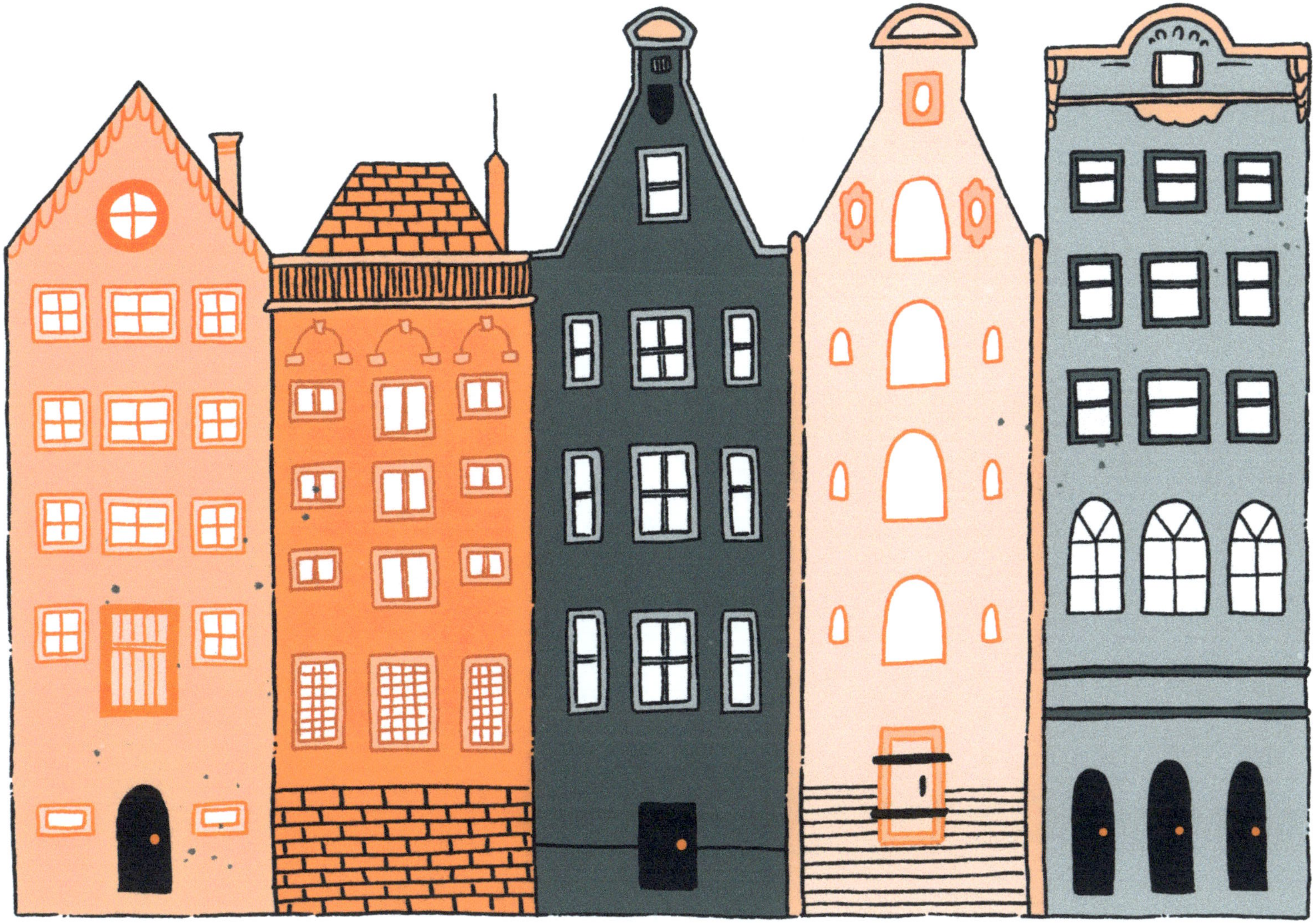

3. Finalize with pen and refine all the details. And color, if you'd like.

SYDNEY OPERA HOUSE

1. The beautiful Sydney Opera House has a very distinctive design. Using your reference and ruler, sketch the cones of the structure—it's okay to overlap in the sketch!

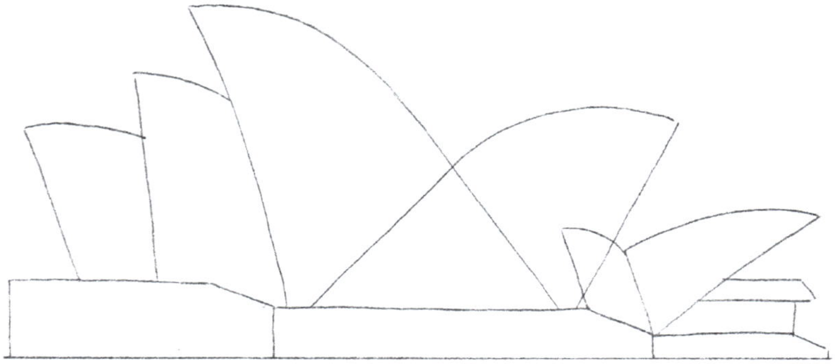

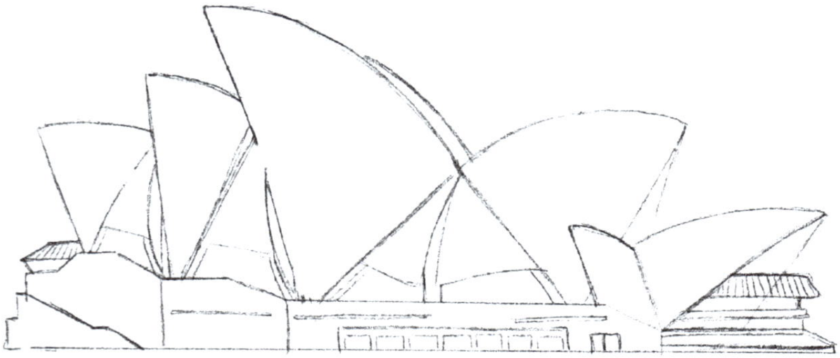

2. Finalize the shapes of the cones, and add the details to the base and arches.

3. With your pen, refine all the lines, finishing with the hatched sections of the roof.

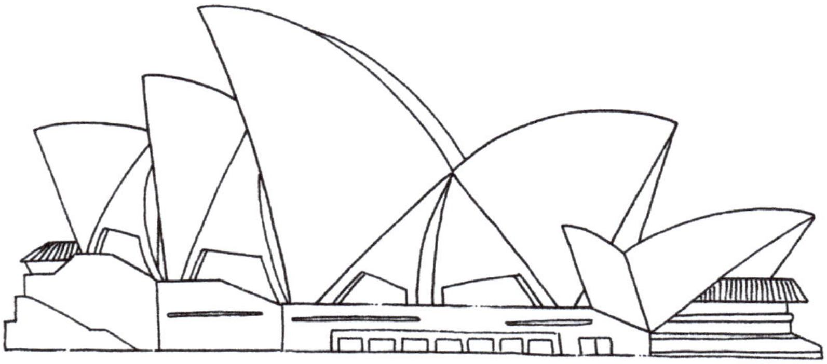

THE COLOSSEUM

1. Build the basic structure using horizontal arches and vertical lines. Add the slanted edges with diagonal lines. Then sketch in the arches.

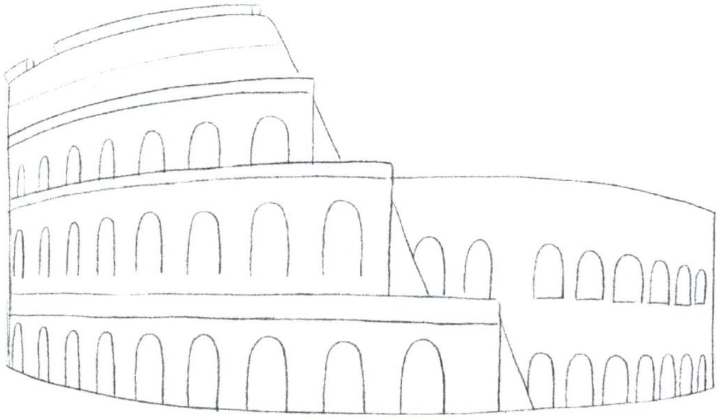

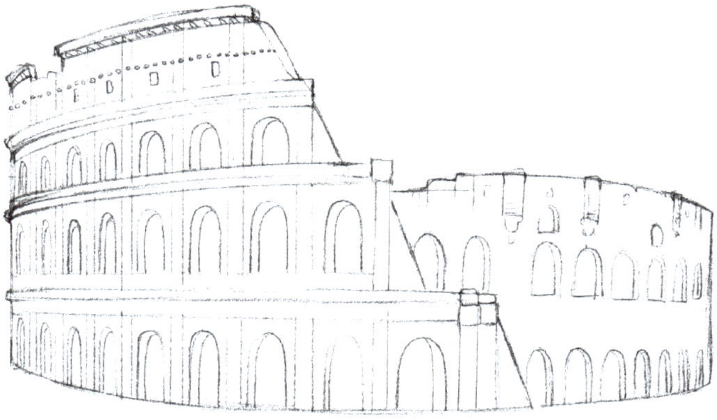

2. Develop the details and add perspective and depth to each arch.

3. Ink and finalize the details. I include a few subtle cracks to give the structure an ancient look.

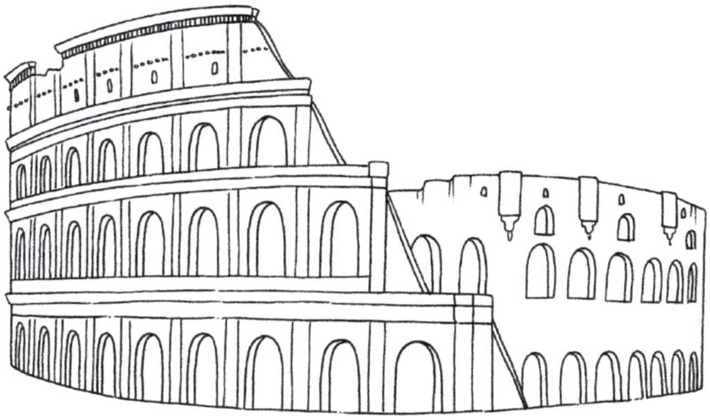

RUSSIAN ORTHODOX CATHEDRAL

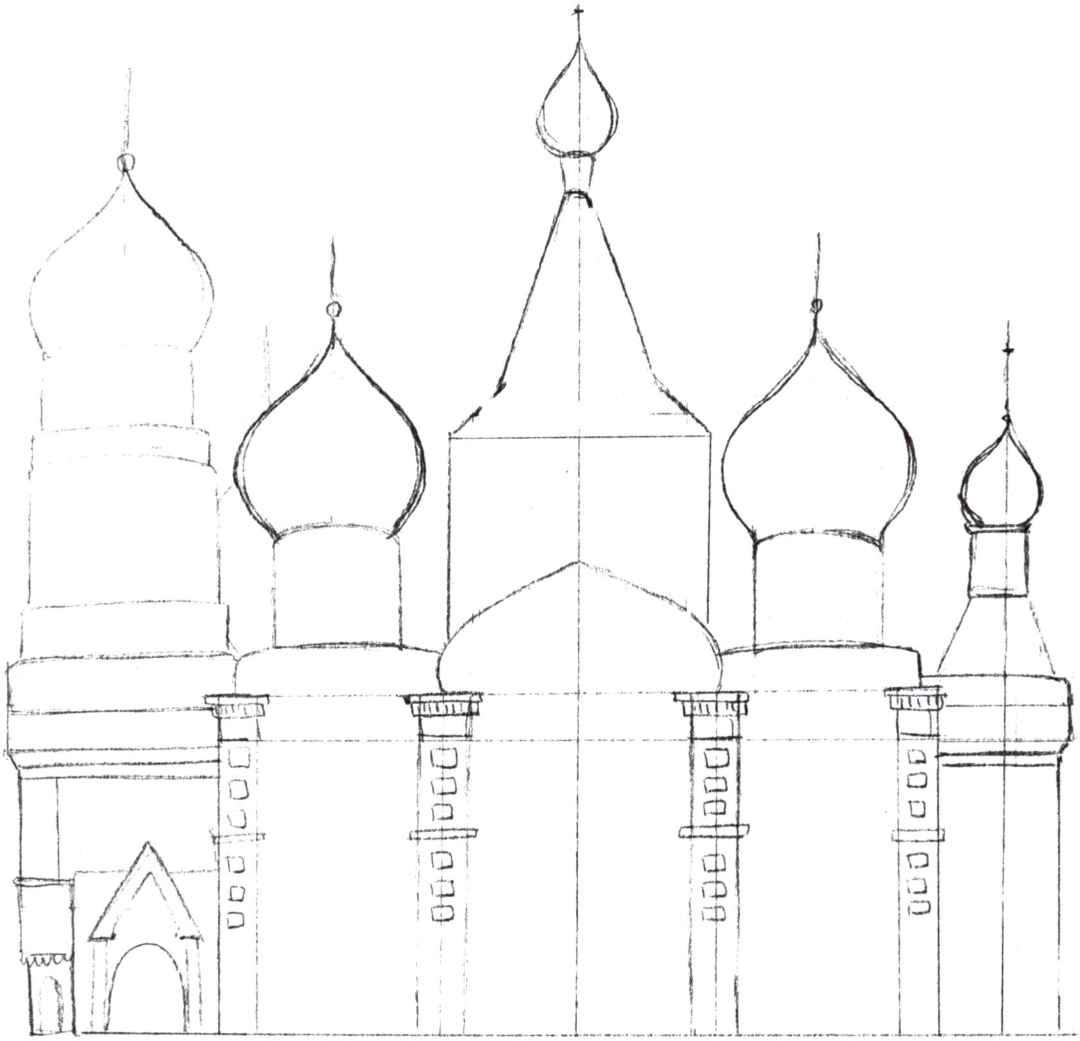

1. The Cathedral of the Resurrection of Christ in St. Petersburg is perhaps one of the most intricate pieces of architecture in the world. Using all of the techniques you've practiced, give this complex building a go! Start with the groundline, and then draw the center cylinder (or turret). On each side, block in a smaller cylinder. The left side of the cathedral has a larger turret, while the one on the right is smaller.

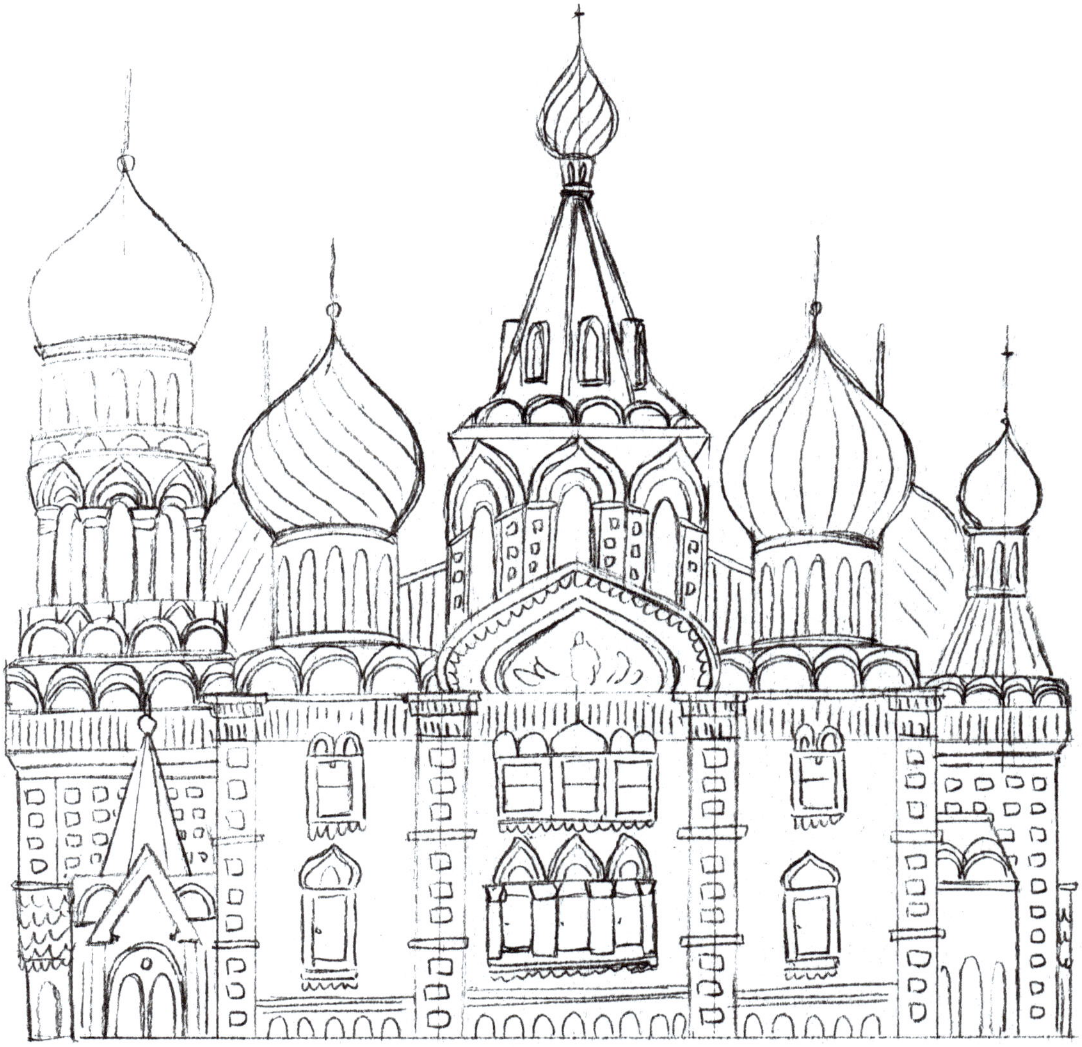

2. Start drawing in the details—don't let them scare you! Start with the main columns in the base, spacing them out correctly. Then move to the details and doors in the turrets. From there, add the windows and the decorative molding on the base of each turret.

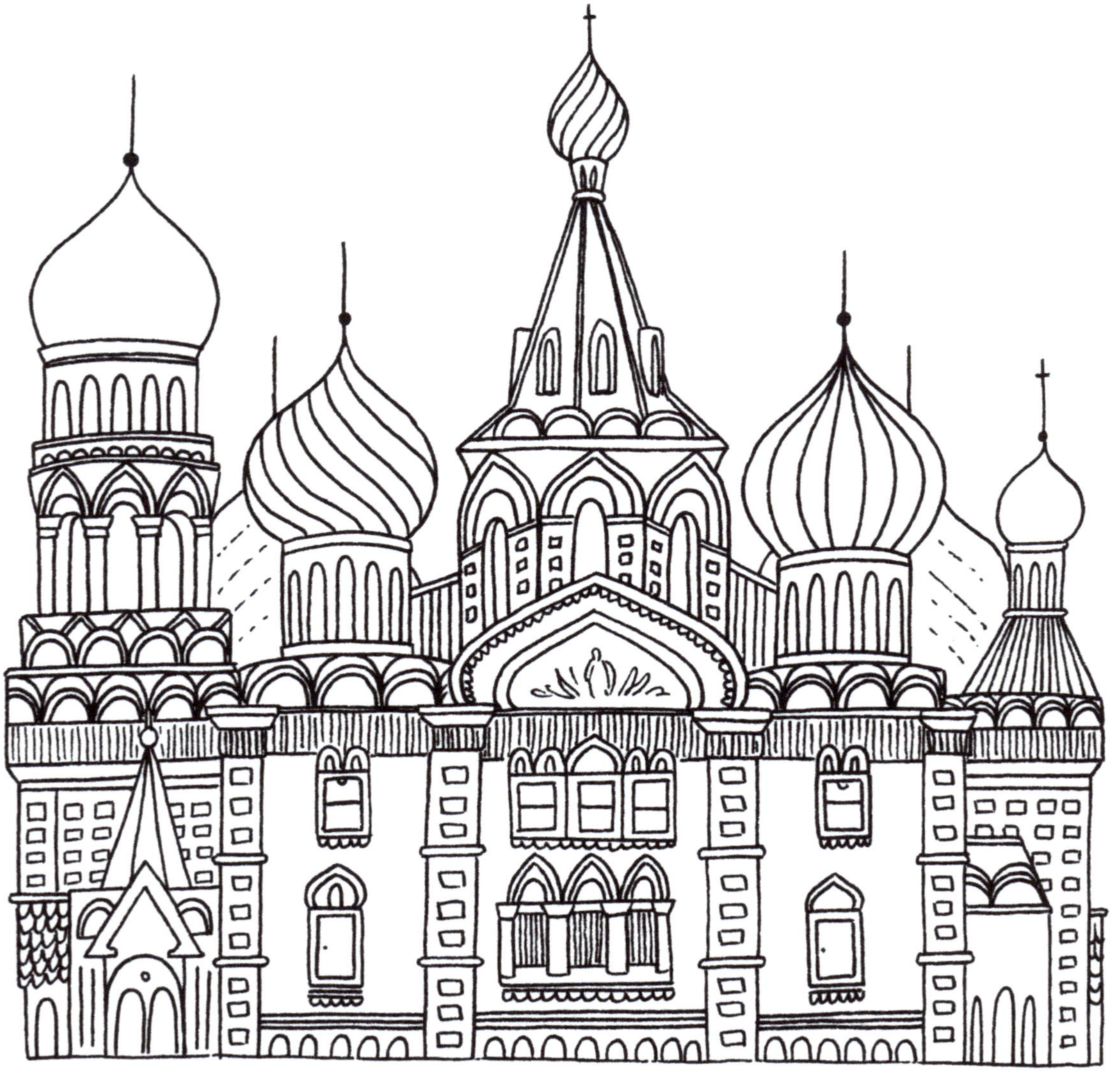

3. Using your pen, ink over your lines. This structure is very detailed, but yields a great result when finished! Don't be afraid to simplify.

SIGNAGE

STREET SIGN

Start with a long, thin rectangle. Draw a thin, perpendicular pole behind the center of the sign. Add the end cap to the top of the pole and a small detail line on the top and bottom of the rectangle. Finish by hatching a shadow and adding the name of the street.

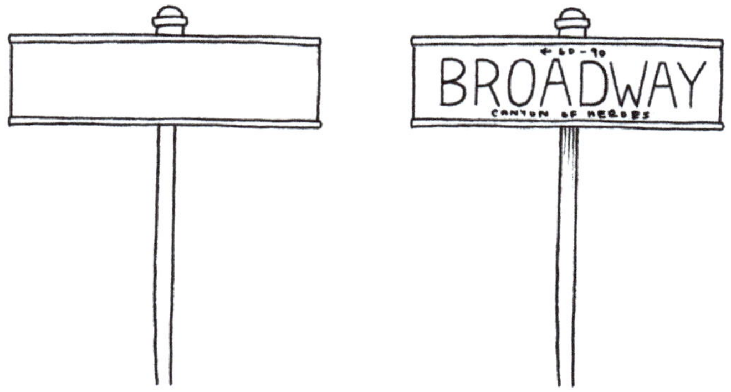

COFFEE SHOP SIGN

For this hanging shop sign, start with a vertical line for the wall. Then draw a perpendicular, horizontal line with a curl at the end. Draw an oval for the sign and a curved, curling line for the ironwork at the top. Draw two little chains for the hanging apparatus. Add thickness to the iron bars and the frame. Add the shop name!

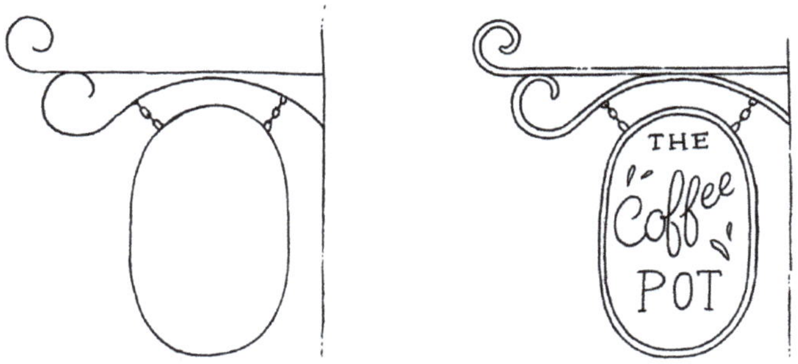

MOTEL SIGN

Begin with a large rectangle. Draw a smaller one above it. Add a center pole and two smaller signs coming off the side. Draw perspective lines to the left side of all signs—make sure they are parallel to one another! This is the secret to good perspective. Add a decorative top and sign details.

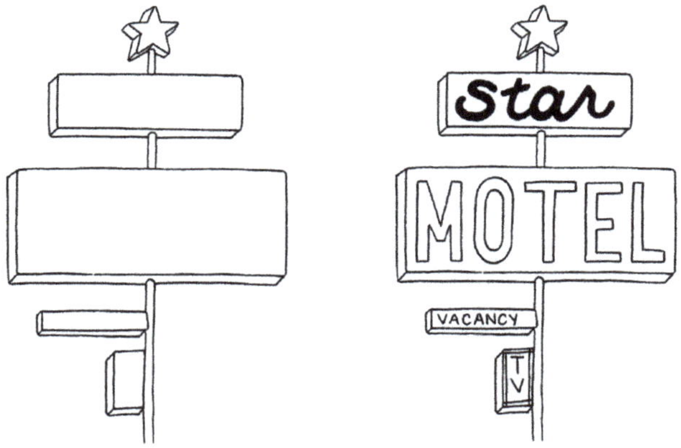

CREATIVE EXERCISE

STOREFRONT

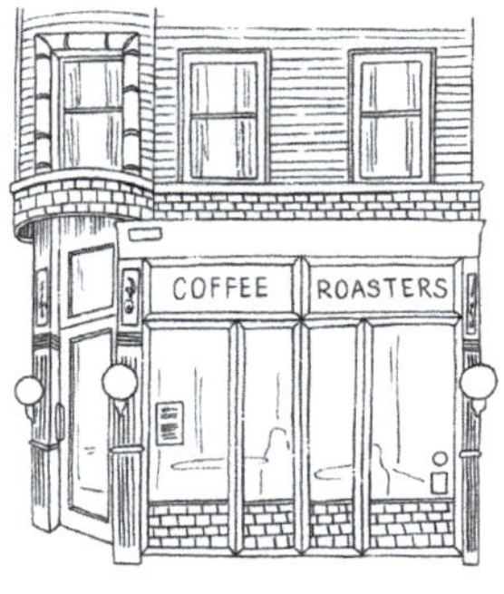

Now it's your turn! Have you traveled anywhere recently? Perhaps you have a favorite coffee shop or store in your hometown? Grab some paper and draw a storefront or building that inspires you!

ANIMALS & INSECTS

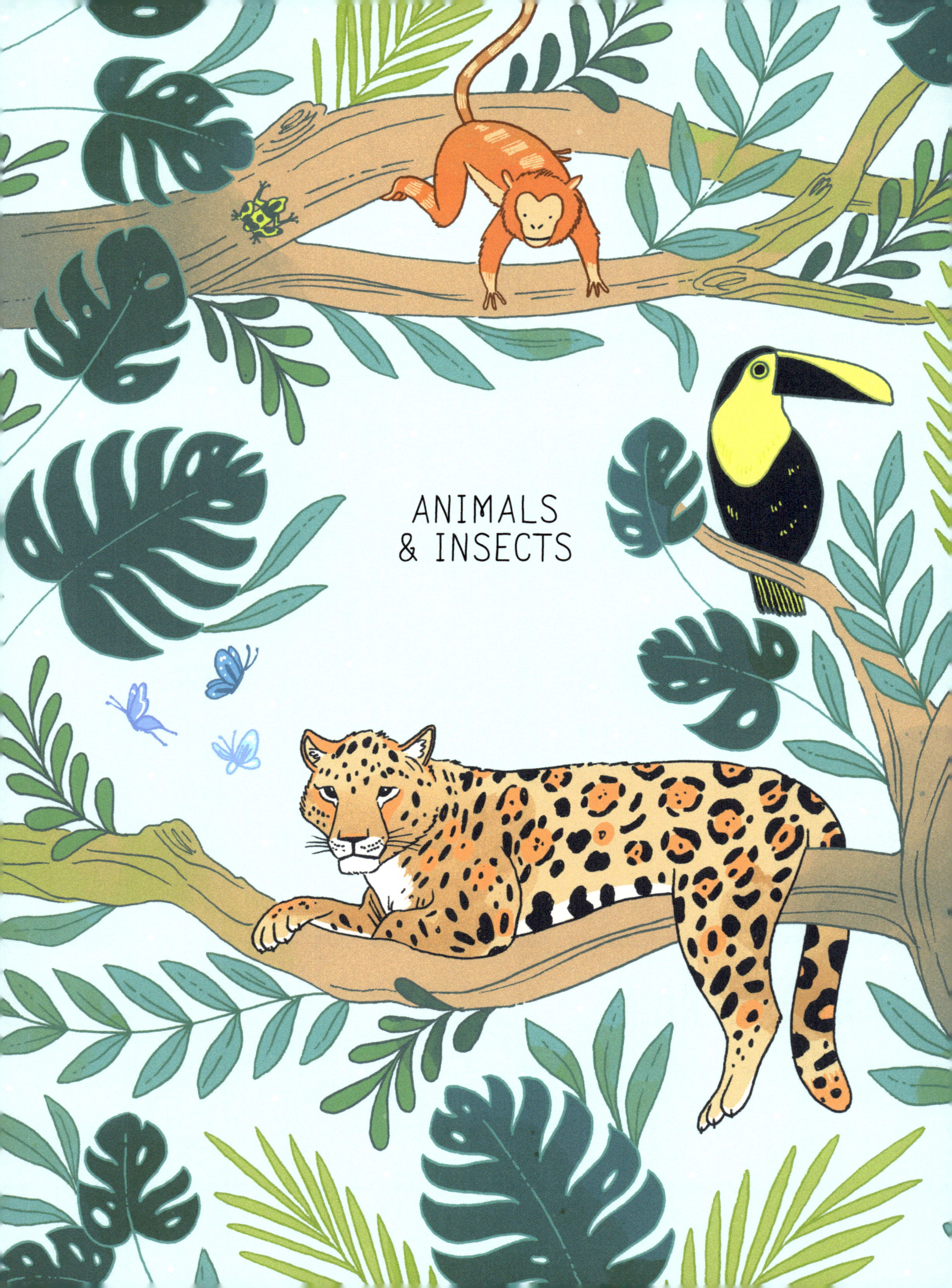

ANIMALS & INSECTS

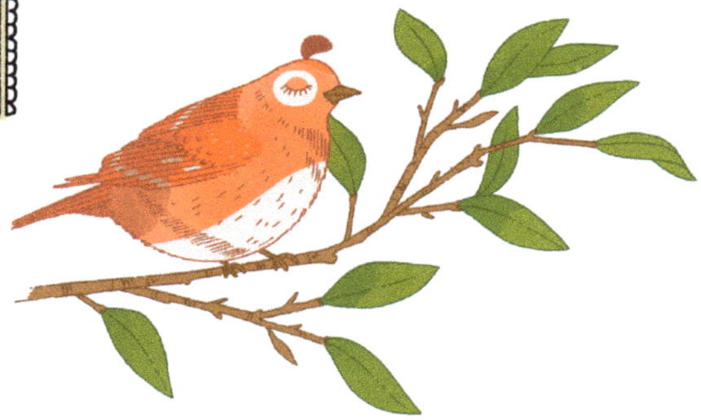

In this section, we'll explore how to draw many types of animals—from household animals, to exotic animals, to creatures of the air and sea, and even insects. Like drawing architecture, you'll greatly benefit from the use of reference images.

We'll start every animal by sketching its main characteristics with form circles. This will help you establish the animal's proportions and forms, making it possible for you to draw any animal!

BIRD

1. To draw a bird, start by drawing a large, egg-shaped oval. Then, on the wider end, draw a small oval for the head. Draw straight lines to delineate the legs and tail.

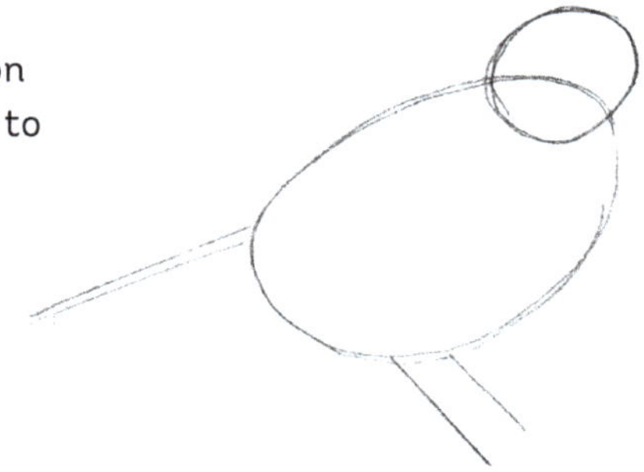

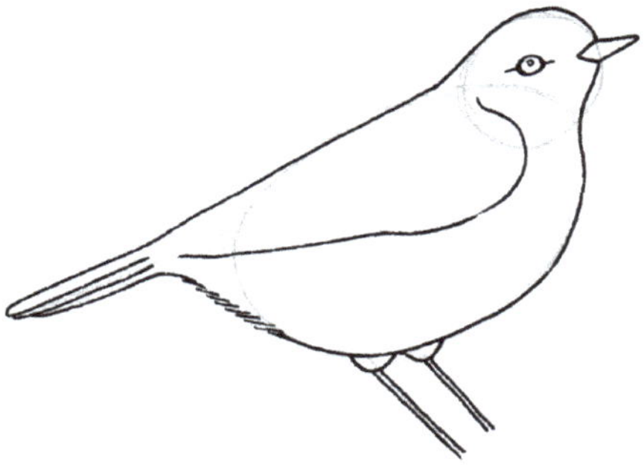

2. Trace the outline with pen, connecting the head and chest with curved lines. Add a beak and an eye, and define the legs and tail.

3. Fill out the wings with feathers and add any special markings.

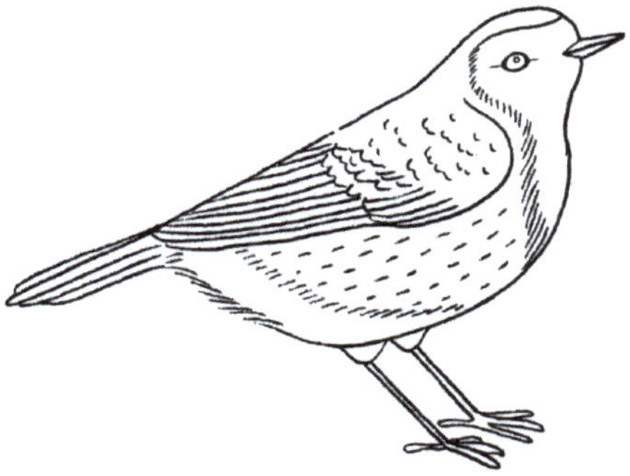

CAT

1. Start with a basic pencil sketch to create the framework. The main body is shaped like a long bean. Sketch a loose circle for the head, about the width of the neck area. If the cat is walking, the legs will most likely be moving in sync on either side of the body.

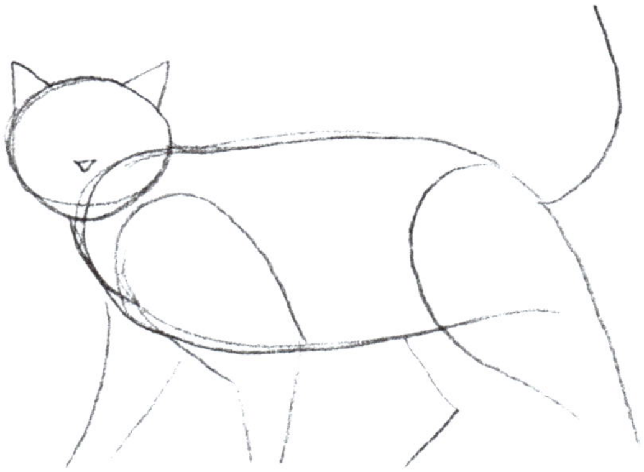

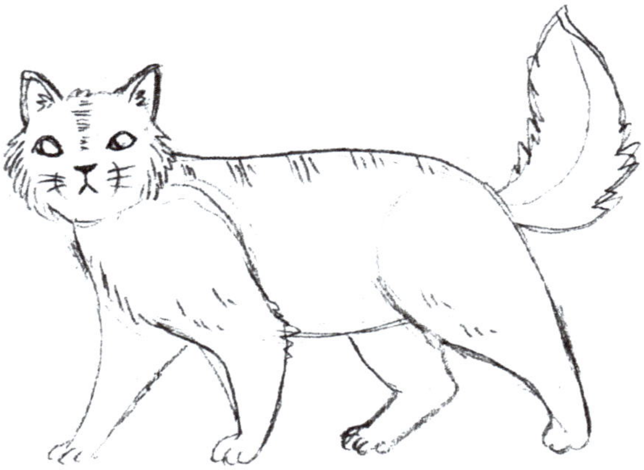

2. Add details to the cat. Create the shape of the face, define the paws, and add a fluffy tail.

3. Finish the cat in pen, adding stripes, fur markings, defined paws, and a sassy expression!

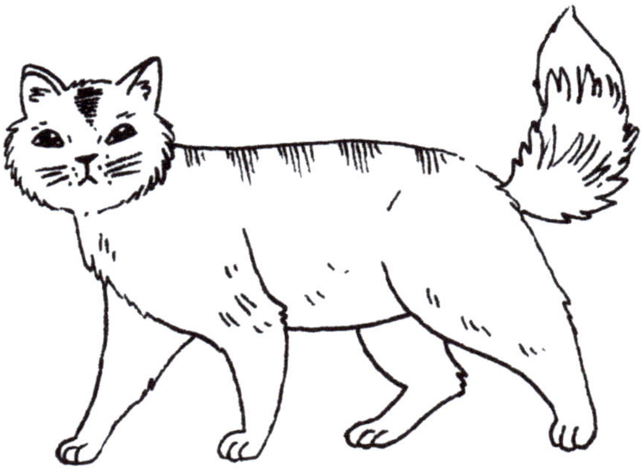

DOG

1. Dogs have a different stance, more limber legs, and different ears than cats. The head is also larger. This dog is standing calmly, facing the viewer, with ears relaxed.

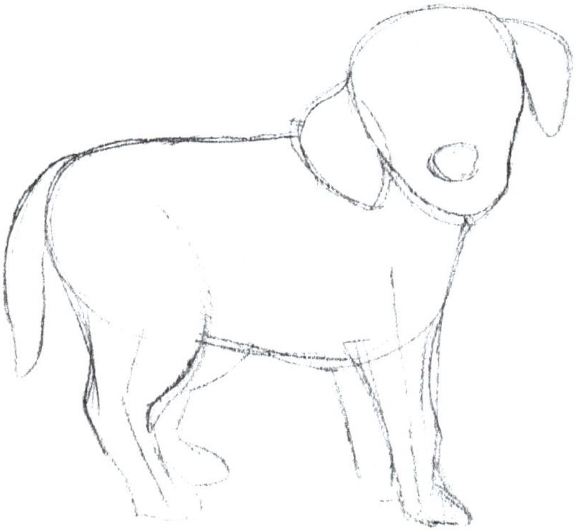

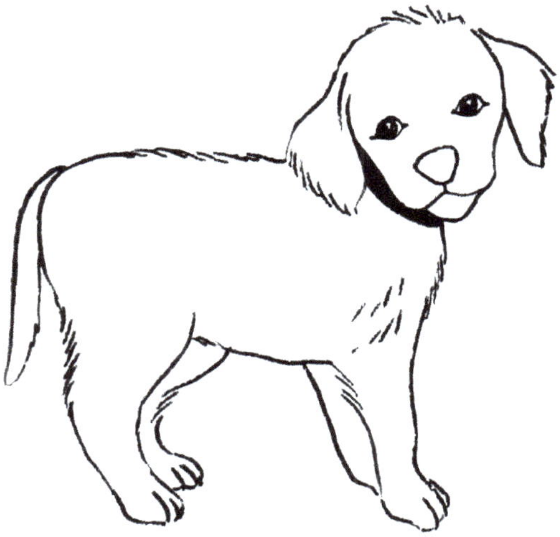

2. Start filling in the details. Notice that the nose is larger, the ears are folded, and the legs are more angular than a cat's.

3. Finish the dog with fur, facial marks, and a collar.

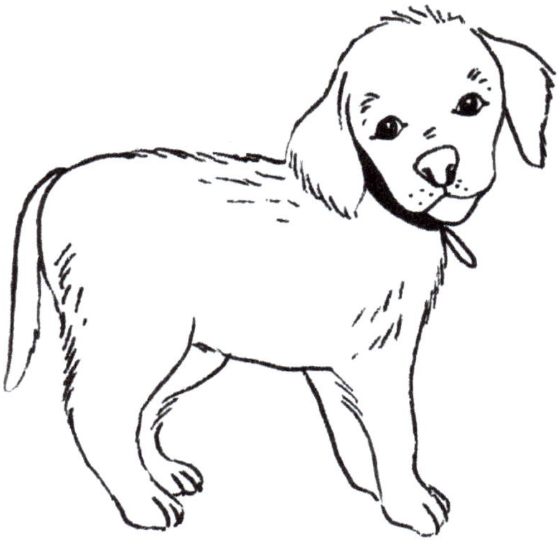

RABBIT

1. Start by drawing a large, egg-shaped oval for the body. Use smaller ovals to place the head, shoulder, and hind legs.

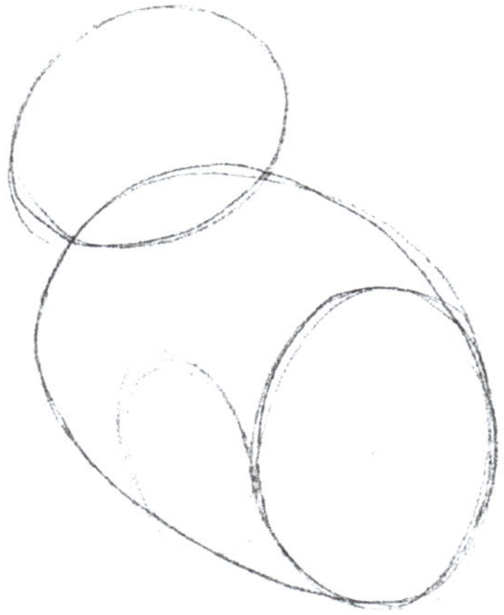

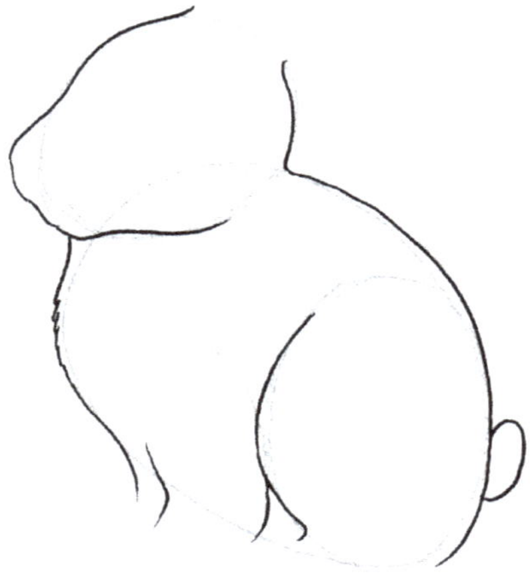

2. Start finessing the rabbit's shape. Note the curve in the top of the muzzle, the protrusion of the chest, and the tail.

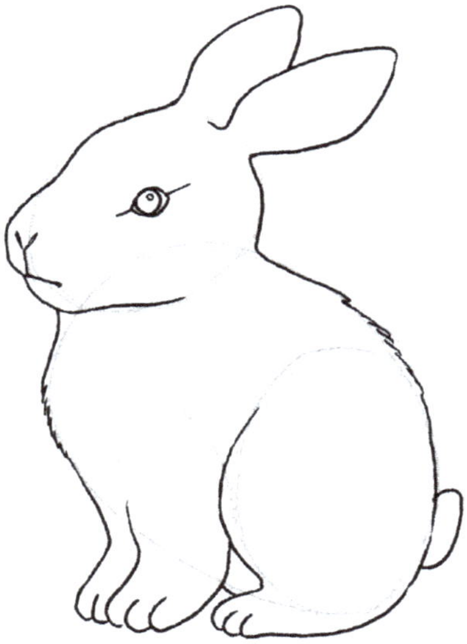

3. Add the ears and the paws. Then add a simple bunny nose and eye.

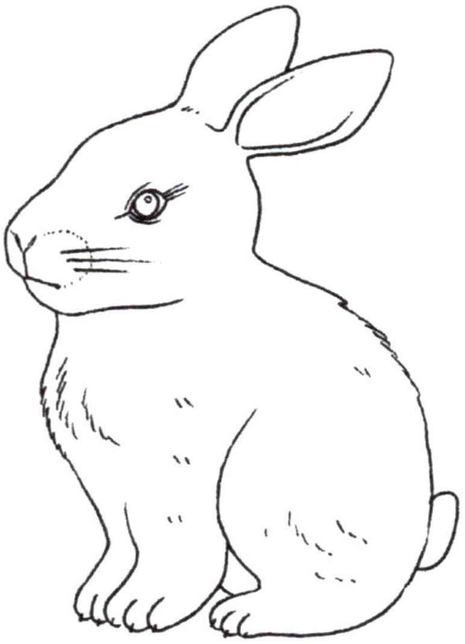

4. Finish by adding fur details, nails, details around the eye, whiskers, and definition in the ear.

HORSE

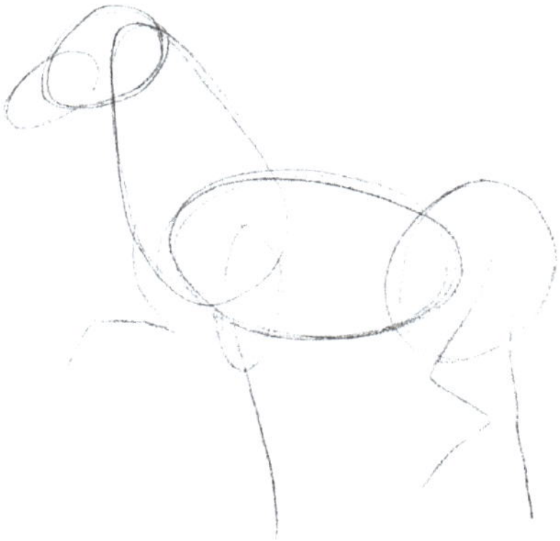

1. Start with a large, horizontal oval for the belly, making one side a bit larger for the chest. From the large side of the chest, draw a wide carrot-like shape for the neck—notice how muscular it is. Then draw two ovals for the head and muzzle. Finally, draw a large oval for the powerful hind legs.

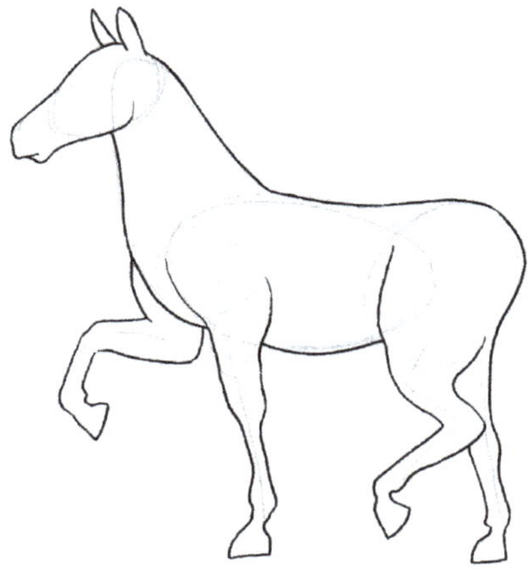

2. Ink the outline of the horse. Notice how the back arches parallel to the belly, how the backside is rounded, and how elegant and curved the neck is. Draw the ears and hooves. The legs can be tricky, so pay careful attention to your reference.

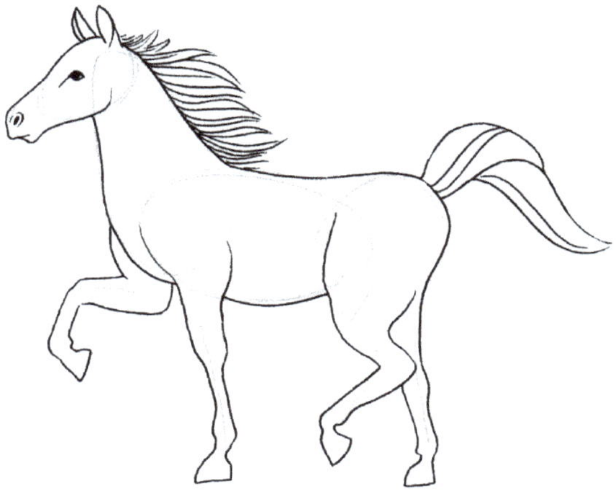

3. Add the nose, tail, and mane. My mane and tail are flowing in the wind. Then add a friendly eye.

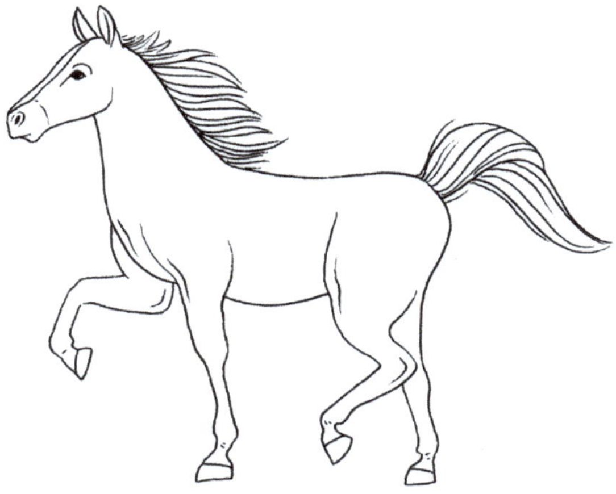

4. Finally, add details to the eye, nostril, and markings on the muzzle. Define the strands of the mane and tail with long, flowing lines. Mark the hooves, and add muscular lines to define the horse's form.

INSECTS

BEETLE

Beetles are complex insects with interesting shapes, so find a good reference for this one! Start with a wide oval. Divide the beetle into three sections: the lower body, the upper body, and the head. The lower body should be the largest section, and the head should be the smallest. Then divide the upper body in half vertically. Use your reference to determine the placement of the legs, mirroring each leg on either side of the body. Finish with shell markings: dashed lines down the lower body and dots on the upper body. Add the "feet" to all of the beetle's legs, and finalize the antennae.

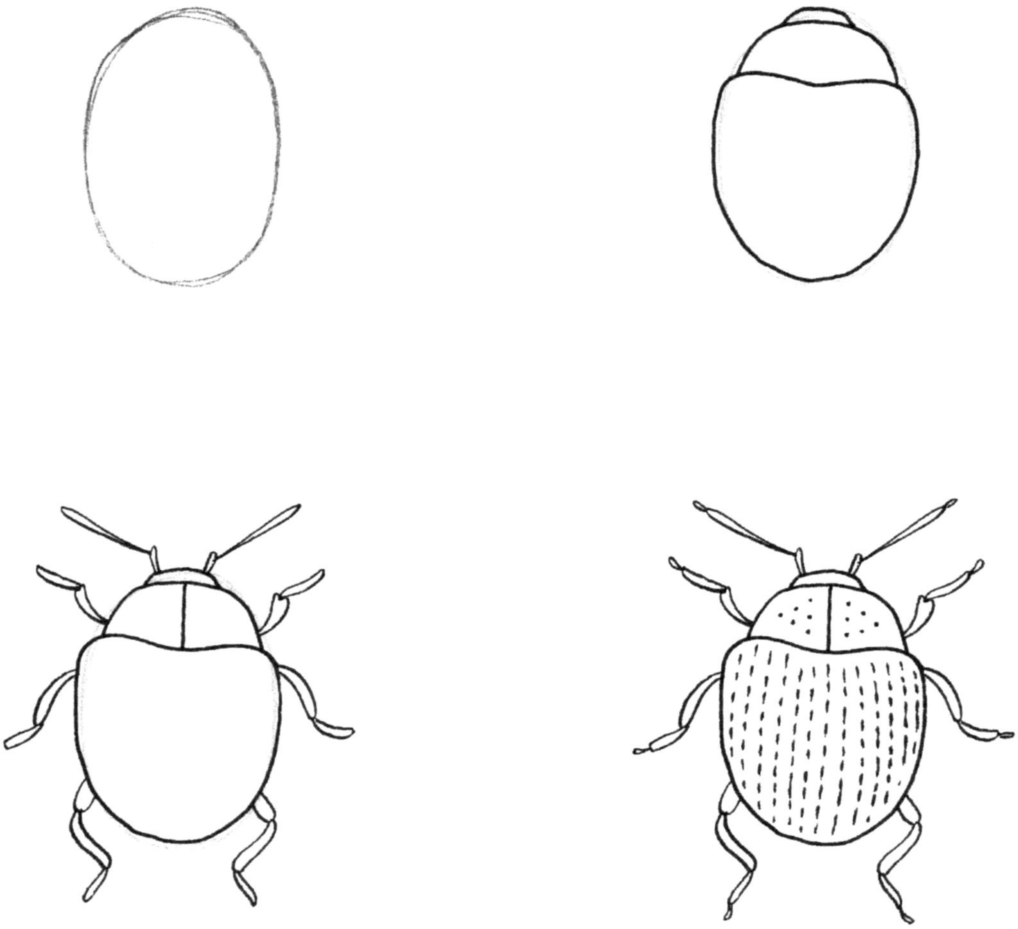

BUTTERFLY

For this monarch butterfly, a reference is helpful to work out the wing markings. Start with a long teardrop shape for the body, with the rounded end at the top. Then draw the upper wings as two symmetrical, rounded triangles. Draw the lower wings as symmetrical teardrop shapes. Ink the butterfly's outline, making the outer edges of the wings wavy. Then add antennae. Draw the patterns and markings in each wing section. The key here is symmetry! The two wings should look exactly the same.

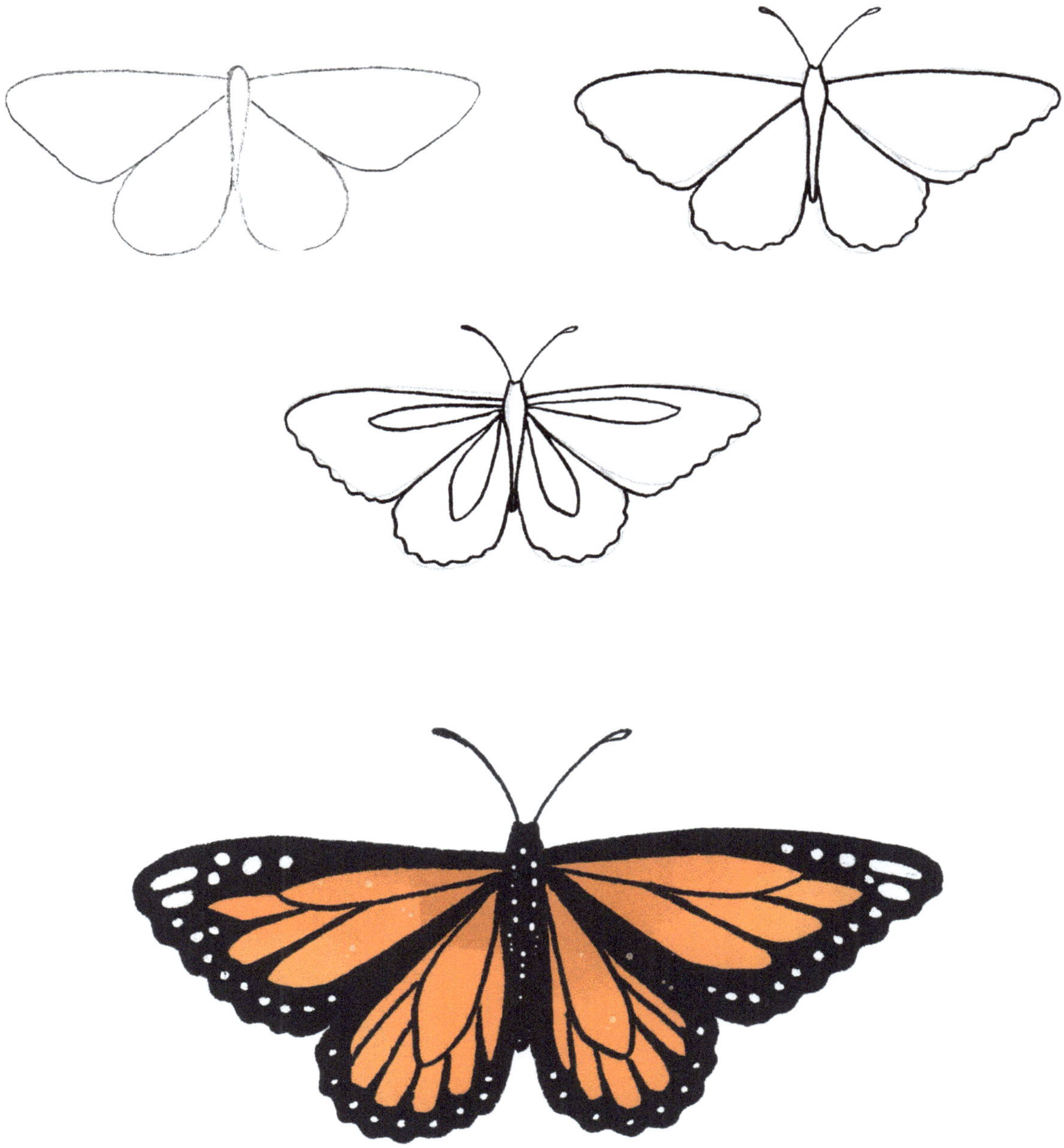

MONKEY

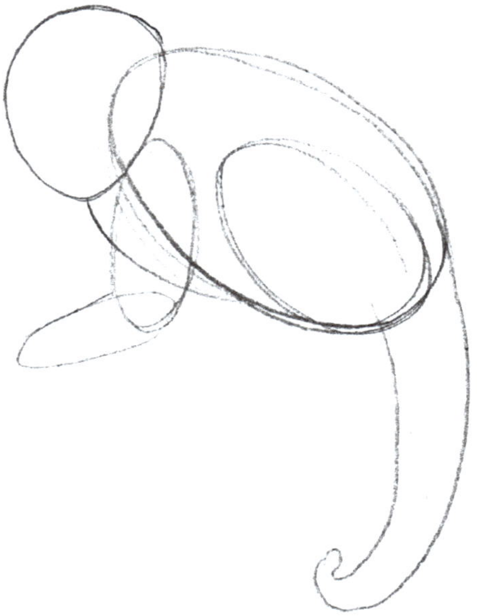

1. Start with a large, egg-shaped oval. On the more tapered side, add a round face. Add a smaller oval inside of the larger oval for the hind leg. This monkey has a thick, curved tail.

2. Monkeys are pretty hairy. To indicate fur, draw the outlines of the monkey with short, broken lines, leaving space for the monkey's face.

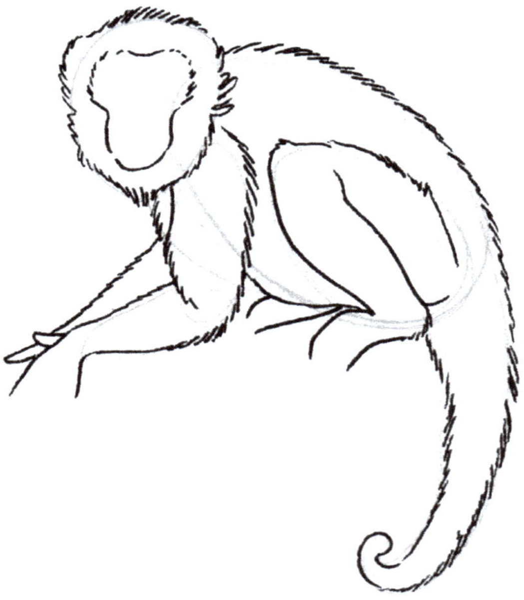

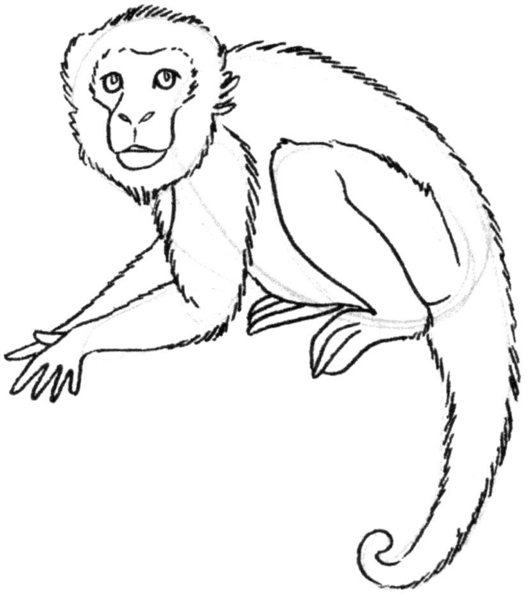

3. Draw the monkey's feet and hands. The face has round, friendly eyes and a slanted nose.

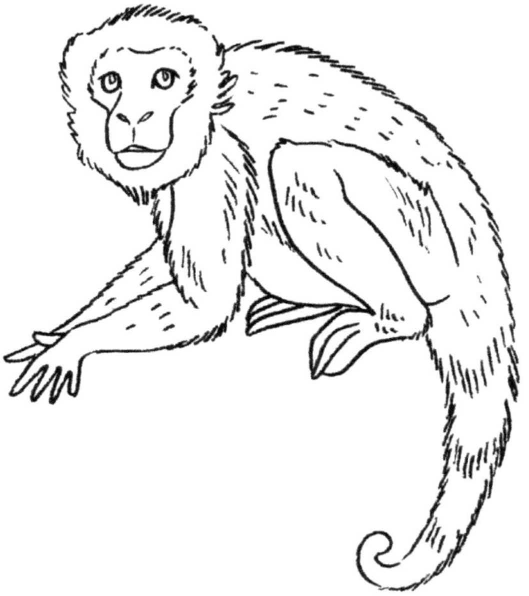

4. Finally, add extra fur lines to show the hairiness of the monkey.

PIG

Start with a large, wide oval. For the head, draw another oval tilted toward the ground. Add ovals for the shoulder and leg.

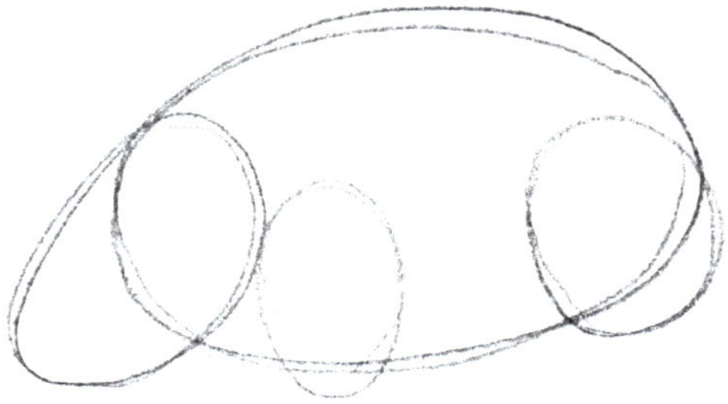

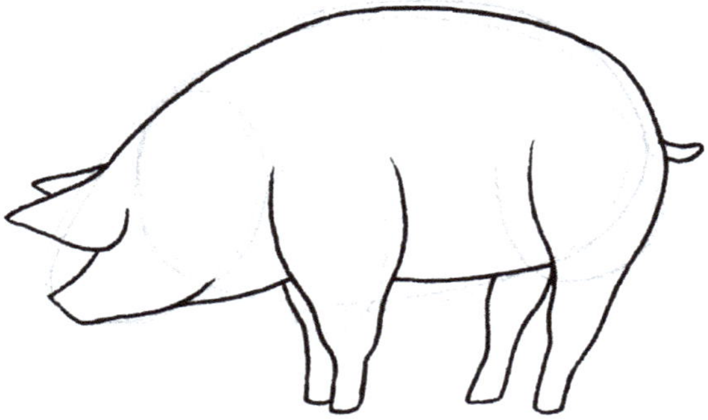

Draw the back with an arched line that continues from the head back to the hind legs. Pigs have pointed ears and snouts, as well as full chins and tapered hooves.

Finish the pig by adding snout details and a mouth, defining the hooves, and adding a few spots.

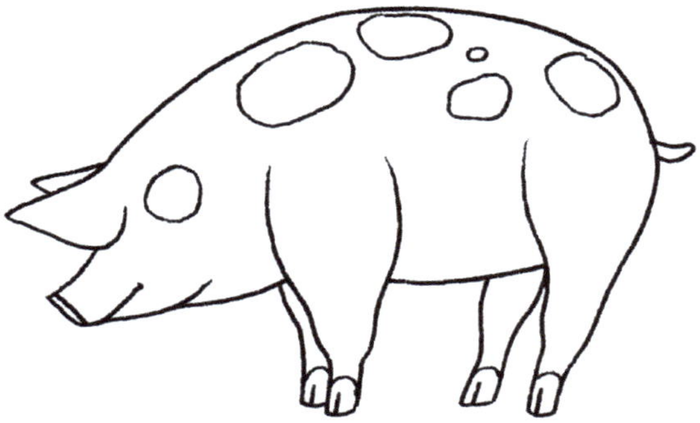

SEA TURTLE

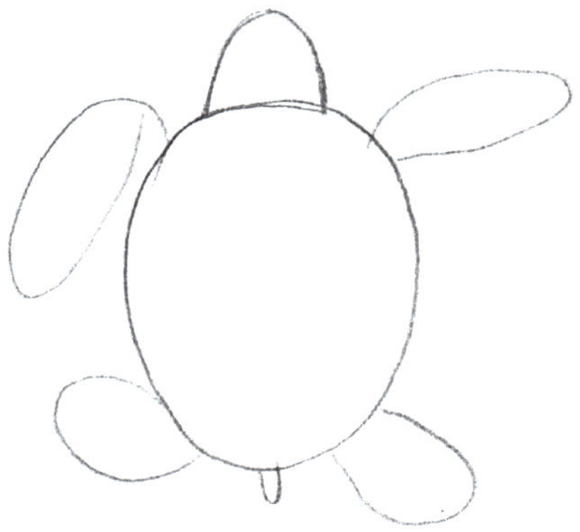

1. Start with a large oval that tapers slightly at the bottom. Then add a small, pointed semicircle for the head. Finally, using your reference, draw bean-like shapes for the arms and legs. The front flippers are longer than the back flippers!

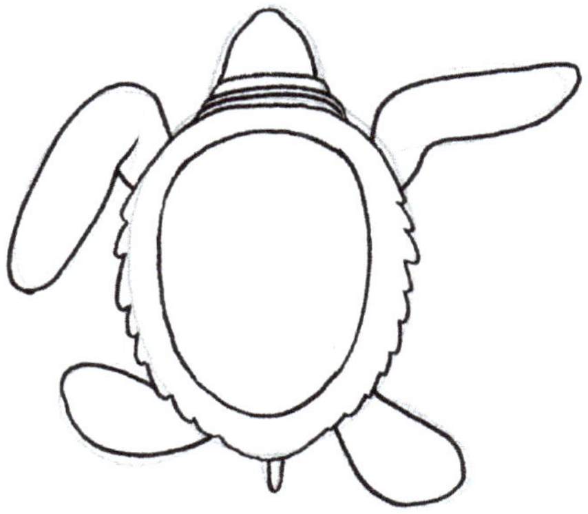

2. Use a pen to define the shape of the shell. Mine is ridged on the outside. Ink the flippers, and add wrinkles to the neck.

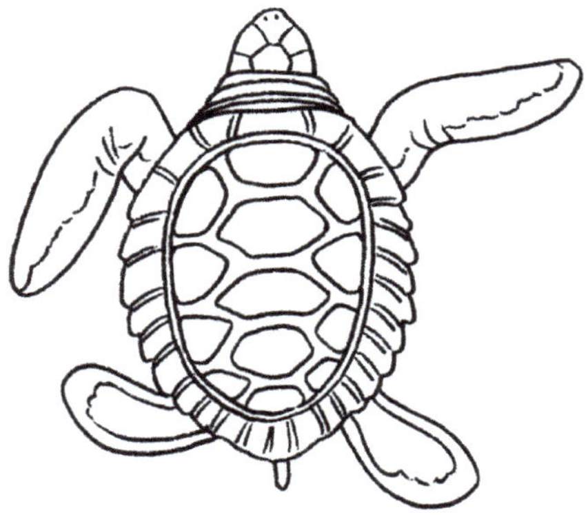

3. Finally, draw the pattern on the shell, following your reference. Add details to the flippers and head. Don't forget the nostrils!

EVERYDAY LIFE

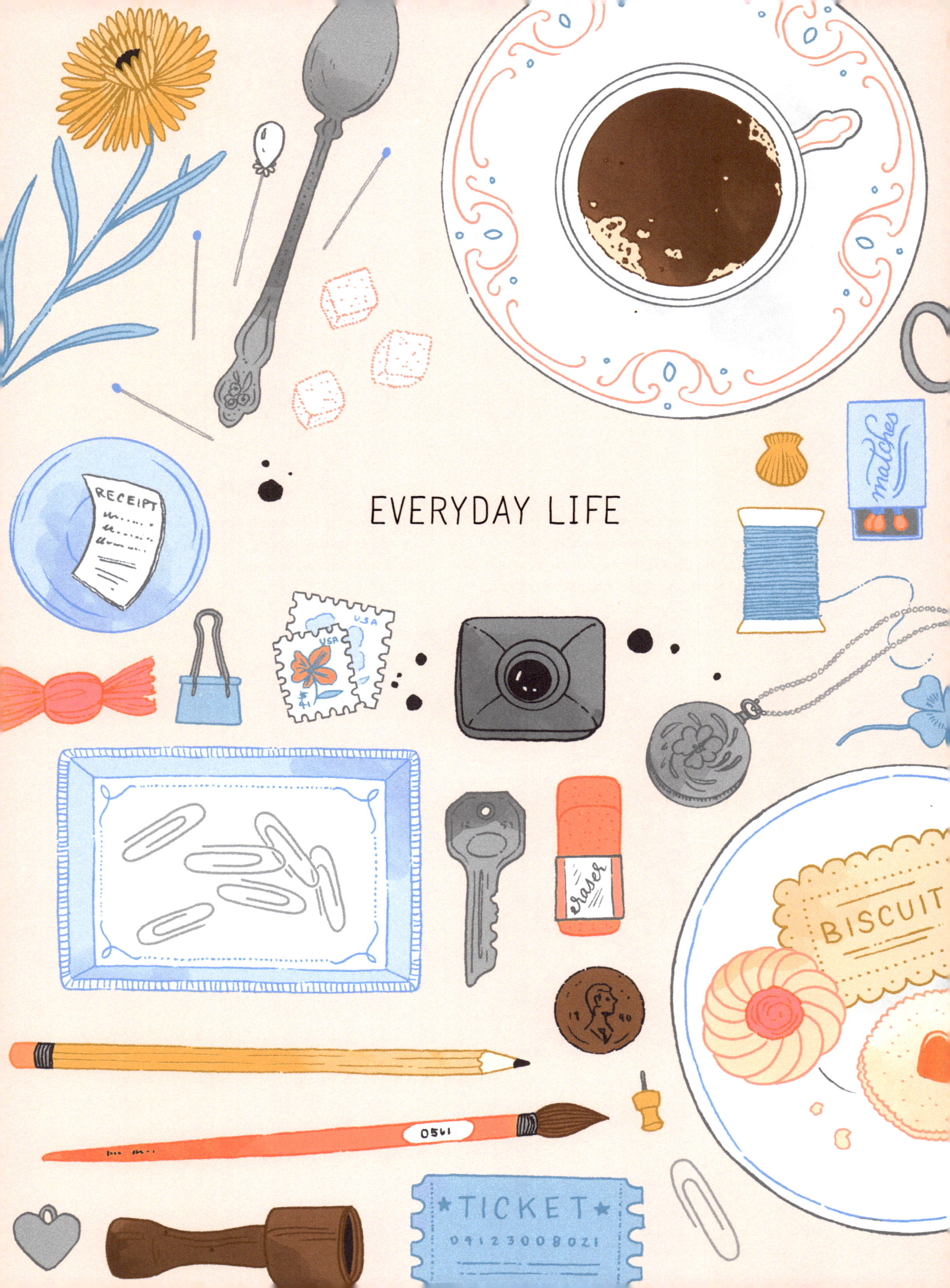

EVERYDAY LIFE

In this section, we'll take a look at many everyday objects that you can find around your own home. We'll learn how to break down complex objects into simple shapes and add convincing details. I recommend gathering a few objects that you own to practice with!

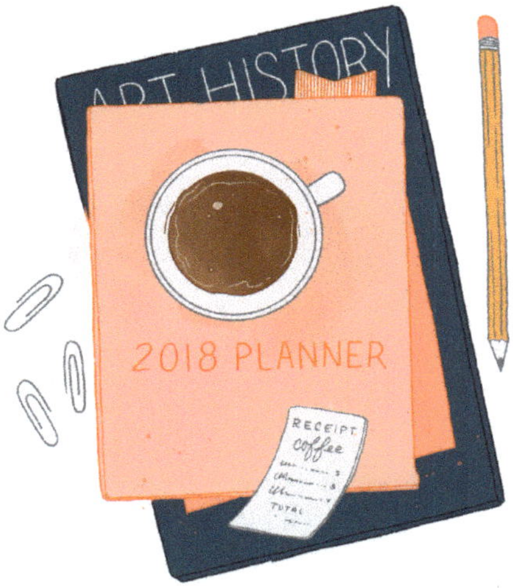

Get started with this easy umbrella tutorial! Start with an open semicircle, and connect it with three curved lines that form two points. Again, using curved lines, connect the top middle of the umbrella to each point. Draw a little rectangle on the top for the spoke and a long vertical handle with a curved end. Finish with little raindrops.

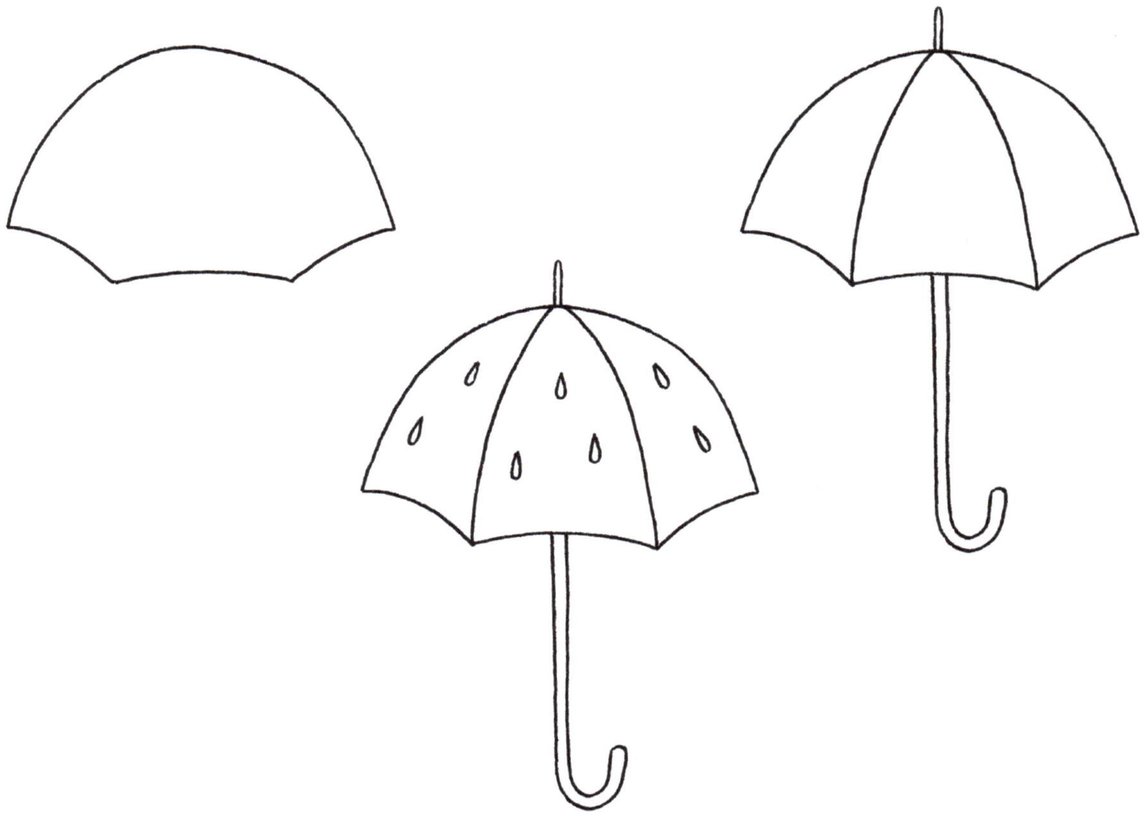

TEAPOT, TEACUPS & COFFEE MUGS

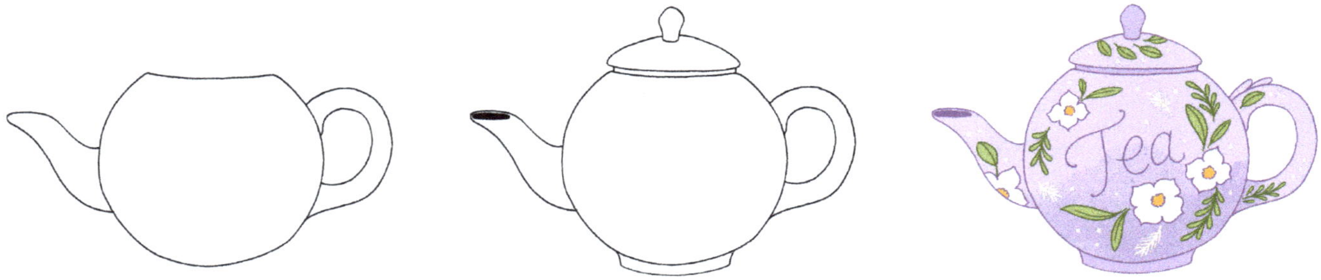

1. Start with a large circle, like a fishbowl. Add a thick handle on the right and a curved, upturned spout on the left.

2. Next draw slender, curved rectangles at the top and the bottom to create the base of the lid and the foot. Draw a mushroom-cap shape and a little knob in the middle to finish the lid. Don't forget to add the hole in the spout!

3. Get creative and decorate! Can you tell that this my favorite part?

To draw your favorite coffee mug, start with a skinny horizontal oval, and add a vertical line down each side. Draw the curved handle, and add two thin lines parallel to the edge of the mug rim to create the lip. Draw a semicircle in the mug to "fill" it with coffee. Then decorate the mug!

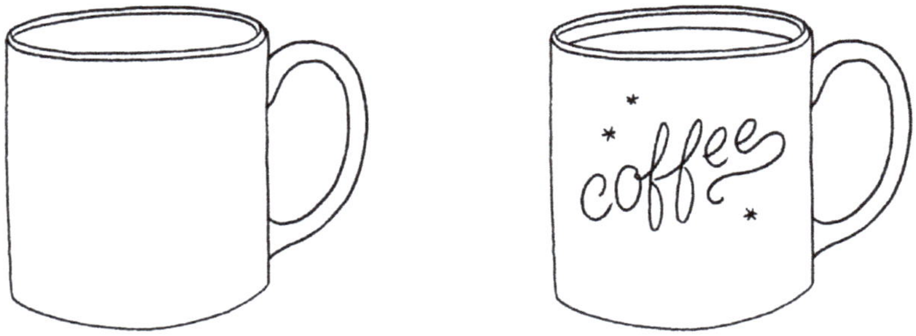

Follow the directions above to draw a teacup. Draw a skinny, horizontal oval, but this time draw a semicircle down from the sides. Add a handle, which should be more delicate. Add a little parallel line for the foot of the cup and the lip. "Fill" the cup again with a simple curved line, and embellish!

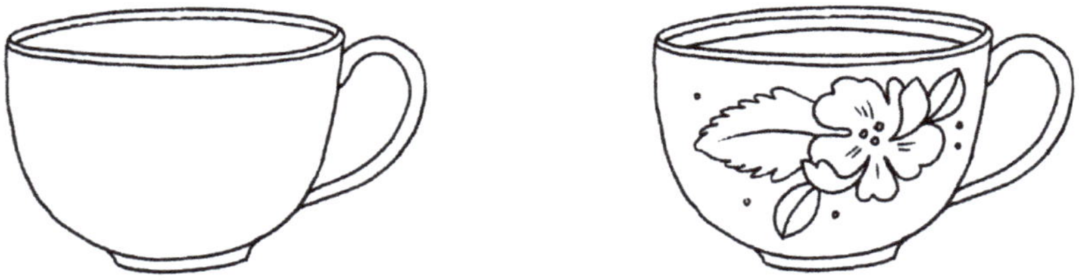

FANCY TEACUP

YOU CAN USE THE SAME STEPS TO DRAW A FANCY TEACUP TOO—JUST ADJUST THE SHAPES!

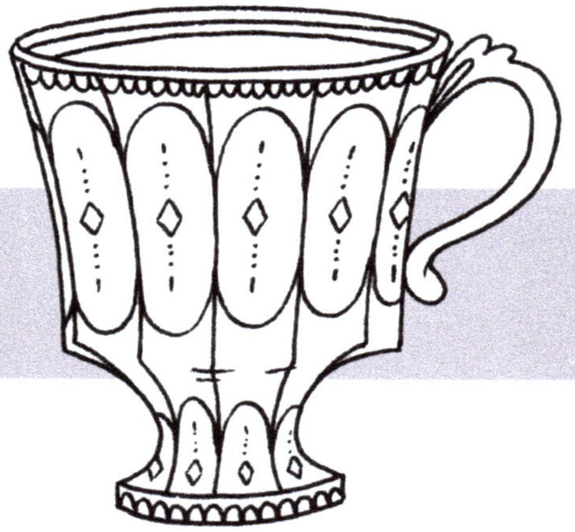

POT

For this kitchen pot, start with a skinny oval for the lid. Then draw a vertical line down from each side, slightly curving them and connecting them at the bottom. Draw two handles on each side and a knob in the middle. Finish the lid.

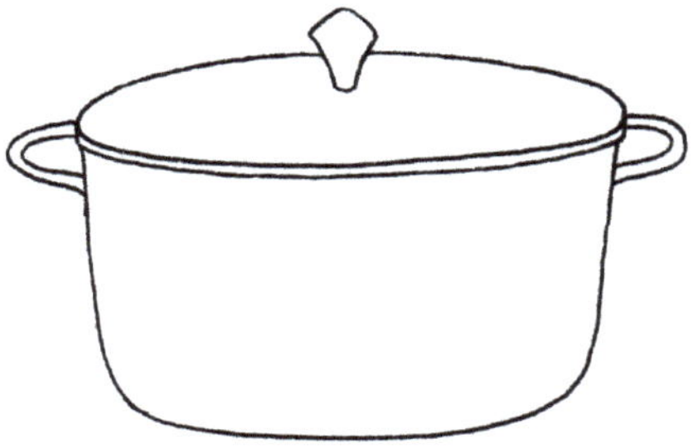

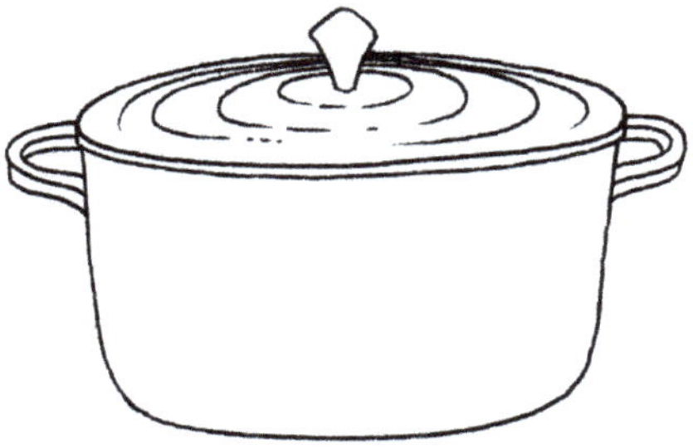

PEPPER

Start with two vertical lines that slant toward each other at the top. Connect the lines at the top and bottom with angled lines, forming two points. Draw a mushroom shape at the top. Connect the lines of the shaker and the top, and add curved lines to suggest metal ridges. "Fill" the shaker with small dots and add shaker holes!

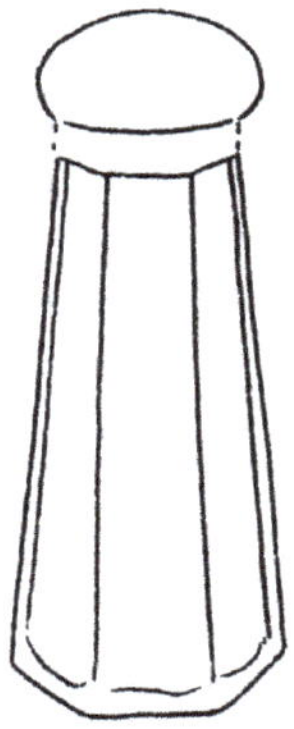

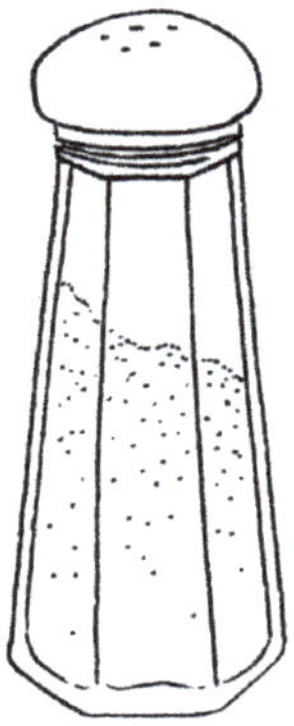

BOOK

1. Start with a rectangle on a skew. Make sure you are working with parallel lines. Draw a straight vertical line down from the leftmost corner of the rectangle. Then draw two lines that mirror the sides of the rectangle below it. Keep the space between them consistent—this is the bottom cover of the book.

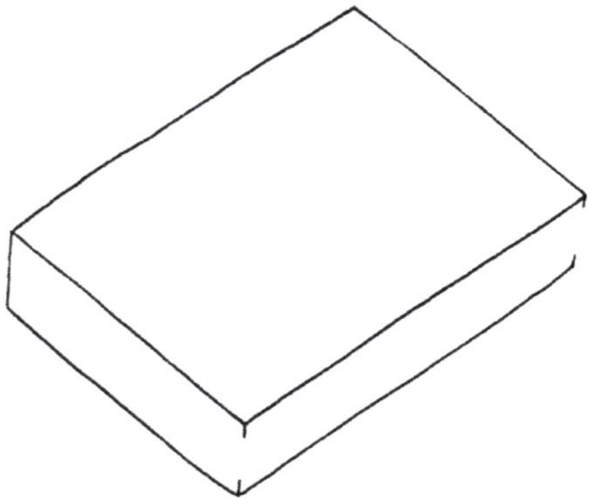

2. Draw another set of parallel lines on each rectangle, keeping the distance thin. Then connect the parallel lines. You have your book covers! Draw a vertical line down from the rightmost corner of the book, but pull it slightly inside of the corner to create the edge of the pages. Then, keeping parallel to the covers of the book, draw the rest of the "pages."

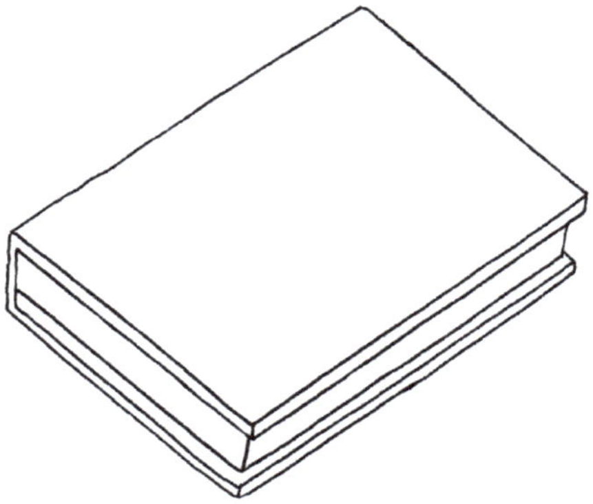

3. Fill the page section with horizontal lines, and finish the book with cover text and a bookmark.

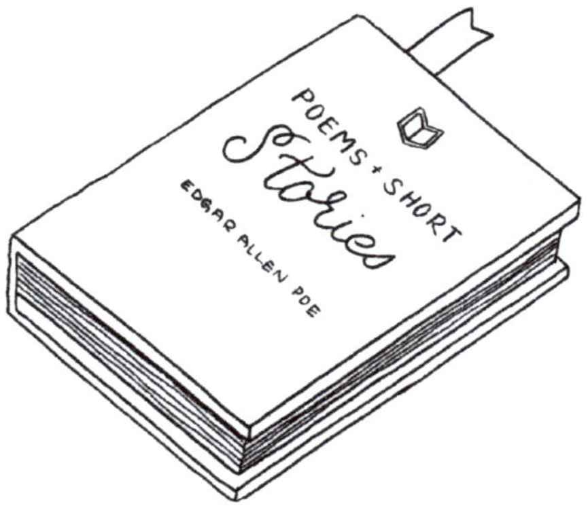

PICTURE FRAME

1. Draw a vertical rectangle on a slight skew. Then draw another rectangle outside of the first, keeping your lines parallel and the same distance apart. Connect the corners with diagonal lines. On the right side, draw two short, diagonal lines in from the top and bottom of the rectangle. Connect them with a vertical line. Then draw a small triangle support at the back, making sure the bottom of it runs parallel to the bottom of the frame.

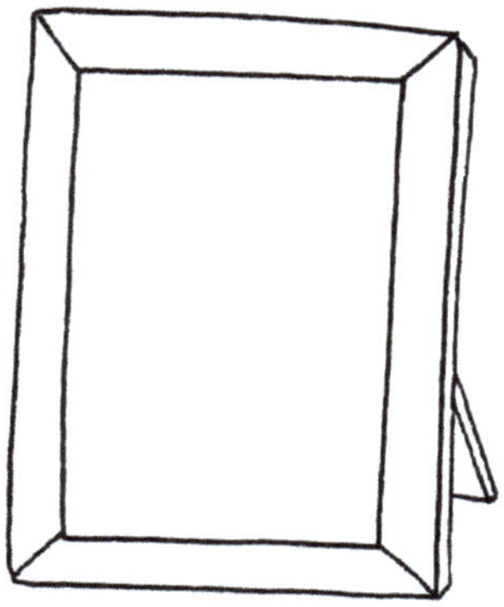

2. Frames come in all different materials. Mine is wooden, so I filled it with woodgrain. Create swirling patterns to achieve this effect. Make sure the grain runs in the same direction as each side of the frame.

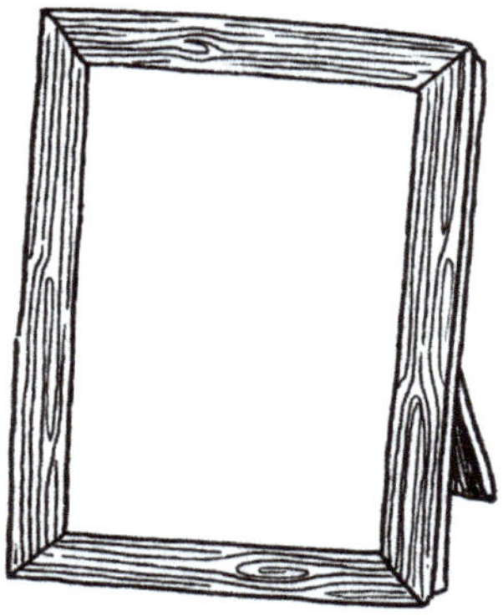

3. Finish the frame with a cute picture inside.

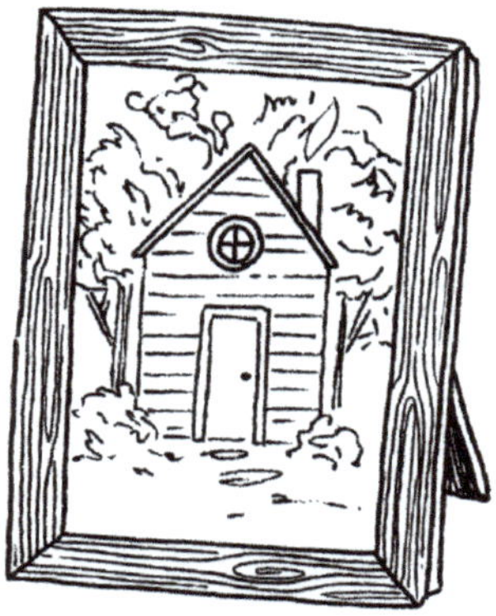

HEELS & BOOTS

1. Shoes are complex, so start with basic pencil lines. Draw a long, slanted triangle, with another smaller triangle for the heel. Then draw a triangle inside the larger one for the opening in the shoe. Drop a vertical lines for the heel stand.

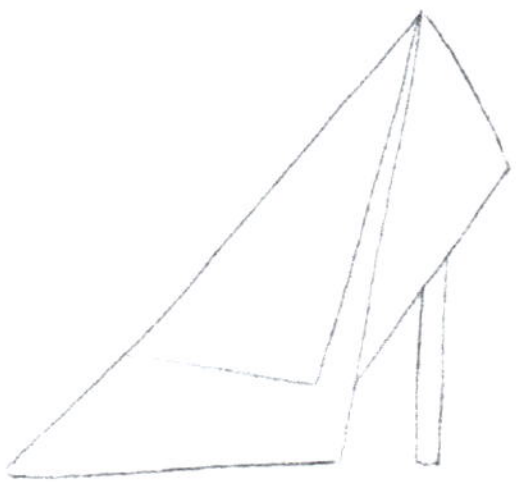

2. Using your pencil guide, draw the outline of the shoe with pen, making the lines wavy to complement the shape of the foot. Make sure the top is pointed, and the bottom is a straight horizontal line.

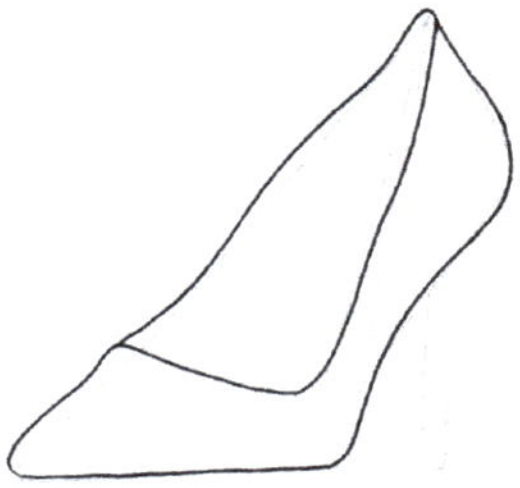

3. Draw a curved diagonal line that follows the side of the shoe to indicate the inside of the heel. Then draw the heel stand.

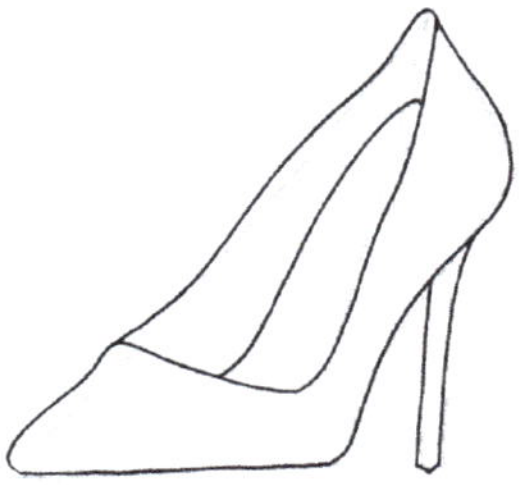

4. Add definition by giving the shoe a rim; then give the heel stand some perspective.

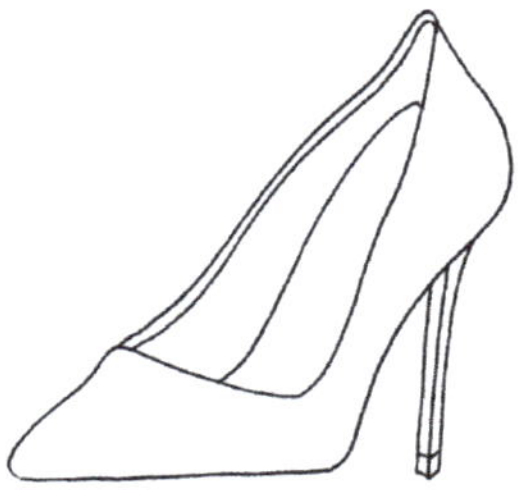

Start with a basic pencil outline. Boots have a taller ankle section, a thinner opening, and a chunky bottom. Divide it into several parts: toe, heel, sole, and flap. Use curved lines. I chose to draw the flap with wavy, bumpy lines to suggest a woolly texture. Add details, such as lines on the socks and to delineate the heel and sole. Finish by adding laces and grommets, notches in the soles, dotted lines for seams, and hatching to suggest the sock hole.

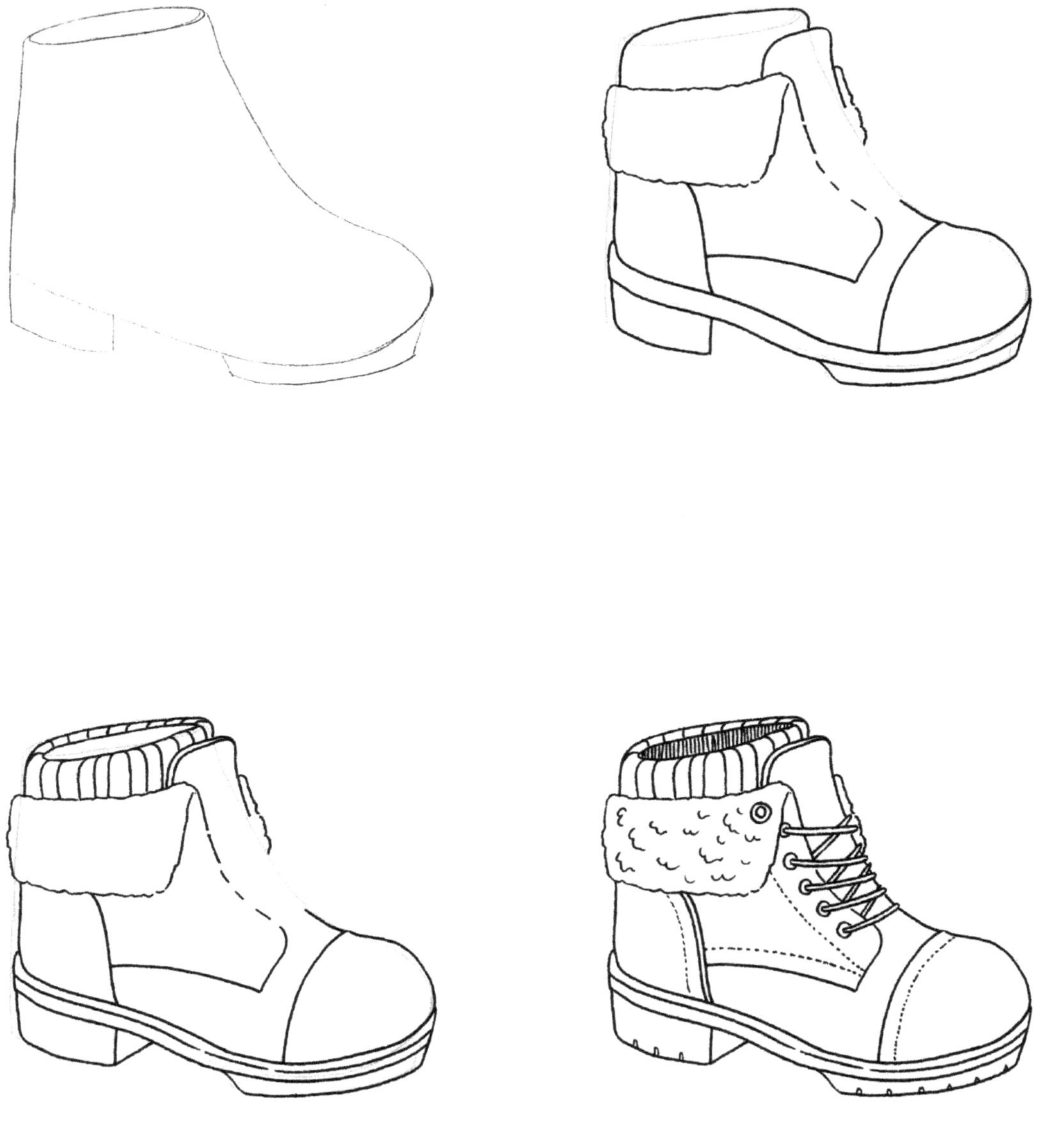

CHAIR

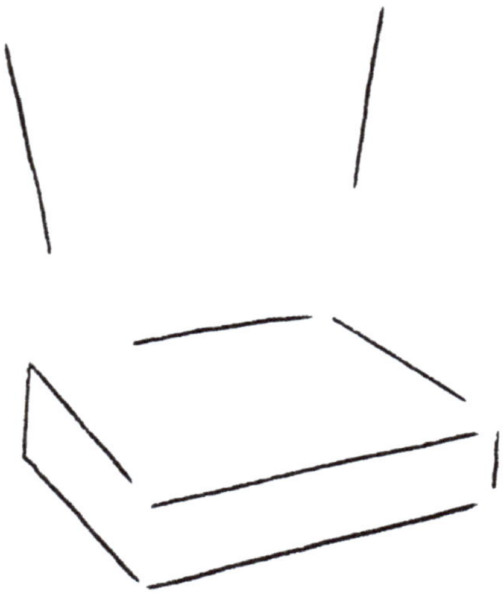

1. Draw a slanted cube, keeping the corners open. Above the cube, draw two vertical, slanted lines.

2. Connect the slanted lines with a dipped line at the top. Add curled armrests on the front of the chair.

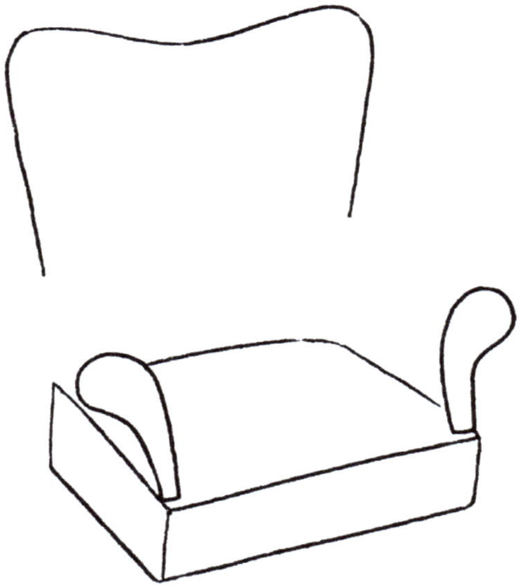

3. Connect the armrests using lines that run parallel to the seat of the chair. From each corner of the cushion, draw vertical lines for the legs of the chair. Make sure each is the same width.

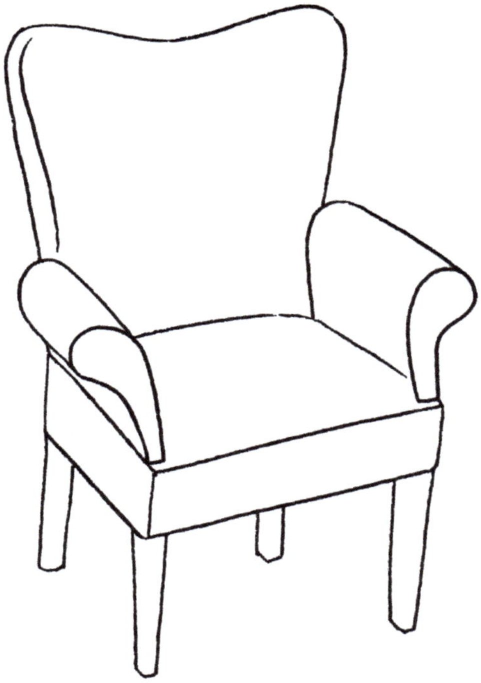

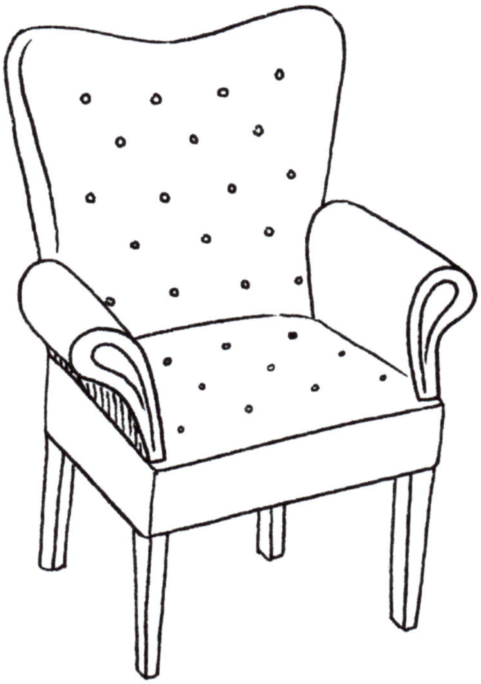

4. Finish the details.

FOLLOW THE SAME STEPS TO DRAW A SOFA!

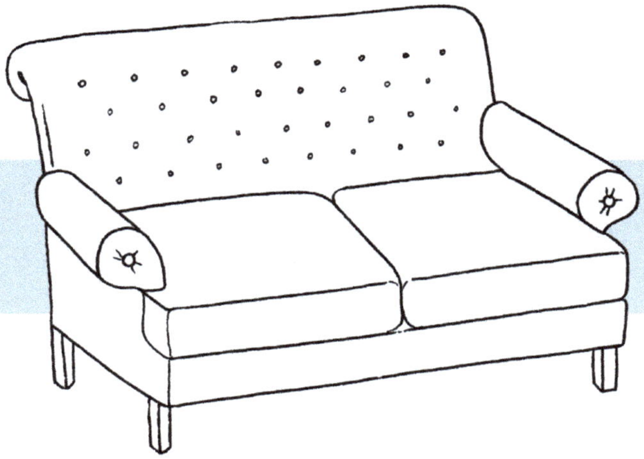

TABLE

1. Start with a skinny oval that isn't closed at the top—we'll add a vase here at the end!

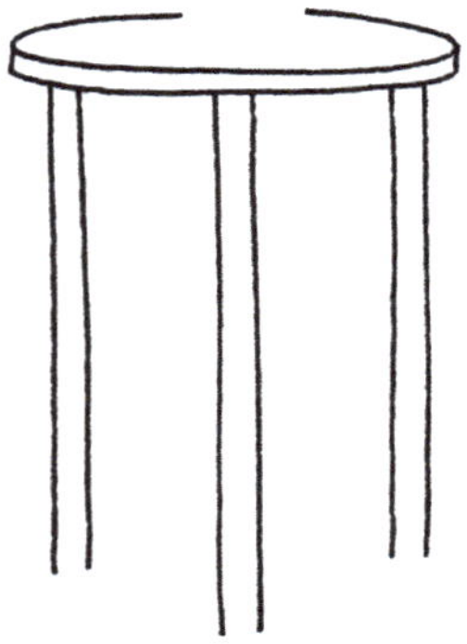

2. Draw a parallel curve below the oval and connect it on the sides with vertical lines for the edge of the table. Then draw three sets of parallel vertical lines for the legs. The middle leg should be the longest, because it will appear in front.

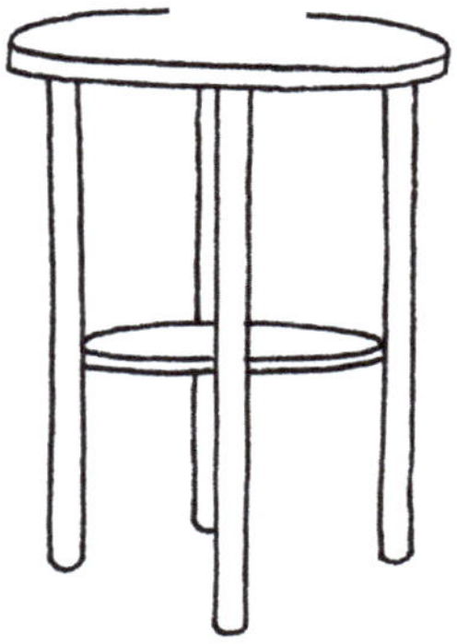

3. Draw a smaller oval halfway down and inside the table's legs. Make sure to add a rim that's the same width as the top of the table! Behind it draw the fourth leg, which is partially obscured by the front leg.

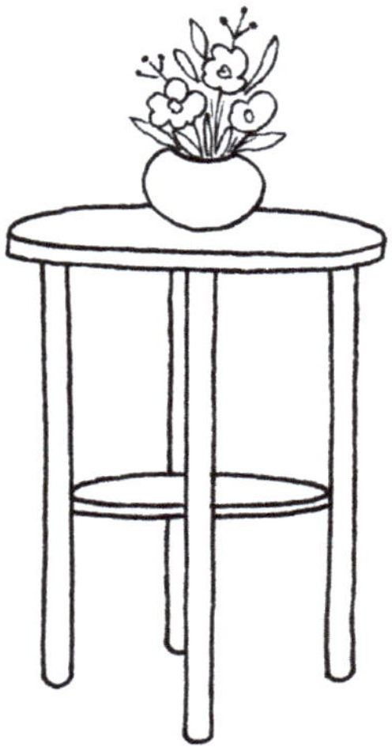

4. Add the bouquet on top and you're finished!

PRACTICE HERE

Now that you've practiced drawing lots of different everyday objects, try drawing your own here!

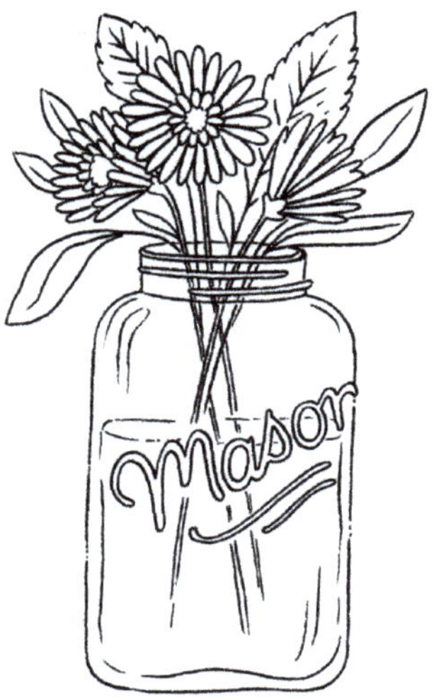

ABOUT THE ARTIST

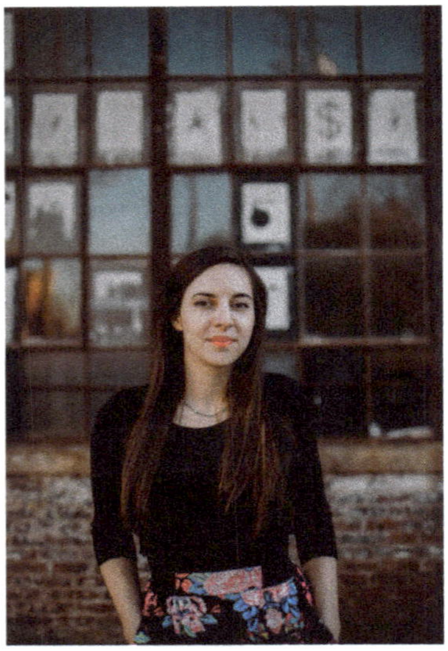

KELLEY RAYE PHOTOGRAPHY

Erin McManness is a full-time illustrator living and working in Atlanta, Georgia. She holds a master's degree in illustration from the Savannah College of Art and Design, where she graduated in 2014. Since, then she has worked in the product design, art direction, and illustration industries, leaving the traditional workplace in 2016 to officially launch her brand, Paper Raven Co., as a full-time endeavor.

Paper Raven Co. started as a small greeting card line, but has burgeoned in less than two years to include a robust assortment of cards, gifts, calendars, notebooks, paper craft, and home decor. Erin's love for pattern and floral aesthetic are hallmarks of the Paper Raven Co. brand, with light moments of humor and animal friends scattered throughout her work. You can find Paper Raven Co. in more than fifty retail stores and boutiques nationwide.

Erin's clients include Minted, International Greetings (for Target, Walmart, and Dollar Major), Greenvelope, Tombow, ChasingPaper, and Casetify, among others. Her work has also appeared in West Elm, Nordstrom, Domino, *HGTV Magazine*, *The Knot* magazine, *People* magazine, and *House Beautiful Magazine*.

When she's not designing, Erin can be found taking walks in the Georgia wilderness with her boyfriend, Daniel, and her Basset Hound mix, Patty. She also loves to cook and has a fascination with true crime and ghost stories. If she wasn't an illustrator, Erin would be a pastry chef or Indiana Jones.

www.ingramcontent.com/pod-product-compliance
Lightning Source LLC
LaVergne TN
LVHW072320021026
849212LV00012B/89
9781633224810